Republic or Death!

Travels in Search of
National Anthems

Alex Marshall

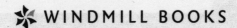

WINDMILL BOOKS

1 3 5 7 9 10 8 6 4 2

Windmill Books
20 Vauxhall Bridge Road
London SW1V 2SA

Windmill Books is part of the Penguin Random House group of companies
whose addresses can be found at global.penguinrandomhouse.com.

Penguin
Random House
UK

Copyright © Alex Marshall 2015

Alex Marshall has asserted his right to be identified as the author of this Work in
accordance with the Copyright, Designs and Patents Act 1988.

First published by Random House Books in 2015
First published in paperback by Windmill Books in 2016

www.penguin.co.uk

A CIP catalogue record for this book is available from the British Library.

ISBN 9780099592235

Typeset in Dante MT by Palimpsest Book Production Limited, Falkirk, Stirlingshire
Printed and bound in Great Britain by Clays Ltd, St Ives Plc

MIX
Paper from
responsible sources
FSC
www.fsc.org   FSC® C016897

Penguin Random House is committed to a
sustainable future for our business, our readers
and our planet. This book is made from Forest
Stewardship Council® certified paper.

To the composers and poets.

Contents

Prologue

Kosovo is more beautiful than you could ever hope a former war zone in the Balkans to be. Plains stretch out wherever you look, hills crowding at their edges, suffocated by forests. Starlings always seem to be swarming overhead, chasing your car, and the sky sits low – a luminous blue in daytime and every shade of red at sunset. It's impossible to ruin a landscape like this, although a lot of people seem to have tried, dotting it with factories and the occasional gigantic obelisk in memory of a fallen soldier, some of the latter complete with oversized photos stuck to the bottom which let you see every spot and blemish on the poor man's face.

I should probably be admiring that view now, wondering how a country that was torn apart by ethnic conflict less than twenty years ago now looks like a postcard. Unfortunately, it's hard to pay attention to even the prettiest countryside when you're being driven at 70 miles an hour down the wrong side of a road. Especially when a car's just appeared in the distance and is heading right for you. The driver of the car I'm in doesn't seem to notice we're moments from collision. He's too busy trying to open the ring pull on the beer can between his legs. To be fair to him, he said he didn't want it, but his boss, a fifty-something, craggy-faced man called Jashar, said he'd be a woman if he didn't drink, and being a woman is apparently the worst insult possible here.

Jashar's told me he's a 'civil engineer', but a few hours ago he drove me around Kosovo's pothole-filled capital, Priština, pointing out businesses he's owned ('Never get into banking,' he said), so I'm starting to suspect that may not be exactly true. He's certainly the first civil engineer I've met with a chauffeur-driven Audi. Perhaps I should have quizzed him on his knowledge of construction, but I haven't had a chance; all we seem to have done during our time together is drink. We've drunk at his house a few doors down from the American embassy – his children brought us whisky and nuts on silver platters, then one stood in the corner holding a TV aerial so we got a better reception of a football match – and we've just finished drinking in a lakeside restaurant. Four beers each. Three shots of grappa. Some savage local brandy to finish.

'Aren't we on the wrong side of the road?' I slur from the back seat.

Jashar laughs.

'Isn't that a car coming?'

Jashar laughs.

'Won't we get arrested?'

Jashar laughs.

'Who would arrest us?' he says, turning to face me. 'You're with the most important man in Kosovo.' From his tone I assume he means himself, but he nods to my left and I look at the person beside me. The most important man in Kosovo is in his mid-fifties, has wiry grey hair and eyebrows so thick they seem to be trying to hide his eyes. He's drunkenly slumped against the window, mouth open, trying to sleep, and he's got a food stain on his top. His name's Mendi Mengjiqi and he's the composer of Kosovo's national anthem.

'But no one likes his song,' I say stupidly, the drink the only reason I'm being honest.

'They will,' Jashar shouts back, sounding serious for the first time in hours. Then he throws me another beer. 'Drink, woman!' he laughs. We're still on the wrong side of the road. God knows where the other car is.

*

How does someone find themselves trapped in a car with the composer of Kosovo's national anthem? In my case, it's all a rapper's fault.

One recent summer, I was interviewing rap's next big thing for a British newspaper. He was sitting on the roof of his record label's offices, London spread out before him as if he were about to conquer it. He had just sold a few million copies of his debut single in the US and was supposedly trying to break Europe, although when I arrived his main concern appeared to be using his new-found fame to get the record label's secretaries to sit on his knee.

When he was ready to chat, he didn't wait for a question, but just started talking about his single, telling me it – a song about being a 'lonely stoner' – was important. Really important. Over and over, he said it. For a while I thought he was going to spell it out for me in case I'd missed his point: 'I-M-P-O-R-T-A-N-T.'

I sat there struggling to see how a song about smoking dope was as life-changing as he said it was, then gave up and started trying to think of songs that actually were. Not ones that people had fallen in love to, or had played at their wedding, or which made them think of their children. I wanted songs that had changed the world; songs that people had fought over and protested against; songs that had made people wake up and decide to build a barricade. The only ones I could think of were anthems.

Right at that moment, I realised I knew nothing about them. I couldn't tell you who wrote my own anthem, 'God Save the

Queen', for instance. I couldn't have sung most of it if the rapper had asked (unlikely, I grant you). I couldn't tell you who wrote America's, Germany's or France's either, or what those musicians had been like, whether they were upstanding citizens or bigamists, racists or criminals. But I was pretty sure that anthems were important – and I-M-P-O-R-T-A-N-T at that. I mean, people had won wars singing them, hadn't they? People had brought down governments with them, right? Somewhere in the world, anthems were being sung in life-changing situations right that minute, weren't they? I wanted to know the answers to those questions, and I wanted to know them more than anything this rapper could tell me. The interview didn't turn out to be my best; I was already trying to work out where I'd need to go to find out if my hunch was right.

*

The song that can claim to be the world's first anthem was written around 1570. No one knows exactly when. It's called 'Het Wilhelmus' ('The William'), and today it's the anthem of the Netherlands. It's slow and steady, the sort of tune you imagine farmers whistling while they plough fields. But in the sixteenth century, it had the impact of punk. The King of Spain, Philip II, ruled the Netherlands at the time and made a fortune collecting taxes from the country and its traders and merchants. But, not satisfied, he decided it was a good idea to step up the persecution of anyone there who wasn't Catholic. The Dutch responded by rioting and so the king executed their leaders and had their heads sent to him in Madrid, neatly packed in boxes. At one point, he sentenced the entire population of the Netherlands to death for being heretics. Literally everyone – even the Catholics. Unsurprisingly, the rioting turned into full-scale rebellion.

That rebellion's leader was a German-born, French-speaking aristocrat, William of Orange – neatly bearded and never seen without a ruff around his neck. He was better known as William the Silent, which hardly suggests he was the most inspirational leader that's ever lived, but it's him that 'Het Wilhelmus' is about. Whether he commissioned it in a fit of egotism or someone wrote it in admiration is unknown, but it's a bizarre song, fifteen verses long and all of them sung from William's point of view. None of those verses are exactly what you'd call anthemic, either. None are a call to arms, demanding people grab their pitchforks and stab a Spaniard in the back. None tell people not to worry, that William and his men will soon win the day. None are even really in praise of the Netherlands, with William rhapsodising about the country's natural beauty, its beer or its canals.

Instead it starts with William all but begging for his life. 'A prince of Orange / am I, free and fearless,' goes the first verse, before quickly adding, 'The King of Spain / I've always honoured' – an attempt to prove William's objection was with Philip's local administrators, not Philip himself. By the end, William is on his knees promising, 'I've never despised him.' It reads like someone who knows he's in trouble and is trying his best to get out of it – a desperate schoolboy running through excuses. Even when he's not trying to show his loyalty, the song's scarcely more rousing, largely him asking God to 'save me from disaster'. But something about the song clearly worked at the time. Everyone sang it: soldiers, maids, farmers, even butchers sweeping blood into the gutters. It made them believe in a cause and want to fight for it; made them realise they'd tried being reasonable, but now had no choice but to stand up to this foreign ruler and kill his men. Within ten years, William had led the Dutch to an (admittedly perilous) independence and created arguably the world's first nation state. Just try to ignore the fact he was assassinated – shot on his doorstep after Philip put a 25,000-crown prize on his head – in 1584.

*

'Het Wilhelmus' was a success – it was sung for decades after William's death as the Dutch and Spanish kept fighting, and it became so associated with the country that it was used by foreigners to welcome Dutch leaders – but national anthems didn't catch on at first. Maybe it was because the idea behind them – that one song could represent a ruler or their people, create hope and defiance – was too revolutionary for most to take in.

More likely, it was because if you weren't from the Netherlands the song was incredibly dull. Kings and queens in other countries would have heard it, nodded off halfway through and then forgotten to ask why it had achieved so much. The world wouldn't hear another national anthem until Britain's 'God Save the King' arrived almost 200 years later, and that came about for almost the exact opposite reason to 'Het Wilhelmus'.

In 1745, George II ruled Britain, but he was known more for his mistresses than for his grip on power, and was facing a crisis: the old Catholic royal family were trying to reclaim the throne, and much of the army who could have stopped them were out of the country. Charles Edward Stuart – Bonnie Prince Charlie, to give him his nickname – landed in Scotland that July with only seven men, but soon convinced thousands of Scots to march with him on London. The French told him they'd provide any support he needed. So what did George do? He didn't seem to panic and immediately call all his soldiers home. Instead he partly took confidence in a song that had sprung up in London and was spreading across the country; one that could help win the war for him. It was a song so simple it reminded everyone who heard it of why they were meant to love him, and it made them think twice before joining the Jacobite army passing through their towns. That song was 'God Save the King'. 'God save our gracious King! / Long live our noble King!' it goes:

Scatter his enemies,
and make them fall.

It struck such a chord it was soon being sung to end performances in theatres in every city, then encored in the nearest pub afterwards. It unified, and it gave confidence – the assumption is that it even motivated soldiers in the fight. The fact Bonnie Prince Charlie's army was also singing it, wanting him 'Long to reign over' Britain instead, apparently didn't matter.

Bonnie Prince Charlie got as far south as Derby, 130 miles from London, before deciding to retreat, realising he didn't have any support further south (his army was eventually defeated at Culloden, near Inverness, and he was forced to flee). George II died of a heart attack fifteen years later while sitting on the toilet. He'd just drunk a cup of hot chocolate. He was, at that point, Britain's longest-ruling king.

'God Save the King' changed the world's relationship with music. That isn't an overstatement. Here was a short, simple song that increased a king's popularity, helped stop an army and helped make everyone in Britain – well, England at least – feel a bit more united. They were no longer Londoners, villagers or serfs under a lord. They were the king's subjects and they could conquer all.

It kept on being sung long after the Jacobite threat had disappeared, and every other king in Europe quickly paid attention to it. 'Why haven't I got a song?' you can imagine Tsar Alexander of Russia thinking. 'Where's my bloody tune?' Frederick V of Denmark might have complained. And so they took 'God Save the King', changed the words to suit themselves, then built nations off the back of it – using these songs to help define borders as much as to foster love for themselves.

As nations emerged over the coming century, anthems became one of the main things that explained to people who they belonged to, what their characters were, what they were meant to strive for, even what language they were meant to speak. The other symbols of nationhood – flags and crests – couldn't do that. These songs brought people together, even if, in the case of the Netherlands, it was only in wondering why they were pledging loyalty to the King of Spain.

By the end of the 1800s, having an anthem had become so natural that even independence movements made sure they had ones ready and waiting. Anthems soon became an everyday part of diplomacy, played whenever a dignitary arrived in a capital. They also became an everyday part of education, taught in schools. And then, just to make sure no one could do without them, they became an essential part of sports. In 1905, a Welsh rugby crowd sang 'Hen Wlad Fy Nhadau', the graceful 'Land of My Fathers', in response to New Zealand's haka, the intimidating war dance performed before matches. It was apparently the first time an anthem had been sung at the start of an international sporting event and the practice soon caught on. In 1921, the International Olympic Committee decided anthems would be played to celebrate every gold medal. From then on, a country literally couldn't go without one of these songs. But, of course, like everything connected with nationalism, as soon as they were penned they were politicised and they became as divisive as they are unifying, and as controversial as they are everyday.

*

'Of course people don't like my anthem,' says Mendi, the most important man in Kosovo. 'It doesn't have any words!'

We're sitting in a restaurant in Priština with a sun-drenched veranda and minimalist black and white paint splattered everywhere. It's not long after I've arrived in the city and it feels as if we could be anywhere from Milan to London. The only way I know we're in Priština is that when Mendi ordered us breakfast

– a stuffed pancake – he spent five minutes quizzing the waiter about whether the meat was fresh.

'How can you like any anthem if it doesn't have words?' he says, driving his point home. 'How can you sing it at a football match? La, la, la, la, la? That'd be silly! How can it be emotional? People hear it and are confused. They don't know if it's good or not, they just know it's not good that it doesn't have words.'

'Why doesn't it?' I ask and Mendi sighs.

'If we put words to it the Serbs would object, or the United Nations would object. This is where the war has left us.'

The war. It doesn't take long for it to come up in a conversation here, even when everyone says they want to leave it behind. The night before, I was chatting to an architect in a bar and he joked, 'So you're here to see a war zone? You're fifteen years late.' I laughed, of course, but the war is actually the reason I decided to start exploring anthems in Kosovo rather than any other country. How can a song mean anything in a place that's so divided, in a country that, due to its separatist origins, isn't recognised by China, Russia or Spain?

The Kosovo War only officially lasted for a year and a half in the late nineties, when Serbian forces tried to force a large proportion of the 1.8 million or so Albanians who then lived here, and who made up around 90 per cent of the population, out of their homes and preferably the country (it was then part of Serbia). The Serbs burned houses, shot families and directed thousands of people to the nearest border.

The Kosovan Albanians – who some argue started the conflict by carrying out attacks against Serbs earlier in the decade, having become fed up with repression – fought a guerrilla war in defence, but the conflict only ended when US- and UK-led NATO intervened. They bombed Serbia so heavily that its president, Slobodan Milošević, was eventually forced to withdraw his troops and leave Kosovo to international forces. But today, the country is still divided. Take the ramshackle, northern town of Mitrovica. It's entirely Serb, and the people who live there have little time for Kosovo's parliament, its stamps or even its beer. Kosovo's brewery has to change the labels on bottles it sends there to remove any hint of Albanian.

Priština is a strange place to visit. The city's main street is called Bill Klinton Boulevard, and on it pride of place is given to an 11-foot-tall bronze statue of the former president, waving. If that doesn't make you realise he's seen as a hero here, there's also a 25-foot poster of him hanging off the apartment block behind, featuring Bill with those come-to-bed eyes, smiling, saying, 'Welcome to Kosovo.' It's just above a coffee advert, though the coffee isn't named after Bill Clinton, which makes you feel they missed a trick. In the middle of town there's also a road named after Tony Blair and another after George W. Bush. There are other reminders of the war everywhere such as burned-out buildings and memorials for dead Kosovo Liberation Army soldiers. But despite the war feeling so close, whenever I try to get Mendi to speak about it, he either gives an extremely short answer or just changes the subject. He's moved on and his anthem is the biggest sign of that, he says.

He actually composed it back in 2008, almost a decade after the war, when the country declared its independence from Serbia. The government announced a competition: two and half weeks to enter; €10,000 to the winner. You could have words if you wanted, they just couldn't be potentially offensive to anyone. It is telling that very few entries included them. Mendi heard about the contest, sat down in his parents' house in the countryside and tried to write an entry. He'd had a melody stuck in his head for years hoping for just this moment – that he could be the one to write Kosovo's anthem – but it didn't quite feel complete, so he went fishing in a small river nearby and for walks in the forest, soon realising that the beautiful country around him was all the inspiration he needed to add the final touches. 'It had to be peace music; that's what I realised,' he says. 'An anthem shouldn't be saying, "Look at us, we are strong." It shouldn't be fight music. I've had enough militarism in my life.'

He genuinely thought the tune he came up with that day would bring the country together, and musically it is a success: strings swoop up and down over timpani rolls like an eagle flying over mountains; horns proudly appear in a middle section to stretch out the melody; then the strings return, lifting the song as high as they can. It's the sort of music you'd normally hear at the end of a film: the hero has just kissed his girlfriend and the camera spirals up until the couple are only a dot on the landscape. It's an appalling cliché, yes, but it still works. I tell Mendi how much I like it – that surely it can't have gone down as badly with people here as he says, even without words. But it's not just the lack of words that's a problem, he says. 'Look at the name: "Europe". Why on earth did they call it that?'

'I assumed that was your idea,' I say.

'Argh, no,' he says, exasperated, and starts telling me it was just the code word he picked for his entry so no one would know it was by him. 'I could have written anything: "blue", "green", "pink". One day I was on a bus listening to some people talking and they said, "Have you heard we've got a new anthem? It's called 'Europe'. Isn't that stupid? Aren't we from Kosovo?" And that was so upsetting for me. Why didn't the government use its actual name, "Hymn of Kosovo"? It was written at the top of the music. If my code word was "pink", would they have told everyone the anthem of Kosovo was called "Pink"?'

Mendi tells this story in one breath, rushing through it as if trying to get to the end as quickly as possible. He doesn't slowly

build up to the end and finish with the punchline like a good
storyteller would, just a shrug as if to say, 'This is Kosovo. What
can I do?'

'How long do you think your anthem will last?' I ask him. It
seems a sensible question. If no one really likes it, or even really
wants this country to exist, you'd think they'd eventually replace
it. But he looks at me with disbelief and laughs for the first time
since we've met. 'Of course it'll last! It just needs words – and
it will get them. When? I don't know, maybe ten years? We have
listened to the Albanian national anthem for years like it's our
own but I think the new generation will think differently. People
will come to my tune. And I know I'm not being modest, but
it's a really good anthem.'

Mendi's optimism is touching, but I think he underestimates
quite what a sad situation he's in: he's written what's meant
to be the most important song in his country's history, yet few
people recognise what he's done. No one in this restaurant has
even glanced at our table while we've been talking. Everyone
has treated him like just another customer; nobody has nudged
a friend to ask, 'Isn't that . . . ?' I doubt anyone here cares that
his anthem perfectly illustrates Kosovo's history and situation
today. In its wordless minute, you can read off everything from
the fact this country is stalled and divided, to the legacy of its
war and the desire to overcome it. It tells a bigger story than
most composers achieve with entire symphonies. The fact it
does, I realise, is enough to make me want to investigate these
songs more. Surely there are other anthems that do the same,
and ones that people actually care about? Surely there are
places where anthem composers are lionised rather than
forgotten? There might even be places where the story of an
anthem is joyful (maybe not the ones for recent war zones,
admittedly).

Excited, I start trying to run through ideas with Mendi for
other countries whose anthems might be worth investigating,

but he only half listens, distracted. 'How about we get some lunch?' he says. 'I have this friend, Jashar. He knows a great place in the country *and* he has a car. Let me call him. We can get a drink on the way.'

La Marseillaise

Allons enfants de la Patrie,
Le jour de gloire est arrivé!
Contre nous de la tyrannie,
L'étendard sanglant est levé! (bis)
Entendez-vous dans les campagnes
Mugir ces féroces soldats?
Ils viennent jusque dans vos bras
Egorger vos fils, vos compagnes!

Refrain:
Aux armes, citoyens!
Formez vos bataillons!
Marchons! Marchons!
Qu'un sang impur
Abreuve nos sillons!

———

Arise children of the fatherland,
The day of glory has arrived!
Against us tyranny's
Bloody banner is raised! (x2)
Do you hear in the countryside
The roar of those ferocious soldiers?
They're coming right into your arms,
To cut the throats of your sons, your women!

Chorus:
To arms, citizens!
Form your battalions!
March! March!
Let the impure blood
Water our furrows!

realise I've perhaps made a mistake. I've been travelling only a few hours now and only twenty minutes of that uphill, but I'm already a wreck. I still have 500 miles to go before I reach the Jardin des Tuileries in the centre of Paris. I've never cycled more than 12 miles in a day before; I've given myself a week. Yes, I think I was rather optimistic with my calculations too.

There's a good reason I'm doing this though. I've set out to cycle the route of 'La Marseillaise', the most famous national anthem of them all. It's a song you can sing from Argentina to Bhutan and everyone will know it. They might not speak French, but they can certainly shout its boisterous tune. It's a song that pushes you to get louder, to pump your fist higher, with every line. It's really the closest an anthem ever gets to a pop song: a melody so simple you can't get it out of your blood after the first time you've heard it. You could play it on a French horn, a violin or even a tambourine and it'd be unmistakable.

Soon after it was written, an English historian wrote, 'The sound of it will make the blood tingle in men's veins, and whole armies will sing it, with eyes weeping and burning, with hearts defiant of death, despot and evil.' A French general used to say it was worth 1,000 extra men in battle. A German poet once wrote that it was responsible for the death of 50,000 of his countrymen. Everyone from Wagner to the Beatles has stolen that melody, and it's popped up, translated, in the US, Brazil and Russia. It symbolises France to the world, even if much of France apparently hates it. A lot of people here see it as vicious and violent – and to be fair to them, they're right. 'La Marseillaise' is a seven-verse call to arms, trying to encourage people to fight by telling them invaders are coming 'to slit the throats of our wives and children'. There's even a children's verse so kids can sing about hoping to share their dad's coffin. It's not the world's most violent anthem by a long way – Western Sahara's repeatedly urges people to 'cut off the head of the invader'; Vietnam's to build 'the path to glory . . . on the bodies of our foes'. But the perception that it is is unshakable. And all in all, it's hardly what you'd associate with the country of love, sex and champagne.

Many people here also think it's an incredibly racist song; a colonial tune. That all comes down to the chorus. '*Aux armes, citoyens!*' it shouts:

> *Qu'un sang impur*
> *Abreuve nos sillons.*
>
> —
>
> To arms, citizens!
> …
> Let's water the fields
> With impure blood.

But then you walk into a French sports stadium and see the pride on people's faces when they sing it. How can you understand such a contradiction? How can you grasp the relationship between one of the greatest songs of all time and what it is to be French? Can an anthem like this still mean something in a modern, multicultural country?

Well, in my opinion, you have to travel across France to get answers to any of those questions. And you have to destroy yourself cycling up hills. Most of all, you have to start in Marseilles.

*

About 200 years ago, in July 1792, 517 men and two cannons left Marseilles, on the coast at the bottom of France, and marched all the way north to Paris. They were responding to an advert written by one of the city's leading revolutionaries, Charles Barbaroux, asking for '600 men who know how to die'. 'You're needed to march and strike down the tyrant,' it said, adding, somewhat obviously, that anyone thinking of applying must know how to hold arms. Volunteers must also know how to read and write, it said, which seem somewhat superfluous skills, but show you he wasn't going to let just anyone get involved.

France was in the middle of the Revolution that would eventually see it get rid of its king, Louis XVI, and his decadent wife, Marie Antoinette. Its government had already severely limited the king's powers (the year before, he'd tried to flee abroad, so horrified was he about what was happening). However, there were fears Austria and the Prussian Empire were about to invade, to force Paris to roll things back to how they used to be. The men of Marseilles wanted to stop Louis reclaiming even a fraction of his former powers and so they set off for Paris. They marched for twenty-eight days straight, first over the Chaîne de l'Étoile mountains and along the Rhône valley to Lyon, and then on and on and on, through fields and the forests of Saulieu, all the way to the capital. And every weary step they sang a song. When they began their journey it was known by a mouthful of a title: 'Le Chant de Guerre pour l'Armée du Rhin' ('The War Song of the Rhine Army'). But not long after they reached their destination, it had become simply 'La Marseillaise', and those 517 men had become legends. Well, 516 of them had; one, Claude Lagoutte, drank too much and died of a 'sudden illness' en route.

I'd decided to follow in the footsteps of these men, though by bike obviously. When I made that decision, I was mighty pleased with myself. I assumed that as long as I avoided drinking like Claude, it'd be easy. I was wrong.

*

Marseilles is the least French of French cities, with a more Mediterranean than Gallic feel to it. You step out of the station on to a wide art deco staircase leading down towards the sea with people stretched out lazing on it, almost asleep. No one is hassling you to buy a knocked-off Louis Vuitton bag or a black-market DVD, unlike outside most other major train stations in Europe. The hills surround the city like a suntrap and the heat has an intensity which says, 'Sit down, have a drink. Relax. Don't worry yourself.' It's hard to picture anyone managing to work hard here, which makes it a little surprising that the city used to be one of Europe's busiest ports, its fortune built on trade. Ships still pour in and out of the dock, but today they are mostly yachts, not container vessels. The city itself hasn't changed much since the time of 'La Marseillaise'. The streets of the old town are still as narrow as they were then, lined with five- or six-storey homes so close together you could practically shake hands with your opposite neighbour each morning. Every building is a different pastel shade – orange, yellow, cream – giving the whole area the dreamlike feel of an Impressionist painting.

Just a short walk from the station, in the courtyard of the Mémorial de la Marseillaise, the city's museum to the song, I meet Frédéric Frank-David, the museum director. He's a neatly bearded, ginger thirty-something and he laughs when I tell him I'm about to cycle the route. 'You do realise the soldiers marched at night, don't you?' he says. 'You'd have to be an idiot to do it in the daytime. See how hot it is here. When are you leaving?'

'In about five minutes,' I reply. It's midday.

Frédéric is meant to be the number one fan of 'La Marseillaise', but he's an odd candidate for the role: he's young and liberal, a man who's as open about the song's problems as he is about its joys. 'The problem with "La Marseillaise",' he says over coffee, 'is that everyone looks at it today, and they see it gets sung by people on the far right – le Front National – and so everyone says it's violent, ugly and racist. But you've got to look beyond that. The song shouldn't mean those things. What it should be is a symbol of revolution. The French Revolution was about giving ideals to the world – liberty, equality. And the song was part of that and is about those ideals.

'When people started looking for independence in South America, they sang "La Marseillaise". In China at the end of the nineteenth century, when they were trying to get rid of Europeans, they sang "La Marseillaise" – in Chinese of course. They sang it in Tiananmen Square too. It's been sung everywhere there's been a revolution.'

The main reason I wanted to meet Frédéric was to try to learn a bit more about the marchers themselves before I set off. But it turns out that little is known. Frédéric can rattle off many of their names – François Moisson, Pierre Garnier, André Carvin – but then it all gets a bit hazy. Their average age was twenty-nine, but there was a fourteen-year-old drummer, Joseph Camas, and a fifty-five-year-old teacher, Etienne Gaugain. Frédéric says the main recruiters were journalists and lawyers, members of the revolutionary Jacobin Club, but the volunteers themselves were more often than not artisans, craftsmen and shopkeepers. The odd merchant. They must have been reasonably well educated given they could read and write. And if they could sing 'La Marseillaise', they were definitely so. In the 1790s, only about 10 per cent of people in the whole of France could speak French, the language of the elite. In Marseilles, they spoke Provençal or Occitan (*langue d'oc*); in the rest of the country languages like Breton and Alsatian. It was a good hundred years before French was basically forced on everyone.

The men were promised 600 livres each for their efforts – the equivalent of twenty-five gold coins. That doesn't seem like much of an incentive for men with decent jobs to risk their lives, but their desire to take part in the endeavour makes more sense when you consider the one thing we do know about them for sure: they suffered from something of an inferiority complex, residents of a city that tended to be the butt of jokes in the capital and had to respond to its every whim. 'There was this feeling at the time that leaving the Revolution to Paris might be a catastrophe,' Frédéric says. 'And their role, their mission to save the Revolution, was very important for these men because they had always had this feeling of being despised by Paris, and of being too far from Paris. This was their time for revenge almost, for reversing the course of things and saying, "Marseilles is important to France. It will keep things together when Paris can't."'

Revenge found its soundtrack in 'La Marseillaise'. The song was sung for the first time in Marseilles on 22 June by François Mireur, a medical student. He was attending a meeting calling for marchers. Why he sang it isn't known, since it had actually been written for an army 500 miles away in east France (more on that in due course). He probably picked up a song sheet off a town crier – the eighteenth-century equivalent of buying a tabloid. Perhaps he was moved by the song's sentiment or perhaps he simply wanted to liven up the meeting. Whatever the reason, from Mireur's lips the song spread through the city's streets, until it had worked its way into every home, every corner. A few weeks later, at 7 p.m. on 2 July, the 517 men met outside a court-house. The Jacobin leaders gave each of them a red hat, one of the symbols of the Revolution, and a leaflet with the words to 'La Marseillaise'. 'The song was there to motivate, to keep them going,' says Frédéric. 'The Jacobins banned every other song. It was a bit of a brainwashing.'

Now, propped up against a crash barrier halfway up a hill above Marseilles, having left Frédéric two hours earlier, I am in such desperate need of motivation myself that I consider singing the song like they did, but I'm just too exhausted, my throat too dry even after slugging back Catherine's water. Maybe if I wait long enough another car will stop, this time with some actual drugs.

*

I eventually manage to pick myself up and get over the hill without the help of 'La Marseillaise' or anything stronger and over the next two days I head north, first to Aix-en-Provence, a town that overflows with cheese, meat and fruit stalls, and then on to Avignon, former home of the popes, where a 6-metre-tall, 4.5-tonne gold statue of the Virgin Mary looks down on the city from her place atop the cathedral bell tower. The papacy was relocated here when a Frenchman, Clement V, was elected pope and refused to go to Rome.

The 517 Marseillais soldiers passed through both these towns on their march – and caused mayhem in each. In both cases, they arrived at first light, unannounced, and immediately demanded the town's mayor bring them all the food and wine he could. Then they spent hours drinking, trying to recruit, swearing about the king and, of course, bellowing 'La Marseillaise'. And then they'd start fighting. They'd fight anyone they thought opposed the Revolution, anyone who refused to join them, and, if they couldn't find any of either, they'd fight each other. They'd only been going a few days, but fearful rumours started racing ahead of them, reaching towns all over France. People prayed they wouldn't visit their town next.

But it's not these towns that leave the biggest impression on me during the first few days of my trip, interesting and beautiful as they are. It's the countryside. The route from Aix to Avignon along the Durance river is all agriculture: orchards so overflowing with apples and pears the farmers don't complain when people stop their cars to pick them; fields full of any vegetable you can name and plenty you can't. The only buildings in sight are the occasional farmhouses, which couldn't look more picturesque. They're slightly ramshackle, with windows that don't quite seem to fit the frames, but they're still postcard perfect. I expect they are the main reason so many foreigners move to Provence: they dream of sitting in those sun-drenched gardens or running their hands along dusty bottles of wine in cool cellars.

That said, living in them at night must be awful. You'd be able to hear sounds from miles away. Every time you watched a detective show, you'd start wondering if the murderer was coming for you that night. As I cycled past these homes, all I could think about was how terrifying it must have been for anyone in them when the Marseillais marched past. It might have been 2 or 3 a.m. when they were woken by the first sound. They'd have ignored it, at first. Fifteen minutes later, they wouldn't have been able to. It would be louder, and they'd be able to tell it was a group of people singing. 'It's probably just some drunks, love. Go back to sleep.' A few minutes after that, the sound louder still, no such explanation would have been plausible. They wouldn't know what the men were singing, because they'd only speak Provençal, but they'd know it sounded aggressive, violent, proud. They would have got up and peered out of the window. And what they'd have seen would have caused them to jump back, and run downstairs to check that the door was firmly bolted: 517 men, flaming torches in hand, dragging two cannons behind them.

No one knows how many times the men sang 'La Marseillaise' each night. It could have been seventy, by my reckoning. That's all seven verses, one after the other, sung for eight hours straight. But then it might have been just a few, only rolled out when the soldiers reached a town, to let everyone know they'd been through. However many it was, it wasn't forgotten.

*

I leave Avignon after having a look at the Papal Palace (now a vast, empty sandstone fortress) and the Pont Saint-Bénezet, a medieval bridge that once gracefully stretched 900 metres across the river Rhône. Today, having collapsed due to flood damage, it stops surreally 100 metres out, almost inviting you to run along it and jump off.

I'm feeling confident. I've managed two whole days cycling, covering about 80 miles. The temperature's finally dropped. And I've met some interesting people; last night I sat at a bar by a waterwheel inside the city's walls, drinking with a young teacher named Olivier Duveau who told me he hated the violence in 'La Marseillaise'. 'France doesn't need a war song any more,' he said. 'It should have a love song, like, er, Edith Piaf's "La Vie en Rose"' (sample line: 'Nights of love no longer finish'). But then he sang 'La Marseillaise' with the biggest grin on his face. He'd just come back from years working in Canada, and singing it was the first time he actually felt French again, he said. So, yes, I leave Avignon feeling optimistic.

That is a mistake.

I'm heading for Châteauneuf-du-Pape, the home of some of France's most famous vineyards. It's only 10 miles away but a few minutes in, as I'm speeding along a main road, a wind starts up. God knows where it comes from. I turn a corner, and there it is, a wall that almost bounces me right into the side of a truck. I've got two panniers on my bike filled with recording equipment, maps, clothes and a range of bike tools I'm clearly never going to use, but it was like none of that weight mattered – the wind simply flung me aside. I start up once more, but just cycle into another wall of air, barely avoiding another truck – and this one had been giving me about three metres' space, having seen the first incident. I get round the next corner, which seems to offer some protection, and am about to breathe out in relief when it starts to rain. It's like the weather itself is trying to tell me this trip's a bad idea. I eventually make it off the main road, and follow some winding lanes to take refuge in a village cafe. The sun decides to come out as soon as I close the door.

It's only 10.30 a.m., but there's already a couple inside having some wine. The man has a big grey moustache and large, flabby cheeks. He sees me walk in, in my cycling shorts, and booms out, 'A lovely day for cycling, no?'

'It is, but the wind . . .' I reply.

'It's the mistral,' he says. 'What'd you expect?'

The mistral is one of the world's strongest winds, intermittently, but powerfully, blowing across southern France, including down the Rhône valley, causing every tree along it to grow bent; some of the people too, I imagine. I'd studied it fifteen years ago in school geography lessons but had obviously completely forgotten about it.

'I'm English,' I say, as if that's a good enough explanation.

'Ah yes, so many English move here. They come in summer when the wind is not so strong and fall in love,' he says. 'Then autumn comes and they can't leave soon enough.' He doesn't stop laughing to himself for some time. When he finally does, he asks what on earth I'm doing on a bike in October.

'That sounds like a great trip,' he says after I explain, 'but why are you following the soldiers? They're not the story of "La Marseillaise". They didn't write it. You should be going to the birthplace of, er . . .' He looks at his wife. 'What's the name of the man who wrote "La Marseillaise"?'

'How should I know?' she replies.

'Rouget,' says the cafe's owner, looking up from behind the counter. 'Oh yes, Rouget de Lisle. You should be going to wherever he was born.'

*

Claude Joseph Rouget de Lisle is the man who wrote 'Le Chant de Guerre pour l'Armée du Rhin'. He did it in one night of genius. That word – 'genius' – is rolled out to describe people far too often, but there's no question it's justified here. Rouget is the greatest one-hit wonder of all time. Listen to that melody. Read those words. You can't be just anyone and knock something like that out. But despite that, he's a man few people in France know about, let alone anyone from elsewhere. The only people who never forgot his name were other composers looking for a tune to borrow: Berlioz, Liszt, Rossini, Elgar, Schumann, Tchaikovsky, Debussy . . . the list of admirers is long.

Rouget was born in 1760 in the small town of Lons-le-Saunier in east France. It's the sort of place where the church dominates the landscape, the patisseries the social lives. Today, it's meant to be the centre of government for the department of Jura, but you'd hardly say the place is overrun with civil servants. It's quiet, feels almost half asleep, and in the 1700s it wouldn't have been much different, little more than a few muddy streets beneath the fat wooden steeple of the church.

Rouget's father was a lawyer and his mother, unsurprisingly for the time, was a housewife. For the first year of his life he was brought up in his father's office, a flat on the town's main street. But by the time he was two, he had moved to the family's house at Montaigu, a village on a hill nearby, where he grew up alongside six brothers and sisters, revelling in the fresh air and the space. Their house is still there, looking like a miniature stately home, its small front courtyard out of bounds behind padlocked iron gates.

Rouget wanted to be a musician. He played the piano, badly; the violin slightly better. But Rouget's dad was having none of it. It was the army or nothing. And so at the age of sixteen Rouget went off to Paris, alone, to military school. He did it with a new name, too. He'd been born simply Claude Joseph Rouget, but his dad bought the 'de Lisle' so that his son appeared aristocratic, officer material (a common practice at the time if you had the money and wanted a boost in status). There's no record of how much it cost.

Rouget spent the next fifteen years being trained, drilled and then shifted around France, but he spent whatever spare time he had trying to impress girls with songs he had written. He probably didn't need to try very hard: he was handsome with swept-back blonde hair curling down to his neck and looked rather like a rugby player who'd avoided being tackled all his life. There's a statue of him in Lons-le-Saunier today, sculpted by Frédéric Bartholdi, the man who designed the Statue of Liberty. Rouget is depicted mid-song, one hand clasped to his breast, and cuts such a dashing figure that he puts the men who actually live in the town to shame.

Rouget would probably have simply trundled along in life, writing the occasional song and fighting the occasional battle, if he hadn't been in Strasbourg on the German border on the night of 25 April 1792. He was there, along with thousands of other soldiers, because France had just declared war on Austria – Louis XVI backing the decision because he thought it would improve his popularity; most others doing so because they wanted to stop Austria rolling back the Revolution and restoring powers to Louis. It was to be Rouget's first proper war – his good looks were under threat for the first time. He seems to have been respected in Strasbourg, though, as that night he was invited to the mayor's house for dinner.

Mayor Dietrich apparently spent the evening boring everyone with his repeated complaints that there wasn't a patriotic song good enough to get the troops excited. Until a thought crossed his mind: Rouget was a musician; why not ask him to write one?

Rouget told a French historian what happened next. 'I went back to my room. I was slightly drunk, but I jumped to my violin, and with the first strikes of my bow those notes came. I had this fever. Sweat was pouring from me – it was soaking the floor – but I couldn't stop.'

There's a simple explanation for how he was able to write the words so quickly; he based some of them on the revolutionary slogans he'd heard shouted in the streets during the previous few years; others he literally stole from the revolutionary posters that were plastered to Strasbourg's walls. That's why the song is such a perfect summation of everything the French Revolution was about: blood, soil and the fatherland.

But that tune – there's no explanation for it apart from, again, genius. Well, there is: he could have stolen it. Some historians are adamant that Rouget didn't do any composing, let alone sweating, that night; that all he did was tweak a well-known tune from the time. But they have no proof. And even if that were the case, just choosing that melody – knowing that it was the one to inspire – there's art in that too. You only have to look at other anthems to realise that. Dozens were written in similar circumstances – when a country was under threat or at war – but none match 'La Marseillaise' as they should if songwriting was such an easy task.

I don't just mean famous anthems like 'The Star-Spangled Banner' or China's 'March of the Volunteers' (more on both in later chapters). Take Bulgaria's 'Dear Motherland', written by a teacher, Tsvetan Radoslavov, as he marched to defend his country from a Serbian invasion. 'Bulgarian brothers, let's go / . . . a heroic battle is approaching, / for freedom, justice,' read the lyrics to a plodding tune that can't make up its mind whether it's a hymn or a march. It's hardly '*Aux armes, citoyens!*'

Romania's 'Wake Up, Romanian!' fares somewhat better. It was written by a poet, Andrei Mureşianu, during his country's 1848 revolution against the Habsburg Empire – the same empire Rouget had been about to fight. 'Now or never, make a new fate for yourself, / To which even your cruel enemies will bow,' goes the first verse, and Andrei goes on to repeat that trick of using an insistent 'now' again and again. 'Now the cruel ones are trying . . . / To take away our language,' goes a later verse. 'Now or never, unite in feeling,' adds one more. '"Life in freedom or death!" shout all.' It's stirring, certainly – it apparently caused thousands to rebel – but it was commonly known as 'the Romanian Marseillaise' and that says it all. If it were anywhere near as good as what Rouget created, no comparison would have been needed.

No, what Rouget did on the night of 25 April is unparalleled among anthems.

The next morning Rouget took the song to Mayor Dietrich. He loved it. Just as importantly, Mayor Dietrich's wife loved it and worked up a proper arrangement on her clavichord. That night the mayor sang it at another gathering. Everyone there loved it too. Before Rouget had time to think, the song was printed up, and put in the hands of newspaper editors and town criers to ensure it reached the armies along the front. Just days after he'd written it, the song was out of Rouget's hands for ever, spreading all over France, and down to Marseilles where it found its way into the welcoming arms of 517 men in particular. That doesn't explain why Rouget's name has disappeared from history, of course. That requires a whole list of reasons, which could fairly be titled 'Rouget's Many, Many Mistakes'.

*

In August 1792, less than four months later, Rouget was suspended from the army and labelled a 'traitor to the fatherland' for refusing to follow the orders of the new, soon-to-be-republican regime. A year after that, at the start of Robespierre's Terror which tore through Paris, he was thrown in prison for allegedly being a royalist. He spent almost a year in there, escaping the guillotine partly because he wrote an awful song to back up his claim to be a true republican. In it, darkness covers the universe and 'impure vapours' take the throne, presumably a reference to Louis XVI, then there are the words 'It rolls . . .', the most undramatic reference to a king's head being cut off you could ever come across.

Rouget was released in 1794, and surprisingly soon let back into the army. Then, a year later, his song became the official national anthem of France – the victory song of the Revolution. But Rouget couldn't walk around Paris milking the achievement, celebrated as the author of one of the world's most famous songs (by that point, it had travelled to the US as well as most of Europe). Once a person was labelled a royalist in revolutionary France, it took a long time to shake off the label. He had to just sit on his hands, do as he was told and bide his time. He got a poor job liaising with the Dutch embassy in Paris.

His life should have got better with the rise of Napoleon, and indeed for a while it looked as though things for him might be getting back on track. He was close to Napoleon's wife, Josephine (there were rumours of an affair), and she nudged her husband until one day he gave Rouget extra work, asking him to ferry gifts to the Spanish royal family like a cut-price ambassador (Josephine used Rouget's appointment to commit fraud, getting him to take Parisian novelties with him so she could avoid export taxes).

Rouget could have simply done a good job and gradually re-established his reputation. Unfortunately, he was a letter writer, the sort of person who thinks nothing of sending a ten-page missive to his boss every time he has a problem, and spends the first nine of those failing to get to the point. Worse, he was a letter writer who didn't get disheartened, a man who believed that truth and honesty would always win out. So when Napoleon didn't write back to his first rant, Rouget simply sent him another letter, and another, and another, getting more wound up with each line.

The letters all started because some Frenchmen stole a Dutch ship along with several million francs' worth of cargo. The Dutch were unable to get their money back, even after going to the courts. A travesty, Rouget thought; the ultimate insult to these brave allies of France. How could Napoleon think he'd keep the loyalty of that country and its 200,000 soldiers if he couldn't even keep their ships safe? So Rouget wrote Napoleon a letter on their behalf, pleading for justice. And that letter led to lots and lots more. And after a few, they stopped saying anything about the Dutch and just became personal.

'Bonaparte,' he writes in one, 'you've lost yourself, and what's worse, you've lost France with you . . . Whatever your plan, you've misplaced it, whatever your projects they've become a catastrophe.' In another he simply says: 'Are you happy? I can't believe it.' Some of the letters are devastating assassinations of life in Napoleonic France. 'The national spirit is nothing but fake enthusiasm,' he writes. 'The national interest has become the interests of one family, the national glory nothing but the foul sewer of sycophancy.' He takes apart priests, generals, judges and officials. They're all liars and thieves, bringers of 'the stupid tyranny under which we're graced'. He occasionally gives Napoleon credit, says he'll be able to turn things around, and pretends he didn't mean anything he'd just said. But those platitudes are tossed in at the end: a few words that clearly aren't going to stop the flames started by the thousands before. It takes some guts – or a spectacular lack of judgement – to write letters like that.

Napoleon, unsurprisingly, didn't take well to any of these missives and he did what anyone would: he disowned 'La Marseillaise', suspending the decree that had made it the anthem in 1795, letting his hatred of it be well known and calling for other songs to be played in his presence instead. The song wouldn't inspire a revolution against *him* and neither would the man who wrote it. By the early 1800s – just a decade after writing the song – Rouget was penniless in Paris and being spied on by the police.

You can pass over the rest of Rouget's life pretty quickly. He kept on trying to carve out a stable career as a songwriter – he wrote over 200 songs and a number of musical plays. Unfortunately none of them were any good. Whatever perfect alignment of inspiration and ability Rouget had enjoyed on that one night seemed to have left him. The musicals were the sort that got closed down after opening night; the songs the sort that couldn't even please a drunk. Rouget was forced to move back to his parents' house. He was then forced to sell it. He was imprisoned for debts. He took up debt collecting. He eventually tried to commit suicide, but failed at that too.

At one point he even went into porn. A few weeks before going to Marseilles, I visited Lons-le-Saunier and was taken around Rouget's childhood home by the town's dapper head of tourism, Dominique Brunet. The flat is now a museum and in a display case I spotted a document, a song manuscript. I could tell it wasn't 'La Marseillaise', but I couldn't make out the words properly, especially as half of them were hidden behind card. I asked Dominique what it was about. He ummed and aahed and looked embarrassed before turning to an assistant, who giggled.

'Do you have to know?' he asked, pained. 'It's about this girl, Rosette. She's beautiful, and she's bathing in a river. Then a man comes along. And . . . well . . . you know . . . they start having sex. Shall we move on?'

While Rouget was trying his hand at smut, Napoleon was at war with most of Europe, trying to spread France's values of liberty and freedom (the freedom to be ruled by Napoleon). But he began to suffer serious defeats in Russia and Germany. Millions died and his power started to wane. As the defeats mounted, he became so desperate he even started tolerating the singing of 'La Marseillaise' again, hoping it, if nothing else, would bring his troops strength. It didn't help: in 1814 he was forced to abdicate and was exiled to a small island off the Italian coast. France reverted to monarchy and the new king, Louis XVIII, banned 'La Marseillaise' completely. You can't have an anti-monarchy song sung in a kingdom, after all, and it had provided the soundtrack for the overthrow of his brother. He chose a tune called 'La Parisienne' as France's anthem instead, a song so stuffy you feel you need to be wearing a powdered wig to sing it.

Rouget did write a song to the new monarch, trying to get in his good books. 'Long live the king [is] the noble cry of old France,' it started. But Louis XVIII treated it with the contempt such desperation probably deserved.

*

Rouget died in 1836, while living in a countess's house in the Parisian suburb of Choisy-le-Roi. Old army friends had found him the room, and he spent his final years there relatively happy, making fake 'original' manuscripts of 'La Marseillaise' to sell for drink money. He didn't even bother writing the original title of the song on them; they all simply said 'La Marseillaise'.

People wanted Rouget's song, not him, and he knew it. Is that the fate of all anthem composers, to be irrelevant compared to their songs? In Rouget's case, I just don't think so. If his personality hadn't got in the way, he'd at least have been far more known in his day than he was, and so maybe now.

You can still see the house Rouget died in today. It's yellow and black, timber-framed, almost medieval in appearance, with a high wall hiding a garden full of 200-year-old yew trees. It's the last thing you expect to see in modern Paris surrounded by dirty tower blocks and dual carriageways. Rouget had the smallest room at the back and its tiny four-paned window would have barely let in any light, even if it wasn't choked with soot as it is now. Today, the building is just a few doors from the Society of Young French Buddhists, whose courtyard has a pagoda in it and is full of men in saffron robes. I doubt any of them are fans of a song as violent as 'La Marseillaise'.

*

I gave up cycling. It happened four days in. That morning I set off from a town called Valence – 136 miles from Marseilles; only 364 miles from Paris. The day started well, with a pretty ride through vineyards where teams of workers were picking grapes, piling them into trucks, hundreds of boxes at a time, so much juice squeezing out of the grapes at the bottom it made me want to stop and find a glass.

But then I hit another hill. A big hill at that. And worse, one with that bloody mistral wind blowing straight down it and into me. The road had large stones at the side to mark each kilometre of the climb. At marker one I got off my bike and pushed. I could feel a blister on my foot threatening to pop with every step. I could hear my knees creaking – and when you're thirty-one, hearing your knees creak is a worrying sign. In an effort to get some energy I ate a preserved sausage I'd bought back in Aix-en-Provence but it was stuffed with olives and the salt just made me thirsty. I put on some music – dance tunes to trick me into thinking I was in an aerobics class and force me up the hill – but one of my headphones had stopped working and being deafened in one ear was hardly what I needed.

It was around that point I realised I had no other option but to take inspiration from the 517 marchers and try singing 'La Marseillaise'. I'd been studying it; I knew all the words now. Ask for any line and I'd give it back to you probably quicker than the French president. Give me the fifth and sixth! *'Entendez-vous dans les campagnes / MUUUU-GIR ces féroces soldats?'* The third in the chorus! *'Marchons! March-ONS!'* If there was ever a time to test the power of this song, it was now.

And so I got on my bike, stood up to pedal the first few metres to build up speed, then straightened my back, pushed out my chest and lifted my head high to sing. I wanted every one of those triumphant words echoing down the valley behind me. *'Allons enfants de la PATRI-E,'* I started no problem. 'Arise, children of the fatherland', it means. I punched out each syllable like a soldier. *'Le jour de gloire est arrivé!'* I went on just as strongly. The day of glory has arrived. My old choir teacher would be proud if he could see me now, I thought. But then I got on to the third line – *'Contre nous de la tyrannie'* – or, more to the point, one word into it, when I turned a corner, saw the road became twice as steep, felt the wind blasting my face with dust, and realised this wasn't for me. I just stumbled off. Pathetically. Miserably. I hadn't even reached the chorus.

My respect for the 517 Marseillais men grew in that moment.

They just kept going for twenty-eight days regardless of the weather. They were willing to march all the way across France for as vague a mission as 'striking down a tyrant'. That one song – just 302 words – drew qualities out of them I can't imagine.

Having said that, as I pulled out my map to find the nearest station, I did wonder what would have happened if they'd had trains back then. It was time to pack the cycling in and get a train to Lyon, I decided; to get back into an environment with concrete and skyscrapers and grime and dirt. The sort of place I'm used to. That decision turned out to be all the motivation I needed to get up the hill.

*

Throughout my time in France, I've been talking to people about 'La Marseillaise', trying to work out what it really means for France today.

I met a man called Didier Cantarel who was working in a wine cellar. Compact and shaven-headed with a big smile, he comically sang the anthem while pouring me a glass of his best red 'for tasting'. He then told me that he was a former soldier who'd served in Kosovo and Bosnia and had had to sing the anthem at too many people's funerals. It didn't mean he hated the song, though, and he insisted its violence has an admirable purpose. 'It's often forgotten that it's a song of values – that it's about protecting liberty,' he said. 'It's important to respect that; we can still learn from it. It is not like liberty has been achieved everywhere.'

I met an old woman in a bakery, who gave me a long lecture about how 'La Marseillaise' is important because it reminds everyone that France once ruled Europe. 'It gives us something to aim for,' she said, delicately picking a strawberry off a gateau ('They get stuck in my teeth'). But then she told me the last thing she actually wanted was for France to become a world power again. 'It'd be too much trouble,' she said. 'Look at the problems the USA has, China has. I'm happy where we are. As long as we can speak our language, I don't mind what happens.'

I met girls who didn't even know the first line to the song, and men who asked to see a song sheet before attempting to sing it. I met a rock musician who told me he loved it but couldn't admit that to his friends. I even met a hippy who told me he'd happily march from Marseilles to Paris today just for the sense of community it'd bring. But the people I hadn't been able to get much out of were those I most wanted to: France's immigrants. The Algerians and Tunisians who'd moved to France after the Second World War. Their children. They make up a good 10 per cent of the population of the country and they're the people who've got most to dislike about 'La Marseillaise' (especially the Algerians, given the eight years of war it took them to gain independence). They're also the ones who have provoked most discussion about it, having booed it at football games between France and Algeria, and between France and Tunisia.

I tried to get them to open up about it, talking to people in bars, in takeaways, in the street – even some kids break-dancing outside a theatre. They were all friendly people, but I got the most dismissive answers when I asked what they thought of 'La Marseillaise'. 'It's the national anthem,' they'd reply with a curt laugh. That was pretty much all they'd say, no matter how many follow-ups I tried. Although some would eventually become angry: 'Why'd you ask me about this?'

That should explain why I couldn't have been more grateful when I got to Lyon and Lahouari Addi, one of the country's leading French-Algerian academics, agreed to talk.

It's 9 a.m. when he swings into the cafe where we've arranged to meet. Unshaven, a scarf tossed around his neck and waving 'bonjour' to the staff, he looks every bit the French professor, not a hint of Algerian patriot about him. But almost as soon as he sits down he immediately starts speaking rapidly about

'La Marseillaise' in the tones of a man who knows an injustice
when he sees one, and who isn't even going to stop for pleas-
antries before railing against it. 'French people who're not aware
of colonial history don't see what is the problem,' he says. 'For
them, of course, "La Marseillaise" is a revolutionary anthem.
It's almost sacred. Just like the US anthem is for Americans.
But for most Algerians, "La Marseillaise" was something else.
It was colonial domination. It's under the aegis of "La
Marseillaise" that the French army tortured, killed, bombed
villages.

'I was in Algeria during the war – I was thirteen at independence – and I was aware that when we were hearing "La
Marseillaise", it was just like the French people hearing the
Germans' Nazi anthem. Just like that. "La Marseillaise", it has
been soiled by colonial domination. That's why no one will talk
to you about it, because they don't want to have to say there's
a problem and harm their relationship with France.'

Lahouari says all this despite being French himself. He chose
to become French after qualifying on residency. 'I respect my
country, my new country. I respect the people, the French way
of life. And I am grateful for them. I want to belong to this
national community and I would like to be faithful. But "La
Marseillaise" is a problem. It's impossible. It's the line about "*sang
impur*", impure blood, that's the biggest issue,' he adds. Lahouari
knows it refers to the people in the eighteenth century, but so
many see it as referring to immigrants today: 'I wish it would
be changed,' he says. I ask how long that could take. 'Maybe fifty
years.'

I bring up the subject of Algeria's anthem, a song called
'Kassaman' ('We Pledge' in English). It was written by a poet,
Mufdi Zakariah, while he was imprisoned by the French for
calling for independence and it's every bit as brutal as 'La
Marseillaise'. 'We pledge . . . / That we'll rise to revolution in
life or death,' it says:

> The drum of gunpowder is our rhythm,
> The sound of machine guns our melody.

By the third verse it's shouting, 'Oh France, the day of reckoning is at hand.' Many Algerians believe Mufdi wrote it using his own blood on his cell walls.

The anthems of other former French colonies don't come anywhere near to the vitriol of 'Kassaman'. Tunisia's 'Defenders of the Homeland' tries – 'The blood surges in our veins, / We die for the sake of our land,' runs the chorus – but it never says anything specific against the French. Others hardly mention the struggle for independence at all, preferring to fill their lines with thoughts of the future and the sort of bland statements usually reserved for greetings cards. 'We salute you, O land of hope,' goes 'L'Abidjanaise', Côte d'Ivoire's anthem. 'Let us live our motto: / Unity, work, progress,' adds the Republic of Congo's 'La Congolaise'. Mali's simply says, 'At your call, Mali, / for your prosperity'.

I read some of the lyrics of 'Kassaman' to Lahouari. 'Isn't that worse than "La Marseillaise"?' I ask.

'No, it's just an anthem,' he says.

But it keeps on saying you'll kill the French, I tell him. It's much worse than 'La Marseillaise' in that sense. 'La Marseillaise' doesn't actually mention any Algerians. Lahouari asks for the translation of 'Kassaman' I have. He reads it through once, twice, smiling occasionally as if remembering treasured lines he'd forgotten. 'No, I don't see it,' he says, finally. 'It doesn't say, "The French are inferior." It says we are enemies, sure. It says we have to kick the French out of Algeria. But that's all.'

I look at him slightly aghast. He picks up the words again. 'I'm sorry, but what's so strong here?'

He smiles, then adds: 'Let me tell you something that may seem ironic. The idea of "Kassaman" was taken from France. The idea of a national anthem is European. It's not from Muslim

countries. The only reason we have one is because of colonialism.'
And with that, he gets up, gulps down the remainder of his coffee
and shakes my hand, the argument apparently won. By the time
he's out of the door, I realise he's right: the fact Algeria's anthem
calls for a few French heads is nothing compared with one that
helped subjugate a country and is still sung by some, no matter
how few, with the hope they could do it again. You can't ever
separate these songs from their context. The fact so many
anthems lust for blood is also really Rouget de Lisle's fault, for
proving you can make such cries catchy. I'm about to run after
Lahouari to apologise, until I realise he's left me with the bill.

*

Lyon is severely underrated, and I can only think that this is
because it's a business city. The Rhône runs through it, but its
sunlit banks aren't for strolling along, hand in hand with a lover,
like Paris's Seine; they're for joggers. The old town with its
traboules – hidden passageways darting under and through buildings – isn't for tourists to gawp at; it's for gourmet ice-cream
parlours and restaurants experimenting in molecular gastronomy,
a treat for people who've spent their week earning sufficient
money to visit them. The city doesn't have art galleries like the
Louvre or Pompidou Centre – stuffed with masterpieces, their
names recognised worldwide; instead most of its art seems to
sit on the fringes, in warehouses which could just as well be
furniture shops.

But for all that, it's a city with a lot of charm, not least because
when you stumble across something unexpected among its sprawl
– tower blocks whose sides have been painted with Chinese dragon
fantasies, or a restaurant that only sells dishes made from blood
sausage – it stands out and stays with you. One of the shortest
chats I had with anyone about 'La Marseillaise' during my entire
time in France took place in Lyon. But it's also one of the most

memorable for that same unexpectedness. I was outside the
Basilica of Notre-Dame de Fourvière, the gothic church that stands
on the city's hill, and saw a priest filling up his car boot with bibles
while kids skateboard around him. He had gap teeth and hair
that stood out in clumps (I presumed it had been cut by another
priest). I approached him, expecting him to fail to understand my
French, or I his, or for him not to want to talk to a random man
in biking gear, but he took me asking about 'La Marseillaise' as
easily as taking a confession.

'I don't sing it because the words are an insult,' he said. 'You
know the history of the French Revolution? For the Catholic
Church that was a time of persecution. It's not the glorious page
in the history of France everyone says it is. There are other pages
you could choose to have a song about. "La Marseillaise", it's
childish. That's how I feel every time I hear it sung. I love France,
but I'd like a different hymn.' He got in his car but then wound
down the window. 'I like the music though,' he said.

That, at least, seems to be something everyone agrees on.

*

A few days later I'm on the outskirts of Paris, having taken the
train to the final place the marchers stopped at before entering
the capital: Charenton-le-Pont. Today it's a suburb that smells of
wealth, where children play in the park and the churchyard is
bustling with young families (the church has carved above its
door the revolutionary line 'Republique Française: Liberté, Egalité,
Fraternité'). The area is full of those four- or five-storey apartment
blocks that line every Parisian street, but here none are tatty;
they are all in pristine sandstone looking as if they could happily
be sitting alongside the Louvre.

Charenton is only twenty minutes from the middle of Paris
by *Métro*, with little more than a ring road, a cemetery and an
incinerator separating it from the city itself. But in 1792, on 29

July, it was a separate town. The marchers stopped here, preparing themselves to march into the capital, hoping they'd be welcomed as heroes and saviours. They were. 'Male and female . . . met them with bravos and hand-clapping in crowded streets,' a historian wrote. 'The Mother-Society [the Jacobins] came out as far as the Bastille-ground to embrace them, and they wended onwards, triumphant, to the town hall to be embraced by the mayor, to put down their muskets in the Barracks of Nouveau France, then towards the appointed tavern in the Champs-Élysées to enjoy a frugal patriot repast.'

Cycling along the route they took through the city is at times magnificent, past 20-metre-high columns topped with gold statues, through grand squares and boulevards, past *Métro* stations whose names seem to ring with revolutionary history: Liberté, Nation, Bastille. Okay, you also have to go along a few streets clogged with grimy cafes and teenagers practising karate in make-shift dojos, with men leaning out of apartment windows smoking dope, but it's not hard to imagine how those soldiers must have felt back then: like they were being given the keys to the city; like they were taking it for Marseilles.

In truth, the Marseillais men weren't treated with much love at first by the Paris authorities, and were split up and shunted between barracks. No one knew what to do with them – they arrived right in the middle of the tensest time of the Revolution, when things were coming to a head between the royalists and revolutionaries, with some very confused people stuck in the middle of it all. On 8 August, Paris's local government announced they would storm the king's palace – the Tuileries, where the royal family had been effectively under house arrest ever since their attempt to flee – unless the king's dethronement was announced. He didn't step down, obviously, leaving the Legislative Assembly, the French parliament, in a state of utter indecision. They wanted change – almost everyone in Paris did – but few of them actually wanted the king's removal and the establishment of a republic.

The decision was soon taken out of their hands. The next day, at midnight, an insurrectionary government known as the Paris Commune was set up. The churches rang their bells as an alarm and all the revolutionaries who'd been prepared for that signal began to march on the palace, emerging from the slums and workshops and bars, and crossing the bridges over the Seine. They'd had enough of the king. They blamed him for bankrupting the country. They blamed him for crop failures. They blamed him for the fact they were poor and hungry. Austria, the home of his wife, was an urgent threat. The king just had to be removed.

And who was at the head of these marchers? The Marseillais, of course, their red hats and their boisterous singing marking them out to everyone. If you hadn't known they were in town already, you did now.

King Louis XVI and Marie Antoinette didn't know what to do. They sat in the palace, while advisor after advisor gave contradictory recommendations and Louis tried to reach a decision. *'Marchons, marchons,'* he apparently said at last, an odd choice of words given the chorus of 'La Marseillaise'. He meant it as an instruction to leave the palace and go to the one remaining place in the city that even offered a chance of safety: the Legislative Assembly. And so king and queen and children got in a carriage surrounded by ranks of gunmen, just enough to protect them, and somehow barged their way out before the revolutionaries arrived.

The Marseillais found out they had left as soon as they reached the Tuileries. But it didn't stop them wanting to storm the building and occupy it to make sure the king could never come back. The palace was guarded by 950 Swiss Guards – in brightly coloured, ballooning trousers, armed with pikes and blunderbusses. The Swiss had been protecting the royals for centuries, and their outfits were meant to look proud, but at the height of that moment they must have looked like an insult to the Marseillais, like the very *'sang impur'* they'd sung about over and over again during their twenty-eight-day march. The Marseillais pleaded with them to leave, and when that didn't work they tried swinging their swords around, mocking them and begging. 'A pantomime', it's been called. But then, depending on whom you believe, either the Marseillais fired their cannons or the Swiss opened fire. The fighting began. The Swiss Guards were soon overwhelmed, hundreds of them quickly cut down. Others ran for freedom, but were chased and caught. They were dragged through the streets, savagely beaten to death. It was like the chorus of 'La Marseillaise' made flesh.

However, the actual events of 10 August aren't as important as the myth created that day, of men who gave their lives for liberty. The battle was not a battle. It was a rout, like a football crowd tearing through a city centre flipping cars. Only twenty of the Marseillais died, and that's not because they were brilliant fighters beating off opponents; it's because their side was over-whelmingly the stronger.

As soon as the battle was over, though, the storytelling began and the magnificence of the act grew with each telling until the truth no longer mattered. All the people of France knew was that a few hundred young men from Marseilles led the charge. Brave and courageous, they brought down the king. And as they did so, they sang a song. It didn't matter that they hadn't brought the king down at all or that they didn't have any hand in what happened next: the king being arrested almost as soon as he got to the Legislative Assembly; France becoming a republic a month later; Louis and Marie Antoinette losing their heads soon after that. The story was better than fact.

Word of the Marseillais soldiers soon spread south and everyone started claiming they knew them. People in Sens, Auxerre, Chalon, Tournus, all the places the Marseillais had marched through: all started asking each other, 'Don't you remember when they came through here? I told you they'd save this country,' regardless of whether they had seen them or not.

Everyone wanted to have borne witness. The fact that some of the Marseillais passed back through these places on their way home certainly helped build the myth, and banquets and spectacles were put on for them in many of the places they went.

There are no signs of the Revolution around the Tuileries today. Only the palace's gardens remain (the palace itself was burned to the ground in 1871), a place tourists stop for an ice cream in between visiting the Louvre and the Arc de Triomphe. Deckchairs are provided, and somehow never stolen.

It's a sunny morning when I arrive and I decide to have a triumphant sing of the anthem. It feels the appropriate thing to do – the way to mark finishing the trip – and unlike my previous attempt I'm confident I can actually get through the whole thing. I start singing and quickly draw bemused looks from the tourists passing by. It's unsurprising. This is what 'La Marseillaise' has become in much of the world – a novelty, a song simply to mean 'France' in films and adverts and on stadium loudspeakers. And here's an exhausted Englishman standing in far-too-tight shorts, singing in bad French. I've probably made a few people's day. But even if I were singing to an audience of French schoolchildren I doubt the reaction would be much different, since the more people I've spoken to, the more I've realised the song has lost much of the power it once had.

'La Marseillaise' meant everything to this country when it was written in 1792; everything in 1830, when the then king, Charles X, was overthrown in the 'Three Glorious Days' uprising (it was brought back as the anthem for a while before the country realised it was still under a monarchy). It meant everything still in 1879, when it became the national anthem for a third time; during the First World War, when German armies advanced across French soil; and during the Second World War, when Germany actually took control of the country. (The collaborationist Vichy government used a song called 'Maréchal, Nous Voilà!' as its anthem, which is quite a jolly piece of French *chanson* if you ignore the propaganda of the words addressed to its leader: 'Marshal, we your boys all swear, / to serve you and follow your path'). 'La Marseillaise' continued to mean something after the war too, when it became a rallying cry to rebuild the country – something to bring out whenever people had had enough of repairing their homes.

But from cycling – and, okay, getting trains – around the country, I'm not sure whether it can be said to carry anything like that meaning now. It's certainly respected – wrapped up with other great clichés of French identity – but fewer people seem to cling to it as they once did. Too many people I met during my trip, your everyday French, said they saw it as much as an overblown piece of fun as anything else and could only um and aah when asked to describe their feelings about it. Yes, it was sung with gusto following the Charlie Hebdo terrorist attacks in January 2015, at rallies across the country, but it wasn't in the all-out way it had been before (there are plenty of videos of people singing it where they look more uncomfortable than proud, as if wondering whether by doing so they were playing into an anti-Muslim and anti-immigrant sentiment they didn't want to encourage).

And yes, in November 2015, following the Paris attacks, there were a few days, weeks even, when it looked like it had become unarguably everything an anthem should be again – unifying and inspiring, a symbol of defiance and solidarity. Even the English sang it. But then far right groups started bellowing it too, and the cracks reappeared in its image, the anxiety it provoked returned, and it fell back to being an anthem some would prefer to do without.

The place that hammers home the song's change in status to me is the last that I visit in Paris: the Invalides, the home of the French military – a huge complex that sits on the south bank of the Seine with both the Tuileries gardens and the Eiffel Tower within sight. The Invalides is a mandatory visit for almost every Parisian child. Around 1.4 million people come here each year to see Napoleon's tomb, which sits at the back of the building's chapel, shut off from the church itself to avoid overpowering it. Inside is a monument fit for any of the great religious buildings of the world: St Peter's Basilica, the Taj Mahal, Istanbul's Hagia Sophia. A huge red granite tomb – big enough to house ten men, audacious even for a self-proclaimed emperor – sits atop a green plinth. On the floor, a yellow sun spreads out from the bottom of the plinth as if to grace all visitors with Napoleon's light.

Visitors aren't actually allowed to approach the tomb, of course; they have to circle it, paying their respects by walking past classical pillars and carvings depicting Napoleon's achievements. He didn't just bring liberty to Europe, freeing it from its old bonds of feudalism and religion, these carvings tell you; he also overhauled France's education system, introduced the metric system, and even set up the Legion of Honour to award France's greatest artists, thinkers and soldiers. The room is almost overwhelming in its grandeur. But just a few yards from here, in the chapel itself, down some steps behind the altar, is another chamber. This one is about as different as you can get from the ostentation next door. It's only about twenty feet long and is almost pitch black, lit by just a couple of weak candles. Along the walls are some graves, each marked by a black marble plaque. Behind those are some bones, bodies, ashes, and in a few cases, hearts.

One of the plaques belongs to Rouget de Lisle.

I stand looking at Rouget's plaque for some time. Given how much he and Napoleon hated each other, I can't help but smile at the fact they're now so close. But it does make you feel somewhat disappointed for him: that this is where he's ended up, hidden away in a dingy half-light, forgotten. I've been told I'm the first person to specifically visit his grave since . . . actually, no one can remember anyone ever visiting his grave.

That said, there are two things you have to know about this resting place. The first is that it might not actually be Rouget de Lisle in there. The rumours are that it's actually a young girl's bones, perhaps those of his own bastard child. His coffin was moved from a cemetery in the Paris suburbs during the First World War, carried in a glamorous carriage and decked in the red, white and blue of the *drapeau tricolore*. It was met by cheering crowds desperate for a wartime morale boost. But the belief among some is that the gravediggers dug up the wrong plot, the coffin's small size being the biggest giveaway.

The second is that whoever's bones they are, they may not stay here long. Rouget's plaque sticks out from the wall, slightly askew, like a painting about to comedically fall off its hook. This is because he's not actually meant to be here – he's meant to be in the Panthéon, the resting place of many of France's great writers and artists. He's not really a soldier, after all; he's a song-writer, and one of the greatest France has ever had, even if he only composed the one great song.

So why hasn't he moved yet? It's politics and bureaucracy, apparently. But I think the real reason is that France doesn't truly need him, or his anthem, right now. It hasn't really needed them since the 1960s when the country got back on its feet. It doesn't need the violence in the song, the ugliness of it. It doesn't wish to be reminded of the many wars it fought, the countries it colonised, or be forced by it to confront difficult questions about its future and identity.

But I think that situation could change, and when it does Rouget will be moved. Hopefully this won't be because France needs the war song again. Instead I hope it'll be because the French make peace with it, reclaiming it from the far right, so everyone – French-Algerians and Tunisians included – simply see it for what it is: a historical song of hope written at a time when the country needed one. When that happens, no one will worry any more about traipsing his coffin through the streets and the reaction it'll provoke. Instead they'll just quietly move Rouget to the Panthéon, to occasionally be stumbled across by curious visitors.

Made of Hundreds of Flowers

सयौं थूँगा फूलका हामी, एउटै माला नेपाली
सार्वभौम भइ फैलिएका, मेची-महाकाली।
प्रकृतिका कोटी-कोटी सम्पदाको आँचल
वीरहरूका रगतले, स्वतन्त्र र अटल
ज्ञानभूमि, शान्तिभूमि तराई, पहाड, हिमाल
अखण्ड यो प्यारो हाम्रो मातृभूमि नेपाल।
बहुल जाति, भाषा, धर्म, संस्कृति छन् विशाल
अग्रगामी राष्ट्र हाम्रो, जय जय नेपाल।

—

Woven from hundreds of flowers, we are one Nepali
  garland,
Sovereign and spread out, from Mechi to Mahakali,
A playground for nature's wealth unending,
Independent and unalterable, by the blood of heroes,
Land of knowledge, land of peace, the plains, hills
  and mountains,
Undivided, this is our dear motherland, Nepal,
Of many ethnicities, languages, religions and cultures
  of incredible sprawl,
This progressive nation of ours, all hail Nepal!

2

Nepal

DEFYING CONVENTION

It's 24 *Baisakh* in the year 2069 – or it might be 24 *Jestha* in the year 2070, I've not quite got a handle on the Nepalese calendar yet, which seems to operate about fifty years ahead of the rest of the world – and I'm sitting in the offices of Nepal's prime minister. They are disappointingly unfuturistic. The Singha Durbar – Lion Palace – sits almost right in the centre of pollution-choked Kathmandu, the only city I've ever been to where the taxi drivers feel the need to wear face masks. If you sneak a glance at it through its iron gates it looks magnificent, with dozens of columns fanning out from behind a long, shimmering pool, rather like the White House if it had been dropped on the site of the Taj Mahal. But up close, any magnificence it once had has long faded. The paint is cracking, a few window panes are missing and sparrows hop along the corridors as if they're used to having them all to themselves.

I'm here to meet Baburam Bhattarai, the prime minister himself (for now at least; Nepal seems to go through them like seasons). He's a handsome fifty-something, with greying, swept-back hair, a thick, brush-like moustache and sunken, inquisitive eyes. Last night, my interpreter, Ram, told me Baburam is the only politician in this country with any intelligence. 'He's very visionary and ambitious for the nation, a hero for many,' he said. 'I think my mother would like to marry him.'

What he failed to mention is that just a few years ago Baburam also happened to be the intellectual figurehead behind a Maoist revolution – an armed uprising that dominated Nepalese life for a decade, caused over 15,000 deaths and thousands more 'disappearances', and led to the overthrow of the country's royal family. It also shattered Nepal's image as that peaceful Himalayan kingdom people visit when they have a midlife crisis and decide they need to climb some mountains. Baburam issued forty-point 'lists of demands', calling for things like 'the invasion of imperialist and colonial culture to be stopped' (that meant banning Bollywood movies, as far as I can tell, India having long dominated Nepalese life), and had to live in hiding because so many people wanted him arrested or dead. His revolution was apparently funded through bank robberies and extortion, and intimidated as many people into supporting it as it truly converted. I'm slightly scared that I'm about to shake this man's hand, to be honest.

But the revolution is precisely the reason I've come to meet Baburam, because whenever the Maoists took over a village, one of the first things they did was stop people singing the national anthem, something many schoolchildren had been doing every morning until then. That song was called 'May Glory Crown You, Courageous Sovereign' and, as the name suggests, it was a one-verse love letter to the then king. 'Our illustrious, profound, awesome, glorious ruler,' it began,

> May he live for years to come,
> May his subjects increase,
> Every Nepali, sing this with joy.

The Maoists made everyone sing folk songs instead, or, better yet, songs crammed with the words 'hammer' and 'sickle'. They even had their own anthem: a bizarre Nepali pop version of 'The Internationale', the great French workers' song ('Rise up, damned of the world!'). When they did finally agree peace, deciding to work within the political system after the public started protesting against the king in Kathmandu, one of their terms was that the anthem be changed. If anyone was going to offer me a convincing argument about the importance of anthems today, chances are it'd be Baburam.

Unfortunately, he's late. Three hours, by my watch. I probably shouldn't complain – the prime minister of Nepal's got a lot of important things to do, I'm sure – but he's left me waiting in a windowless, strip-lit office filled with underlings and we seem to have run out of conversation. For a moment, I think about trying to start a discussion about the benefits of Maoism compared to Marxism, Leninism or even Marxist-Leninism, but instead I tell them a story about two friends of mine who visited Nepal right in the middle of the revolution.

Alan and Tricia, a polite middle-aged couple, were trekking in the Himalayas one day in the early 2000s when they stopped to camp for the night on a school field. They'd just set up their tent and were getting ready to cook when two dozen Maoists ran out of the trees straight for them; an equal mix of men and women, all in perfect formation, all in uniform and all with guns pointed straight at the camp. As soon as they reached the tents, they shouted at Alan and Tricia's Nepalese guides, forced them to the ground and searched their pockets for money. Then the female soldiers marched Tricia off. It seemed like minutes passed. It was probably just seconds. Finally, a young commander strode up to Alan. 'Can I have your money?' he said in English. Alan was terrified – what the hell was happening to his wife? – but at the same time the question seemed strange. Why is he asking for my money rather than just taking it? Alan wondered. So he took a risk.

'No,' he said. The commander looked confused.

'Er . . . Okay, can I have your camera?'

Alan said no to that too. After a lot more of this back-and-forth, the Maoists left with just some food and medical supplies.

The couple were about to celebrate the simple fact they were alive when the Maoists came running back out of the woods, guns raised once more. They headed straight for Tricia and she prepared herself for the worst.

'You are the first woman we've done this to,' they said. 'Could you tell us how we can improve the experience for next time?'

I finish the story and look around at the staff – all Maoists themselves – who'd been listening intently. They start rapidly talking to each other, the ones who understand English translating for the others, occasionally pointing at me. I expect a few snatches of laughter here and there, but everyone stays stern-faced and I realise what a stupid thing I've done. I've basically spent five minutes calling them incompetent, haven't I? Oh God, they're going to call off the interview. Maybe they'll rough me up a bit before chucking me out. Do they still have guns? They fall quiet then one turns to me. This is it.

'We know your friends!' he says, breaking into a grin and reaching out to clasp my shoulder. 'They're famous across Nepal. They're the only ones who ever said "No". In ten years! You must give us their address so we can send them a letter. You wait until Baburam hears this!'

*

Nepal is often thought of as the most spiritual country in the world. The birthplace of Buddha, it's the country where you go to find enlightenment, either by watching the sun rise over the Himalayas or by bowing down before a golden stupa, with monks chanting nearby and the *clack-clack-clack* of prayer wheels echoing around you. Tibet may have once rivalled it, but then the Chinese moved in. India once did too, but every skyscraper that goes up there seems to dent that position.

Anyone who visits may wonder how Nepal has managed to maintain its reputation unblemished. On my second day here, I went to Pashupatinath, one of the world's holiest Hindu sites, a maze of intricately carved temples dedicated to an incarnation of Shiva, with monkeys jumping all over them. People go there to cremate relatives before pushing their ashes into the polluted Bagmati river. I watched from the hillside as one family cremated their father, his widow wailing as she covered him in bright yellow and orange powder before setting his head alight, men rushing to put wood under him to get the fire going. But as the family wept, struggling to comfort each other, a group set up a disco opposite and started playing thumping pop music. A group of sadhus – holy men – appeared, dreadlocks piled on heads, faces white with make-up, and started dancing up and down the river-bank trying to get tourists to pay for pictures or dance with them, as if the cremation was little more than an annoyance.

But despite almost every visitor witnessing events like that, Nepal's image doesn't change. Perhaps because some things are geared to protect it. The country's anthem, for one, seems almost made to reinforce that image: it's beautiful and uplifting, like the mountain views you get as soon as you leave the capital. The song is called 'Sayaun Thunga Phool Ka' ('Made of Hundreds of Flowers'). Lyrically, it's eight simple lines about how the 28 million Nepalese – all 130-odd ethnic and caste groups – are actually one garland, 'woven from hundreds of flowers'. 'Of many races, languages, religions and cultures of incredible sprawl,' it goes, '… all hail Nepal.'

But it's not the words that make Nepal's anthem unique; it's the music.

*

You can split anthems into four main musical types. By far the largest group is anthems that sound like church hymns. 'God Save the Queen' has a lot to answer for, as does colonialism. If you travel around Africa or Asia you'll stumble across dozens of anthems that sound as if they were written by a priest after a walk in the dewy English countryside. Some of them even turn out to be actual hymns. Take Zambia's, Tanzania's and South Africa's. All of those are based on a song called 'Nkosi Sikelel' iAfrika', or 'Lord Bless Africa', written by a Methodist school choirmaster, who, in turn, allegedly stole the tune from a Welsh hymn. The worst songs of this type are found in the Caribbean and the small islands that dot the Pacific, many of which are so filled with religion there's no room left for anything else. You only have to read the title of 'Tuvalu for the Almighty' ('Be our song for ever more!') to know what its two verses focus on, while Samoa's anthem claims the country's flag 'is the symbol of Jesus, who died on it for [us]'.

The second type of anthems are those that sound like military marches. Russia's is a prime example. Stalin chose the tune himself to be the anthem of the Soviet Union – the only music people would hear as they languished in his gulags. It has a striking staccato melody and it doesn't take much to picture rows of soldiers, tens deep, marching through Moscow to it, turning as one to salute their beloved leader. Unsurprisingly, a lot of dictators tend to go for this type of anthem. (Russia's was actually dropped following the collapse of the Soviet Union, but Vladimir Putin brought it back shortly after he first became the country's president.)

Alongside the hymns and marches, you also have fanfare anthems, once particularly common in the Middle East. These consist of little more than a few trumpet flourishes (Jordan's and Saudi Arabia's barely last thirty seconds), which may seem apt for Islamic countries where music is sometimes more tolerated than encouraged but tend to be found more often in the Emirates. This type raises the obvious question of how something so short could inspire anyone to patriotism, but for a sultan they probably answer the bigger question of how he can get through official ceremonies as quickly as possible.

Finally – and saving the best for last – you have the epic anthems of South America. These are tunes that seem to ignore every convention of anthem composition. They're not short (FIFA, football's governing body, demands anthems are under ninety seconds, but these don't even think of stopping for four, five or even six minutes – at matches they only play the intros), and they're not easy to sing either. Instead they're set out like mini-operas, with rollicking openings in which every part of the orchestra seems to try to out-play the others; melodramatic middle sections where oboes and flutes whimsically take the lead; and huge, over-the-top finishes, with multiple false endings. They're songs that feel as if they were written for the stage, to accompany scenes of lovers being torn apart then explosively reuniting, or scenes of family feuds ending in gut-wrenching deaths. It's not a surprise that opera composers wrote most of them, although perhaps it is that most of those composers weren't from anywhere near the continent. Chile's fantastic anthem, for instance, was written by a Spaniard, Ramón Carnicer, who'd never set foot in the country (Chile's London ambassador begged him to write it because the anthems his country's own composers had managed weren't up to scratch).

*

So you have your hymns, your marches, your fanfares and your epics, but then you have Nepal's. There isn't a brass instrument or rattling snare to be heard in 'Sayaun Thunga Phool Ka'. There's no trumpet flourish for a king, or stately rhythm for soldiers to parade to. There's no cymbal-crashing ending and nothing that could be hummed in four-part harmony. Instead there's a folk tune, and one that, in the version you hear throughout Nepal, is played on the cheapest of Casio keyboards at that. It's little more than a few synthesised strings bouncing up and down an addictively sweet melody and the sound of some hand drums tapping out a bassline. And because of that simplicity and difference, it's wonderful. It's the sort of music you imagine schoolgirls singing as they skip to class or farmers using to pass the time while stood thigh-deep in water in the middle of a rice paddy. If you heard it in a restaurant here midway through a plate of lentils, you wouldn't look up – it'd fit in perfectly with all the other songs coming out of the radio. It couldn't seem a more fitting song for this country. Although, obviously, if you heard it at the Olympics, or at a palace, you'd think something had gone seriously wrong.

Nepal isn't entirely alone in having an anthem that actually sounds like the country it comes from. Most of the 'Stans' of central Asia have anthems that sound as though they couldn't have come from anywhere but former Soviet states. They trudge along in minor keys, like armies across the steppe. Mauritania's, similarly, is an astonishing piece of music that's like a trip into the Maghreb's most menacing souk. Then there's Puerto Rico's 'La Borinqueña', which has a certain heat to its trumpets, a remnant of the fact it was originally a dance tune called 'Gorgeous Brunette', written for swinging partners around rum-soaked music halls. But on the whole you'd be surprised how rare it is to have such local character in an anthem. There are no rumba rhythms in Cuba's, for instance, and no bossa nova in Brazil's; there's no oud being plucked in Iran's and no highlife guitars in Ghana's. It's as if everyone's afraid of sounding unique – as if they heard 'God Save the Queen' and 'La Marseillaise' and decided, 'This is the music that means patriotism, let's copy this,' even when their musical heritage couldn't be further from the West's.

But even bearing that handful of examples in mind, no one has taken the leap into local music quite like Nepal. It's surprising that a country this small is the only one to have had the guts to stand up to 450 or so years of anthem history and pick such a unique tune. It's also a surprising choice for another reason:

'Sayaun Thunga Phool Ka' isn't at heart a peaceful song as the music and lyrics imply, but a song of revolution and struggle. It's also one with a far from gentle story behind it, one that involves four men: Baburam on one side; the former king, Gyanendra, on the other; and two poor composers – one poet, one musician – trapped in the middle.

*

Pradip Kumar Rai is, I'm almost certain, the only man to have met his wife thanks to an anthem. On 1 December 2006, a poem Pradip had written – under the pen name Byakul Maila – was chosen over 1,271 others to become 'Sayaun Thunga Phool Ka', Nepal's new anthem, and help end over 200 years of devotion to Nepal's royal family (Nepal was created in 1769 when a family called the Shahs came down from the hills to conquer a host of princely states; in 2006, King Gyanendra was still on the throne, but the Maoist agreement meant it was clear the monarchy would soon be abolished).

From that day, Pradip, then a shy thirty-four-year-old from a one-road village in the eastern mountains, became a celebrity. He got invited to events all over Nepal, where people would drown him in garlands made from bright orange marigolds, piling them around his neck until he could barely see, or else they'd ask to touch his feet, the most respectful gesture a Hindu can make. People would come up to him in the street ('They always recognised my moustache'), while bus drivers would refuse his fare. Once he crashed while driving in Kathmandu, smashing another car's sidelights. The driver demanded all the money Pradip had, until he realised who he was.

'Wait, aren't you Byakul Maila?' he said. 'I can't charge you anything.'

As the plaudits built up, a family friend, Nanu, kept calling him to ask how he was doing and where he was going next, to tell him she was so happy he'd brought attention to their home region. Pradip didn't get the hint until one day she came to his house to say thanks in person and asked to greet his wife. 'I haven't got one yet,' he said. She blushed.

Pradip tells me all this with a proud grin on his face. We're drinking milky spiced masala tea in the front room of the house he rents in Lalitpur, a city just to the south of Kathmandu. His daughter is sitting on his knee in a pink dress, pulling faces and throwing a Barbie doll around, while Nanu is hiding in the kitchen cooking lunch, embarrassed to hear herself mentioned. The walls are covered in silver plaques and a portrait of Pradip – prizes he's been given for writing the anthem. It feels like the home of a genuinely content family and that's the story Pradip would like me to tell. But the problem is his tale of overnight success isn't as straightforward as he makes out. Pradip finishes talking then looks at me expectantly, asking me what I want to know next. I tell him I'd heard he almost had the anthem taken away from him as quickly as he won it; that everything he has today almost didn't come about. 'What happened?' I ask.

Pradip struggles to keep smiling.

*

Pradip came to Kathmandu to study law. He hadn't wanted to, but his older brothers had decided it would be a good course for him. It was here he started writing poems, feeling lost and homesick in a city of about a million where there's no escape from the honks of car horns and the whirr of generators. He was a fan of the country's then king, Birendra, as most Nepalese were. Birendra was your archetypal 'man of the people' – a king who wore thick-rimmed, oversized glasses that looked as if a doctor had forced them on him, and who was known more for serving drinks in plastic tumblers at parties than any extravagance. He'd once held almost total power, enabling him to act like a god among men – some thought he was actually the living incarnation of the Hindu god Vishnu – but in 1990 he allowed political parties to form and elections to happen. Some of the politicians who came to power proved so venal many started to wish he hadn't.

But Pradip's pro-royal outlook changed somewhat in 2001. On 1 June that year, the royal family gathered for dinner at their palace in Kathmandu. One of Birendra's sons, Crown Prince Dipendra, suddenly fell down, apparently drunk. He was taken to his room, helped to bed and left with some cigarettes filled with a substance no one's ever identified, probably cocaine. But he soon reappeared, walking back into the room where everyone was drinking, only now dressed in army fatigues and carrying an assault rifle, a Glock pistol and a shotgun. He smiled at one of his uncles and then shot Birendra three times in the chest. He then briefly left the room before returning to shoot his brother-in-law and an uncle, then left and returned a third time and shot Birendra once more in the head. Birendra's last words were apparently, 'What have you done?' Dipendra then shot another uncle and several aunts, his sister, and some family friends. Other guests saved themselves by cowering behind a sofa. He then walked out into the garden, his mother, the queen, one of those chasing after him. Perhaps she wanted some kind of explanation or just to hold him and try, somehow, to make it all right. But he shot her, then shot himself.

There are many explanations for why he did it – that Birendra had disagreed with his choice of wife; that some past members of the royal family had suffered from insanity and he'd inherited their genes – but it feels like no explanation could ever help anyone understand that evening.

You can visit the palace today. It's now a museum with royal knick-knacks everywhere, including a china dog collection. The rooms where the massacre took place have been knocked down, and all that's left of them are a few small stone walls, making it look rather like an archaeological excavation site. There are signs pointing to spots on the ground that say things like, 'Queen Aishwarya fatally wounded here.' Nepalese queue to take photos.

After the massacre, Birendra's brother Gyanendra was named king (he had actually been king once before, for a few weeks at the age of four, when the rest of his family fled to India fearing they were about to be killed). Fat and with a drooping mouth, Gyanendra was known as a hard-nosed businessman with interests in everything from turpentine to incense sticks. He had an air of arrogance, disdain even, and was far from popular. Many Nepalese actually assumed he was behind the massacre, trying to secure the throne for himself with the help of Indian security forces. The fact he was not at the dinner that night was apparently all the evidence they needed; his wife might have been one of those shot, but that was clearly just a ploy to divert people's attention. (The Maoists tried to encourage this conspiracy theory, Baburam writing in a newspaper that no one should accept Gyanendra as king and suggesting they'd been negotiating peace with Birendra all along.)

When Gyanendra received the crown, the Maoist uprising had already been going for five years but had been confined mainly to the western hills. It had begun with Baburam's forty demands, which were issued in a very polite letter in February 1996 (Baburam was the group's second in command behind a military leader called Prachanda). The letter pointed out that over 70 per cent of Nepal's population was in poverty, then called for everything from the abolition of the royal family's 'rights and privileges', to Nepal being declared a secular state; the confiscation of landlord's property to free medical care. 'If there are no [positive moves] we would like to inform you we will be forced to adopt the path of armed struggle,' it added, politely. The 'people's war' began a few days later. The next few years saw attacks on police and government offices, mixed in with periodic ceasefires. But after Gyanendra assumed the throne, the rebellion stepped up a gear. The Maoists killed forty policemen on his birthday – an unwelcome gift if ever there was one – and a few weeks later they attacked the army for the first time.

It was about this time that Pradip first learned that the Maoists were banning the old royal anthem. 'I was at home and I read in the newspaper they were making people sing communist songs instead and it made me feel that maybe there was something wrong with it. "Why would they ban it?" I asked myself. "Was there a problem with the king or not?"' It was the first time he'd ever questioned the monarchy.

Gyanendra went on to do everything wrong in his quest to stop the Maoists. He called in the army to attack them. He repeatedly dissolved parliament. In 2005, he took full power for himself, then started banning newspapers and cutting off phone lines and internet access. He also started having anyone who showed opposition arrested. At one point, he declared a curfew and ordered those who broke it to be shot. Because of all this, he soon didn't just have the Maoists against him, but most of the rest of the population too. Baburam knew an opportunity when he saw one. The Maoists announced a ceasefire and began to work with the existing political parties to create a future without the royal family in it.

On 3 May 2006, Nepal's government and the Maoists jointly announced an end to the uprising. The king's days were numbered (although he somehow scraped along with his title until May 2008). Two weeks later, the anthem was scrapped. A few weeks after that, the competition for a new one was launched and Pradip started to write his song. The rules to the contest said the new anthem should be a maximum fifty words; the description of what it should be about – 'Nepal's natural beauty, its special cultural identity' and so on – ran to twenty-seven, not exactly leaving much room for creativity.

*

I can tell we've reached the point in Pradip's story where things are about to go wrong when I ask him a simple question: 'So, were you always patriotic?' It's the sort you'd expect the briefest of answers to: 'Of course! Why would I have entered the contest if I wasn't?' But once Pradip starts answering, he seemingly can't stop. He talks about his childhood and the day 'I literally touched the soil and decided I'd never leave'. He talks of listening to patriotic songs on a radio an uncle bought for him. He talks about everything he did to improve the life of his village, and his work in a lawyer's association fighting to improve people's rights. And then he talks about attending protests against the king in Kathmandu, getting shot at with rubber bullets and having to hide in a ditch. He speaks for so long my tea gets cold and my interpreter Ram's voice starts to crack from talking so much. It's as if Pradip feels he needs to prove his credentials to himself, let alone to me, which is somewhat understandable given what happened after he was named as the lyricist of the country's new anthem.

For almost two weeks, Pradip was one of the main news stories in Nepal. The national newspapers were filled with comments about him; it was the same on radio and television. He was famous. But it wasn't all the overwhelmingly positive attention he might have hoped for. Much of it was instead people arguing about whether he should have won or not. There were the kind of complaints you'd expect: people who didn't like his words, who complained he didn't mention the 'martyrs' who died during the people's war, or who, conversely, complained he'd used the word 'blood' and who felt the country needed to move on from the fighting. Then there were also those who complained about his ethnicity – Pradip is a Rai, a group that makes up just 2 per cent of the country's population. One of the main reasons the Maoists had risen to popularity was by promoting minority rights, saying people could speak their own language and celebrate their own culture rather than having to follow the traditions of the dominant high-caste Brahmans. Giving Pradip the anthem was clearly just a sop to them, some said. 'I was the victim of a dangerous ethnicist contraction,' claimed the competition's runner-up, despite none of the judges having known Pradip's name, let alone his ethnicity, until he was into the final three.

All of this was, by and large, silly – jealousy mixed with conspiracy – that was always going to die down as soon as people ran out of breath. But there was one accusation that couldn't just be shaken off: that Pradip was a monarchist. It took journalists all of a day to discover he'd once edited a poetry collection that included a poem by Gyanendra. 'We are very proud to have the opportunity to include a composition by His Majesty,' Pradip had written in that book's introduction. That one sentence – fifteen short words – was like a match to paper.

The level of scrutiny became such that it wouldn't have been much of a surprise if people had been found going through his bins, or breaking into his house hoping to find hand-drawn pictures of Gyanendra with hearts around them. Few people seemed to ask why a monarchist would enter a competition to create an anthem for a new, soon-to-be-republican Nepal. And fewer still pointed out the book had been published years before, when practically everyone was a monarchist. To their credit, Pradip's publisher did. 'If we are going to ask questions about [him] on the basis of one sentence, who among us is pure?' they said in a letter to Nepal's main newspaper. But a few weeks later, Pradip's anthem was still 'in quarantine'. He had won the competition, he was due a £4,500 prize, and he was being invited to ceremonies and getting phone calls from his future wife, but there was seemingly no guarantee his words would become the anthem. Pradip was just left anxious and confused, unable really to relax for months: the committee didn't approve the final anthem until the following April; the government until a few months after that.

I try to get Pradip to talk about this time, but it's clearly hard for him to do so. It's what he's been trying to avoid ever since I walked into his house. He looks at the floor and speaks quietly. 'The attention, the interviews, all of this went on for so long. It was like being stuck in a black hole. I had heart pains, headaches. Everything was hurting. Obviously it was a stressful time, but I tried to suppress my anger and fear and fury with what was happening. I was trying to be a man! Maybe I had some short-comings and weaknesses, but I told myself I had always done the right thing. One of my uncles was so shocked he said, "If I were you I wouldn't tolerate this – just say, 'Let it go. Mine won't be the anthem.'" But he knew I wouldn't listen.'

Pradip finishes saying all this, then looks at me expecting another question. He seems pained as if dreading what's about to come and I decide I can't put him through any more. The smile of relief that appears on his face when I say I'm finished couldn't be wider.

*

After speaking with Pradip, I go to meet Benju Sharma, a middle-aged poet who was one of the fourteen judges of the contest, and the only woman. I want to check that the judges were really affected by the controversy.

Benju smiles fondly at the memory of the first time she met Pradip. He was called in for interview after making the final three. 'This really rustic-looking guy came into the room, tiptoeing like he was afraid, and it was amazing to think he'd done this. We were sitting there wondering if this guy could even be a writer, he was so simple and naive.'

She loved the song – 'This anthem can unite all the religions and languages and cultures here. It can make everyone feel Nepali, and it is working' – but even she had her doubts when the controversy built up. She started calling everyone she knew from

Okhaldhunga, Pradip's home region, and it was only they who convinced her he wasn't a monarchist. And it was only her assurances that convinced the prime minister to approve the anthem. She looks through a file and pulls out her original copy of Pradip's entry. She'd scored him eight out of ten.

*

A few days later, I finally get to meet the man who's the reason I wanted to write about Nepal's anthem in the first place: Amber Gurung, the musician who was asked to come up with a tune for Pradip's words, and who decided that some beautiful, bewildering Nepalese music was as deserving of being a national anthem as any brass flourish or stately hymn. So many people have told me he's Nepal's greatest musician and made him sound like a towering figure, larger than life, that it's a shock to find he's in his mid-seventies and suffering from Parkinson's disease, which has made his face and neck rigid and causes his hands to shake slightly.

'Oh, it was so hard to write the music,' he says, once his son, Kishor, has made sure Amber is comfortable and happy to talk. 'They told me this song should be so simple that even an old man or small child could sing it and that idea got stuck in my mind. I became really conscious of it; found it very hard to compose. It's very easy to make difficult songs, you know; it's very difficult to make easy ones.'

Amber was one of the judges who chose Pradip's words. The government then asked him to write its music, having failed to get a good enough tune out of the army or police bands. Everyone expected him to knock it out quickly. It would take him a few hours, they were sure. A day or two at most. But he started and restarted tunes for weeks, writing a melody then giving up halfway, having an idea then scrapping it in doubt. 'It was making me sick. One day my family took me to a resort to see the mountains, and left me there with a harmonium to get inspiration. I stayed for two days and when they came back: nothing. I couldn't even sleep, I was so restless with worry.'

Somehow he eventually wrote thirteen and a half songs, all in different styles. Most of these he's forgotten about, but he remembers the final three he offered the government. The first was your typical run-of-the-mill military anthem, of the kind that you hear the world over and that would never have made Nepal stand out. Amber's inspirations for that were 'God Save the Queen' and 'Jana Gana Mana', India's anthem – both of which he'd had to sing as a child while studying at missionary schools in Darjeeling. His second potential anthem was a raga – the classical Indian style of music, the kind of tunes you hear in films whenever the director's trying to sound mystical. His final suggestion was the song you hear today, the folk song.

I ask Amber how the government chose between the three, but he doesn't really explain, instead getting philosophical. 'This is not great music,' he says. 'Anyone could have done it, and any government could have accepted it. But it's a lucky tune. Time made this song the anthem, not me.'

As if sensing his father is flagging, Kishor comes into the room and suggests we end it there. But before I go, he invites me up on to the roof of their home for a drink. It's covered in multi-coloured prayer flags fluttering in the wind and there's a breathtaking view over Kathmandu's northern suburbs. The sun is setting behind a mountain in the distance, spraying orange and red light over the city, making the metropolis seem peaceful for the first time since I arrived. There are children playing chase on a roof opposite. On another a man's feeding some birds. I feel as if I could stand there for hours, as if Nepal's spiritual image might have some truth to it after all.

Kishor points to a road below and tells me that during the final days of the revolution it was flooded with peasants who'd come from the countryside and got lost trying to find their way into the capital to protest against the king. 'They'd walked two or three days just to be there. That's the grip the Maoists had on rural people,' he says. 'Over half the people in the countryside live in poverty and the Maoists had given them so much hope in their speeches.' He asks how I got on with his father, and I tell him the only thing Amber didn't explain was how the government chose between his final three tunes. I want to know if they ever came close to picking something far less unique. Kishor laughs.

'The selection process, now there's a story,' he says. 'I went to a small office in the Singha Durbar – my father asked me to go on his behalf – and all the ministers gathered to hear the songs. I was about to press play when one of the ministers took out a CD. He'd brought his own song to play! I couldn't believe it. The guy must have been out of his head. But then another did the same thing, saying that *his* song should actually be the anthem. That man was one of the Maoists and – I don't know if I should say this – but his song had words like, "Wake up, rise from every village. Wake up, rise from every town. Wake up and rise with hammer. If you don't have a hammer, rise with fists." And no one told them not to be stupid. They played the music!' He shakes his head. 'Sometimes the politics in this country is something else.'

*

There is of course one person central to the anthem's story, whose views about it I've yet to mention at all: Gyanendra, the former king – the only man alive who's had an anthem that was effectively about him, stripped away. He's someone who still carries an air of regality – I've been told to address him as His Royal Highness if we ever meet – and he seems to still cherish secrecy as if he's a ruling monarch too. He just doesn't want to talk to me. I've been chasing him for over a week now, ever since

I arrived, trying to orchestrate even the briefest of meetings, but I've got nowhere.

I should probably have given up on my very first day in Nepal. I got a phone call from his assistant turning down my request for a meeting: 'The anthem's just too sensitive a matter to discuss.' But then I stumbled across an old English émigré in a cafe off Patan Durbar Square, the heart of one of the old princely states that used to make up Nepal, its huge space littered with red and brown pagodas surrounded by flocks of pigeons (some of the pagodas were tragically destroyed in the 2015 earthquake). This man was about sixty, in white khaki trousers and wide-brimmed hat, and looked so comfortable speaking Nepali to the waitress, I could tell he'd been living in the country for decades. I guessed he was a former British army officer who came over once to recruit Gurkhas and never left, but he could just as easily have been a cleaned-up hippy, someone who came to Kathmandu's 'freak street' in the seventies and then realised he could make a fortune if he stopped taking drugs and ran a travel agent's instead.

'Oh, it should be easy to arrange a meeting with the king,' he said. 'You're just going about it the wrong way. Requesting meetings: that's not how business works around here. You need to pay.'

'What? A bribe?' I asked.

'Well, that's a very vulgar word, but you've got to grease the wheels. Just go to one of the posh hotels – they're all owned by his relatives – and make an offer.'

'I could spare about eight thousand rupees,' I said (about £50).

He looked at me with pity. 'Yes, perhaps it's not for you.'

But that conversation did give me an idea. I started bothering any of Gyanendra's relatives I could find; any people I knew he'd done business with. One of the latter, Prabhakar Rana, told me, 'What do you expect? Of course it's sensitive. If he says he dislikes the new anthem, it will anger people. If he says he likes it, it will anger people. Plus, he is still working out his options.'

'What do you mean by "options"?' I asked. 'He wants to come back to power?' Prabhakar laughed awkwardly and changed the subject.

I even went to Pokhara, where I'd heard Gyanendra has a summerhouse. Pokhara is Nepal's second city, far smaller than Kathmandu – the sort of place where cows run across roads forcing cars to jam on their brakes. I thought while there I might just hang around the gates to Gyanendra's house and see if he went for a stroll one afternoon around Pokhara's famous lake. He didn't. But one morning I met a few students watching a football match. They were all halfway through their degrees and were meant to be taking exams, but a lecturers' strike meant they couldn't. I asked them about the anthem and one, Suman Gautam, told me he preferred the old royal one. 'I sang it when I was young so it means more to me, but also, in my opinion the king is better. The politicians are just chasing money. He never did that. He tried his best.' The old song also sounds like an anthem, he added. 'The one now is like a pop song,' he said, dismissively. 'It doesn't have any power.'

Despite his view, Suman offered to take me to his old school to watch the pupils sing that 'powerless' anthem and so the next morning drove me there on his motorbike, bouncing over potholes and swerving between buses. In the schoolyard, several hundred children were lined up in crisp white shirts and blue ties, midway through their morning calisthenics: putting their hands on the shoulders of the person in front of them, stepping left, stepping right, then doing three short claps. When they were finished they sang the anthem, the younger ones only joining in for the words 'Nepali' and 'Nepala' that finish the main lines, the oldest shouting every word. I couldn't stop grinning: it was funny and touching and that music, played by the teacher on a harmonium – the nineteenth-century equivalent of a Casio keyboard – sounded amazing. Yes, like a pop song, and yes, without the pomposity you might expect, or even want, of an anthem, but like Nepal.

Once it finished, the headmaster whispered in my ear, asking if I'd like to hear the old royal anthem too. I said I was surprised they knew it – most looked too young to have even heard it. 'Oh, they know it,' he said, with a conspiratorial smile, and led me off to a classroom where he sang it boisterously, while the thirty children mostly looked confused. 'I'm not saying I'm a royalist,' he said afterwards, 'but there's a lot wrong with this country today and the anthem's part of it. It doesn't make you feel proud like what we had before.'

That moment seemed to sum up my whole time in Nepal. When I spoke to people about the anthem, anyone who'd welcomed the Maoist revolution and felt freed by it – basically anyone from a minority or a low caste, or anyone who supported their campaigns against drink and patriarchy – told me it inspired them and that they loved singing it. But anyone who still had royal ties seemed to cling to the old song. Often they'd criticise Amber and Pradip's effort – either the music wasn't bombastic enough, and was too weird to be an anthem, or the words weren't stirring. I'd explain how unique it was, and how brilliant it was that they hadn't just copied a Western march, that to my ears it couldn't be better, but they wouldn't listen. The anthem seemed to be a small reminder of a change they regretted, even if they'd never say that openly but only with a nod and a wink. And then they'd go into a long list of ways the country had gone nowhere since the revolution and perhaps talk about moving away to somewhere better like Delhi.

*

I was still in Pokhara and about to give up hope of getting anywhere close to Gyanendra when my phone rang. It was a secretary from the Hotel Annapurna in Kathmandu, one of the city's oldest, situated a stone's throw from the royal palace. 'Shreejana Rana will meet you tomorrow,' the secretary said. I didn't know who Shreejana Rana was, but hastily agreed, then pulled out a book I'd bought that contained a copy of the royal family tree. I started at Gyanendra and went down through his children. No luck. I slowly moved further and further away, checking the names of relative after relative, until I found her, sitting quite alone: Shreejana Rana, the wife of one of Gyanendra's second cousins. Her stepmother had been at the royal massacre in 2001, somehow getting out with only a bullet wound to a hand. Shreejana was not a royal. She wasn't a princess and she definitely wasn't a queen. I doubt she'd even run our meeting past Gyanendra's assistants. But if this was the only opportunity I was going to get to speak to a member of the Nepalese royal family, I'd take it with both hands.

*

'We're very much commoners,' Shreejana says, for the third time since we've met, before blowing on her tea to cool it down. We're sitting in the cream-coloured cafe of the hotel she runs which has the air of an imperial tearoom, with suited waiters speeding around carrying trays of white china and crisp cucumber sandwiches. 'We don't hold any titles. We run a business,' she adds. 'Of course my mother-in-law was one of the victims of the massacre, but . . .' She doesn't bother finishing the sentence; the massacre was so long ago, it's not worth talking about. Instead she starts happily explaining her relationship to the former royals. Of course she used to go to the palace, she says.

'Did you ever hear the anthem played in front of them?' I ask.

'Oh, very much so. Nothing started without the national anthem. There was a lot of protocol just like with the British royal family. Wherever the king went, even weddings, the ceremony would start with the anthem and everyone would stand up and sing. Not the king and queen of course. Now the royal palace is no more, you hardly hear it. When do they play the new one? State's day?'

We have a few minutes of such polite conversation, then she gives me a piece of paper containing answers to some questions I've sent through in advance. 'I prefer to get my thoughts down in writing,' she says. 'This should tell you all you need to know.' I look at the list.

'How did you feel when the anthem was replaced?' I'd asked.

'The anthem has to reflect the political reality and status of the country. It had to change,' she's written, very on-message.

'What do you think of the current anthem?'

'It is too new to arouse patriotic sentiments, or any sentiments at all. It is a ditty which ends rather abruptly, leaving one standing, literally.' It's a little more revealing; maybe she will be open after all.

And then the key question: 'How do you think Gyanendra would have felt about losing the royal anthem? It was about him, after all.'

'One cannot presume to know how His former Majesty feels,' she's written. 'It might be strange to put it this way, but I am glad His late Majesty King Birendra was not alive to suffer this change.' I read that last sentence several times, initially disappointed that she's batted away the key question, until I realise that it says a lot. Birendra, the man of the people, didn't deserve to lose the song people sang at him with love. Gyanendra never had that love to lose.

Of course, that still doesn't explain how he'd have felt. I try to find out in a roundabout way. 'Do you think he's happy being a commoner?' I ask.

'Look, what I really admired about him was that he said, "I'm Nepali. I have a right to live here and I will,"' she says. 'Because a lot of kings, when a monarchy has been abolished, they leave.

But he said he would never do that. I think that was the best way to show his acceptance of the changes. To be honest, I think he is happy leading the life he used to, that of the businessman. I mean, how many years was he king? It was only, like, five.'

I think about asking why, if he was happy to be a businessman, he fought so hard against the Maoists to stay in power, but I know she won't answer, fearing being misinterpreted and having already explained that rumours start far too easily in this country, and that she doesn't want to start any more. But after she leaves, I look back over the sheet of questions and see I've missed one other question: 'What do you feel the future of the monarchy is in Nepal?'

'A country of diverse peoples, cultures, traditions, languages and aspirations is now in the process of actively examining its priorities,' she has written. 'When this comes to a natural conclusion, the citizens will decide what institutions – old and new – will be retained, reinstated or abandoned.' I know I'm just seeing what I want to, but that word 'reinstated' seems to stick out, almost as if she's typed it harder than the rest of the sentence.

*

Baburam Bhattarai, the Maoist prime minister of Nepal, races into his official meeting room. Literally. He's going so quickly he has to swerve to avoid falling over a leather sofa and crashing into the intricate woodcarvings of dancing deities and snakes eating their own tails that decorate the walls. 'I'm sorry I'm late,' he says, somehow composed. He's wearing a blue suit, open-necked shirt and the traditional triangular Nepalese hat called a topi, which sits bolt upright on his head. For a man in his fifties, he looks vibrant and youthful – every bit the game-changing politician. He offers his hand. This is the moment I've come to Nepal for. This man spent ten years at the head of a revolution – hundreds of thousands devoured his every word and were inspired to fight in the conflict that went on to claim some 15,000 lives. Now he's a trusted statesman, turning that revolution into a respectable government. He's not become a dictator or a laughing stock like so many revolutionaries before him. I reach forward, half afraid, half excited.

He has one of the limpest handshakes I've ever come across.

We sit down and he doesn't even wait for me to ask a question. 'Every national anthem reflects the aspirations of the people and should reflect the unity of the country,' he says, as if rattling through a prepared speech. 'In that way, an anthem is historically specific. That means it should keep changing according to the political and historical situation in a country.

'Here, we had absolute autocratic monarchy for more than two hundred and forty years. So when the people's war was launched and the people's struggles were waged against that monarchy, one of our slogans was of course, "Abolish this so-called national anthem." It wasn't a national anything – it was just praising the ideology of the monarchy. So when the monarchy was abolished, it was natural that the anthem would be changed. This new anthem reflects the circumstances of the country today. It's about republicanism. It's about democracy. It's about the socio-political diversity of Nepal and the unity of our country.'

'I've been told you wanted a much stronger anthem,' I say quickly, before he has a chance to get going again. He 'mms' as if to say 'Go on'. 'One that reflects the people's war better and the struggles people had?' He 'mms' once more. 'One that perhaps had slogans like "arise workers" and "march on" in it?'

He pulls a quick, wry smile. 'Of course if the anthem had been written by the revolutionary forces, they would have written a more revolutionary song,' he says. 'If we had our own way we would have created a better anthem than this. But we've had to compromise on many issues since coming to power and this is one of them.'

Do you feel pride when you hear it then? I ask.

'It's okay for the time being. Personally I'm quite happy with it.'

We talk a bit about his background. He claims to have been politically awakened at school, partly because he had to sing the anthem every day – 'a slavish eulogy to one man'. He didn't feel he'd found an anthem for himself, he adds, until he sang 'The Internationale', 'the song of workers all over the world'. I decide not to mention that his background isn't one shared by many workers – Baburam came from a peasant family but spent most of his youth doing degrees in India – and instead tell him I was surprised to learn just how important music was to the people's war. The Maoists didn't just stop the anthem, they also tried to ban Hindi music and to get people singing songs in their own ethnic languages.

'Of course it was important,' he says. 'We used music to arouse the feelings of the people and to inculcate in them a political consciousness. It's a very effective tool. All Nepal's different ethnicities, its women, and the so-called lower caste, none of those groups used to be able to express themselves, and so we encouraged them to show their cultural identity. They liked us for it; no one had done that before.' He says that's the one undeniably good thing about the new anthem: it sounds Nepalese. It sounds like the country expressing its identity rather than copying other people's.

At this point we've been talking all of six minutes, but Baburam's press secretary looks as if he's going to have a heart attack. He keeps leaning forward trying to get my attention so he can draw the interview to a close, only to slump back in annoyance when I ignore him. He looks as though he's having to strain every muscle in his face to stop himself from shouting, 'STOP TALKING! WE'RE IN THE MIDDLE OF A CONSTITUTIONAL CRISIS!' (They actually were, I learned later: Nepal's Supreme Court having ordered Baburam's government to agree a new constitution within days.) I realise I'm pushing my luck, so I say I have one final question.

'When you said earlier the anthem's "okay for the time being", does that mean you'll one day replace it?'

'Everything is temporary in the world, nothing is absolute. All the world keeps on changing,' he says, sounding oddly like a Buddhist monk for a supposedly anti-religious Maoist. And with that he gets up, grabs my hand for some photos – the photographer's flash so strong it forces me to close my eyes, ruining them all – and then he's gone: the most intelligent man in Nepal; one of its heart-throbs. As I'm walking out, I bump into one of his underlings from earlier. 'Did you tell him about your friends?' he asks, excitedly. 'Did he know them too?'

*

It's several months and several thousand miles later, and I'm in Folkestone, Kent, the heart of England. I'm in a community centre full of Nepalese getting drunk on cheap lager. Most of them are connected to the Gurkhas, the Nepalese regiments serving under the British army nearby. But up on stage is Pradip Kumar Rai, under his poet's alias Byakul Maila. There's a queue of people waiting to put garlands around his neck, although he's got so many around him already he appears to have grown to twice his size, becoming comically obese.

The Nepalese anthem – his anthem – is playing on a loop over the speakers; a recording of some high-pitched women singing over Amber's keyboard and drums. That music seems completely out of place in the cold hall, especially after someone puts the disco lights on, but it doesn't appear to bother Pradip or anyone else. Everyone is smiling. In this room, finally, the anthem doesn't mean politics, or conjure images of kings and uprisings. It just means home.

It's the music that's key to that. If a trumpet flourish was looping out of those speakers now, everyone would feel as though they'd have to stand to attention, waiting to boredly salute whichever dignitary was passing through. But thanks to Amber's tune, no one's looking bored. They're swigging from super-strength beer cans, they're singing to their children and getting them to clap and dance along. It could be any Saturday night. It could be the final of a Nepalese talent contest, Pradip declared the winner for a beautiful poem. I stand there and make a little wish that one day this tune *is* played at an Olympics. Everyone in the stadium would be utterly confused, but they'd feel a little happier for having heard a song so different and so uplifting.

The Star-Spangled Banner

O say can you see, by the dawn's early light,
What so proudly we hail'd at the twilight's last
  gleaming,
Whose broad stripes and bright stars through the
  perilous fight,
O'er the ramparts we watch'd, were so gallantly
  streaming?
And the rockets' red glare, the bombs bursting in air,
Gave proof through the night that our flag was still
  there,
O say does that star-spangled banner yet wave,
O'er the land of the free and the home of the brave?

3

America

AN AD-MAN'S DREAM

Nashville is little more than a handful of skyscrapers rising out of the Tennessee countryside but, as a great many billboards tell you, it's the home of country music. So many people have made their names here – Elvis, Dolly Parton, Taylor Swift – that it's no surprise everyone you meet is either a singer, an aspiring singer or someone who, y'know, writes a few songs now and then, just for fun. It doesn't matter if they're young girls in fifties shades and leopard-print hot pants, or sixty-something men in suits and ties, sweating in the heat – they'd all grab a guitar given half a chance. Some people have even crossed continents for a shot at making it. Last night I saw an all-Japanese country band in a bar on the east side of town. They looked completely incongruous in their rhinestone-studded boots and red tasselled shirts, the frontman tipping his Stetson after every number, yet they somehow had the drawl of true Southerners, and their songs made them sound as if they'd gone through three wives each and just as many jails. They were fantastic.

But I'm pretty sure Nashville would lose all its allure for that band if they were with me now. I'm standing in the city's base-ball stadium, home of the Nashville Sounds. It's a beautiful March morning, sun streaming down from a cloudless sky. Two groundsmen are on the field: one watering the grass, creating rainbows with flicks of his wrist; the other carefully rolling sand into place. Freight trains are passing in the distance, the sound of their horns drifting across the stadium. It's an idyllic scene, the sort that makes you think you've at last found that mythical 'small-town America' (despite being in a city of 700,000). Or at least it would be an idyllic scene, if it weren't for the sound coming from behind the batting cage – an out-of-tune wail that seems to be growing louder and more piercing with each second.

'O say can you SEEEEEEEEE,' it starts, the singer somehow managing to hit five different notes in that final one-syllable word, 'by the dawn's early LIGHTTTTT.'

The girl making this racket looks all of eight years old. She's wearing a pink polka-dot dress, and has her hands nervously clasped in front of her. At any other time, the audience would be smiling and nudging each other – 'Ain't she cute?' – and when she got to the end, they'd give her a standing ovation just for having the courage to get up in front of several hundred people and sing her country's anthem.

Unfortunately for her, everyone here has spent the last hour and a half watching people mangle that anthem, 'The Star-Spangled Banner', over and over, and over again. We've watched children lisp their way through it and groups of soccer moms with matching scarves struggle to sing it in harmony. We've watched jocks grind to a halt after three lines, the words slipping embarrassingly from their grasp, and we've seen gospel singers add twists and turns to it, to the point it seemed like it'd never end. No one has any charity left. Each of those people was auditioning to sing before one of the Sounds' home games this season.

One of the judges turns to me. 'Shoot me now,' he whispers. I look at his judging sheet. We're only on number 51. There's at least 100 to go. I decide not to tell him I'm due up in an hour.

★

Americans play their anthem so much it sometimes feels as if they're worried they'll forget it. 'The Star-Spangled Banner' is sung before baseball games, basketball games, American football and ice hockey matches, at political rallies, school bake sales, even supermarket openings. When someone sings it brilliantly, it makes the news. When someone sings it horribly, it stays news for days. Thailand is the only country that seems to come close to that devotion. There, their anthem is played every day at 8 a.m. and 6 p.m., leading to strange scenes of people standing to attention in train stations and shopping mall food courts. But those renditions are required by law; they're not voluntary and spontaneous, like you get here.

Before coming to America, I'd decided an audition like this was the best place to witness this apparent love for the song. I was sure the stadium would be filled with super-patriots: women who'd take the stage in dresses stitched out of the flag, or who'd break down in tears halfway through, overcome with memories of family who'd died in service. I'd leave the stadium with stories of heartbreak and bravery, maybe even some romance ('We met singing it. I can't resist a man who nails his anthem'). Unfortunately no one I've met so far has lived up to that fantasy.

I've met patriots, of course – men in Vietnam War trucker caps who've told me that 'when someone butchers the anthem, it's like they're trampling on the flag' or who've complained that no one's wearing a suit ('Where's the respect?'). But most people have simply been singers desperate to win one of Nashville's prime talent contests. The only real exception has been a scruffy thirty-something librarian called Gib Baxter, who I found sitting at the back with his blue-haired, bubblegum-blowing girlfriend. She'd forced him to come. 'It's a "Get out, conquer your fears" thing,' he said. 'I'm quite an anxious person.' He held up his hands. 'I'm trying to stop biting my nails too.' I decided not to point out he was only succeeding on three fingers.

Perhaps I should actually have expected this crowd. 'The Star-Spangled Banner' may be an everyday occurrence here, but it's also a song that's difficult to love, no matter how patriotic you are. For a start, it's bloody hard to sing. It has a range of an octave and a half – something few other anthems get close to (although South Korea's used to reach such heights that in 2014 they changed its key to make it easier for post-pubescent boys to sing). That means you have to start uncomfortably low or finish uncomfortably high, whoever you are. That range almost stopped it becoming the country's anthem. Days before it was chosen, Congress ordered the Navy Band to come to Washington and prove it was actually singable. They wisely took along a professional.

The song is also full of olde worlde language – words like 'o'er', phrases like 'foul . . . pollution' – that hasn't been used in everyday speech since the time it was written. And there are just a lot of other patriotic American songs around begging people to love them more: real heart-grabbers like 'America the Beautiful', which glides across the landscape from 'amber waves of grain' to 'purple mountain majesties'; or 'God Bless America', which any three-year-old could learn to impress their grandparents ('God bless America, land that I love'). Sometimes you get the feeling most Americans would be happiest if Bruce Springsteen donated 'Born in the USA' to the country in his will (the chorus only, obviously). It makes you wonder if 'The Star-Spangled Banner' really does have a hold on people here, or it's simply a tradition that can't be shaken off; whether the people who stand for it every day are doing so because it's the most important song in the country, or just because they've been nagged so many times by their mums.

*

It's taken me all of ten seconds to realise I'm not as good a singer as that eight-year-old girl. I'm standing behind the batting cage staring up at the three judges, and all of them are looking at me pleadingly as if to say, 'Please, just stop singing.'

'Ooooo sayyyyy cannnnn youuuuu seeeeeeeeee,' I bellow, far slower than you're meant to. It's like I've suddenly developed a speech impediment. The judges and the audience must think I've forgotten the words and am dragging each one out to give myself time to think. 'Byyyyy theeeee dawwwwwnnnnn'sssss earrrrrrllllllyyyyy lighhhhhttttt.' I realise my hands are shaking, my nerves coming to the surface. I dread to think how large the sweat patches are on my shirt. 'WhaTTTTT so proudly we hailed at the TWIlight's last gleaming,' I manage, finally picking up pace but my voice now wobbling wildly for some reason, like it's about to break. And this is only line two. I've got six to go. Unless something changes soon people are going to start booing. But then an idea suddenly pops into my panicked head – the crowd. There are several hundred people out there. Get them to hide the disaster this is becoming. So I pump a fist as if I'm actually getting into it, and I wave at them to stand up. I point the microphone at them too as if to say, 'C'mon, sing with me . . .'

And magically – wonderfully – it works. Well, sort of. One person joins in. She's middle-aged, with platinum-blonde hair and gaudy shades that cover half her face. She's probably the mother of an equally bad auditionee, but I don't care. She claps. She shouts, 'USA! USA!' She waves at everyone to join her; everyone laughs. I fix my gaze on her as though she's my first girlfriend and I don't let go until I reach the end. That takes another minute or so, but when I finally sing, 'The land of the FREEEEEE and the home of the BRAVVVVVE?' straining to hit those high notes, I finish an exhausted, exhilarated mess.

'How did I do?' I shout, running up to the judging table suddenly filled with adrenalin.

'Ten out of ten for the words,' one replies.

'And . . . how about the actual singing?'

'Yeah . . . er . . . um . . . We'll get back to you,' he says, with a wry smile.

*

Nashville might be a great city in which to sing 'The Star-Spangled Banner', but if there is really a place to explore its history and meaning, it's Baltimore, just off the Chesapeake Bay, in the corridor between Washington DC and New York.

Baltimore used to be thriving and energetic, one of the world's most important ports, sucking in anything that could be grown or manufactured in the eastern US and shipping it out. Today, after decades of decline, it only seems to make it into newspapers for riots or in connection with the city's appalling reputation for drugs. Baltimore is now apparently all crack and meth, re-ups and corner boys, and is dominated by the projects – large estates filled with the city's poor, places you don't go to unless you want your car stolen.

When you step out of the city's train station and on to a bus downtown, that reputation seems deserved. Within two minutes of getting on one myself, I'd seen my first addict, shuffling up the aisle in a stained Michael Jackson sweater, hunched over and missing a few teeth. He didn't ask for money, perhaps assuming everyone else was in as hopeless a situation as his own.

But give Baltimore a little time and it opens up to you. It's a city with some extremely obvious problems, but it also has a youthfulness and vibrancy to it, like a cut-price New York. You can be skirting a project one minute, the next be walking along a tree-lined road with bustling Mexican cantinas and gentrified terraced homes. You can go to one end of the waterfront and be shocked by homelessness, then head to the other and join the people gazing enviously at the yachts moored in the bay. And it's also here, at a red-brick and white-timber fort on the city's southern edge, that 200 years ago 'The Star-Spangled Banner' was born.

*

Before you can tell the story of 'The Banner', as everyone in Baltimore seems to call it, you need a brief lesson about the War of 1812. It was fought between Britain and America. It lasted three years. It was also one of the strangest wars in history, with its biggest battle fought long after peace had been signed. Yet hardly anyone's heard of it.

The US had been independent for just thirty-six years when that war began. In nationhood terms, it was still a baby barely able to make out shapes, and it was trying to be sick all over its parents. To be fair, the British had given it enough reasons to want to do so. Britain was at war with France at the time and so was trying to strangle America's trade with the French: stopping American ships mid-ocean, taking their cargo or even throwing it into the sea. The British navy was also in desperate need of men and so had developed a habit of boarding American ships to look for deserters, then taking anyone it liked the look of – British or not. As real as these grievances were, some Americans wanted war for other reasons, such as to open up the west (Britain had been arming some American Indian tribes) or thinking it would present a good opportunity to make Canada part of the United States. With the British busy fighting the French, there'd never be a better chance. Soon the five-foot, four-inch president, James Madison, realised he couldn't keep away from conflict, and on 18 June, he signed a declaration of war. There's no record of when he started to regret that decision, but it was probably, at most, three days later.

The next two years passed in a series of embarrassments and mishaps for the US army, which, it turned out, wasn't really capable of invading anywhere. It had few proper soldiers. Those it had were poorly paid. And some of those refused to fight anywhere but their home states – they'd happily march up to the Canadian border as long as they didn't have to cross it.

The British, meanwhile, could only really sail up and down the coastline, raiding the odd town, bombing the odd city, what with most of its troops occupied elsewhere – hardly the behaviour of a global superpower. Things didn't become anywhere near dramatic until the summer of 1814, when Britain, having finally seen off Napoleon, sent thousands of troops across the Atlantic, all of them angry and embittered that they couldn't just go home to their wives. That August, there was a large battle at Bladensburg, a village that today sits in the middle of Washington's commuter belt. President Madison turned up to give orders, the last president to set foot on a battlefield. But half of his cabinet decided to come along too, shouting at the generals and contradicting each other. The Americans had the numerical advantage, and they occupied the high ground, but with such confused leadership, and relying on militias easily scared by British rockets, it was unsurprisingly soon a rout. Thousands of Americans fled, the British giving chase in their distinctive red coats. Madison was forced to jump on a horse and gallop for his life, while a messenger was sent to the White House calling for his wife 'to quit the city immediately'. She carried off their silver in her handbag.

That battle has been called the 'most humiliating episode in US history', but what came next seems, in some respects, worse. The British got to the White House and found a meal for forty laid out in the dining room: decanters of wine chilling in ice on the sideboard and food in tin-warmers (they thought it was a victory banquet, but it was actually that day's dinner). So they ate wolfishly – gluttonously, apparently. You can imagine them letting the fat from the meat drip down their chins and slopping wine on to the floor. Then they burned the White House, and most of Washington's other public buildings, to the ground.

Then they turned their attention to Baltimore.

*

You can tell that some people are going to be heroes. They're a certain type: men and women whose hair appears to be blowing in the wind even on still days, whose names are never far from words like 'magnetic' or 'debonair'. Francis Scott Key, the man who wrote 'The Star-Spangled Banner', was never meant to be a hero.

In September 1814, Key was a thirty-five-year-old lawyer and father of five. He had a long Roman nose and hair that fell around his face in curls. He was in demand for his work, by all accounts, but he hardly stands out from anyone else from that time. If you dig around for exciting anecdotes about him, you come up desperately short. He liked to go to church – a lot. And he liked to write poems with titles like 'To my Steed' and 'To a Rose-bud'. The most interesting thing about him actually seems to be his confused views on slavery: he owned slaves, but he argued cases on behalf of freed ones; he thought the answer to slavery was to encourage freed blacks to go back to Africa (ignoring the question of whether they'd come from there in the first place), but he vehemently opposed abolition. That's pretty much it – apart from the fact that he wrote one particular poem, or rather song, which became very famous indeed.

In Baltimore, I met Burt Kummerow, the portly president of the Maryland Historical Society, which owns Key's original manuscript, but he, too, was unable to tell me one good story about Key. He tried desperately, searching his memory, flicking through books for something amusing or interesting to say, but he just kept slipping into stories about different people entirely. 'Do you know Key's son, Philip?' he said at one point. 'He was this well-known rake and at some time he was having an affair with a Latin ingénue, the wife of a congressman. She was evidently "raising the shade" whenever her husband went out. But the congressman somehow learned about it, confronted Philip in front of the White House, pulled a pistol and murdered him. Just shot him right in front of everybody! You should really look him up.'

'But Key himself, there's nothing about him that stands out?' I asked.

'Er, let me think a minute,' he said, looking off purposefully. Then he suddenly brightened. 'You know, he *was* friends with a guy called John Randolph of Roanoke. Now *there* was a character . . .'

The only person who gave me a different picture was Lisa Sherwood, Key's great-great-great-great-granddaughter and the most sparkling seventy-three-year-old you could ever hope to come across. I met her in a sunny courtyard in the middle of the city and with her blonde bob and mischievous smile she could easily have passed for twenty years younger.

Lisa had no stories about Key himself – her parents hadn't passed any down – but she almost pleaded with me that he couldn't have been as staid as he seems. 'The paintings I've seen of him, he looks – what's the word? – debonair,' she said, 'like he's about to flash his cape about.

'And his wife, Polly, was lovely, beautiful, a real prize. Her father was the richest man in the whole of Maryland so Key must have had a lot of charm – or *something* – to catch her. And he wrote her these wonderful, romantic letters. I guess I think of him as a bit like my own father, who was extremely exuberant and mischievous and energetic and passionate.'

Whether he had any heroic characteristics or not, Key was clearly respected, since about a week after the burning of Washington he was asked to sail out to the British fleet near Baltimore and help negotiate the release of a prisoner, Dr Beanes. Beanes had been 'punishing a bowl of punch' with some friends one afternoon, celebrating the British leaving his town, when he discovered a desperate British soldier in his garden trying to steal food. They took him prisoner then went in search of more stragglers to lock up, a somewhat foolhardy idea given the British would clearly find out about it. The British came for the men the next day, and took Beanes off as well, not even letting him pick up his glasses.

Key reached the British fleet on a Wednesday, 7 September. He was deeply pessimistic about the trip, believing that even if he argued for days he would still have next to no chance of convincing the British that Beanes had done nothing wrong. But it turned out to be surprisingly easy. He was harried and messed about, but then he produced letters of gratitude from British soldiers Beanes had cared for throughout the war, and that was it: Key was given his man.

But the pair weren't allowed to leave. The British were planning to bombard Baltimore's Fort McHenry, the only thing stopping them sailing straight into the city's harbour, and Beanes and Key had seen the preparations being made. They also knew that a simultaneous land assault was planned. They couldn't be allowed to just sail off and warn everyone. So the British made them wait – and then they made them watch.

*

Fort McHenry today sits in a beautiful park filled with Lycra-clad joggers and chihuahua walkers from the up-and-coming neighbourhood nearby. It couldn't feel more peaceful or genteel, so it's probably not a place where you should do impressions of bombs going off. Vince Vaise, a thirty-something park ranger who has agreed to show me around, doesn't seem the slightest bit concerned about shattering the calm, though.

'The British were firing mortar shells from two MILES away,' he says, throwing his arms out towards a bridge in the distance. 'And these shells were filled with THIRTEEN pounds of high explosive black powder, so when they exploded – BOOOOOOOOOM! – they would shower down fragments. You'd have heard them for miles. BOOOOOOOOOM!'

Vince is the sort of tour guide you dream of stumbling across when you visit a historical monument like this. He lives and breathes Fort McHenry. He also, without any self-awareness, acts out everything he says, his arms swinging, his legs apparently forcing him to jump on to things or crouch behind them whether he wants to or not. And he RANDOMLY shouts WORDS in every sentence, like a comedian who can't remember where the punchline is.

The reason I wanted to meet Vince was to get an impression of what Francis Scott Key would have gone through with the British, and what he would have seen from his ship. It would have been far from pretty, Vince insists. On 13 September, at 6.30 a.m., the British stopped just out of range of the fort's cannons and, like the most ungodly dawn chorus, then pounded it with about 1,500 mortars and 800 rockets (the rockets were barely controllable, there as much to scare as to hit anything). 'The bombardment lasted twenty-five hours, and don't forget it was in a thunderstorm too, so you had WIND and RAIN and LIGHTNING. I don't think anyone got ANY sleep that night,' Vince says.

Key was stuck pacing his ship's deck, watching those bombs, trying to make out the condition of the fort by the light of the explosions, to see whether the flag was still flying or a British one had been raised in its place. That flag would have been easy to see during the day as it had been made deliberately huge – 42 feet wide and 30 feet high – so the British couldn't fail to see it, a cocky gesture by the fort's commander to give his soldiers the confidence to take on the world's biggest navy. The flag was so large that when it was made it had to be laid out on the floor of a brewery, and was so heavy it took eleven men to lift it. It was actually taken down during the battle to stop it getting damaged by the storm but even the smaller flag that replaced it was vast: 17 feet high, 25 feet wide.

*

'Key is a FASCINATING person,' shouts Vince, as if trying to get the passing joggers interested in him too. 'He was quite an Anglophile before he went out there. But the British gave him a pretty hard time and really turned him off. I mean, it's not surprising – a lot of the British high command came from the ARISTOCRACY, so they were used to looking down on their OWN people, let alone Americans.'

Vince starts talking about some of the British logbooks he's seen. In one an officer wrote, 'The work of destruction is about to begin and this must distress the Americans as much as it delights me.' In another, Alexander Cochrane, the admiral in charge, says the Americans were a 'whining, canting race, much like spaniels', and had to be smacked on the nose and made to heel. He'd hated the Americans for years, ever since they'd started burning villages in Canada (the burning of Washington was partly retribution for that). 'We know the negotiations were in the admiral's cabin over wine,' Vince adds, 'so after a few drinks I'm sure the talk got a little LOOSE. I'm sure they told Key exactly what they thought about him and his country.'

Key stood on his ship's deck on the morning of 14 September, his spyglass trained on the fort. The rain had stopped, but he still couldn't see a lot – there was too much smoke from the cannons drifting over the water, and it was still too dark. 'You may imagine what a state of anxiety I endured,' he wrote to a friend shortly afterwards, saying his mind had been jumping throughout the night, one moment thinking the city's cause was hopeless (he partly thought God would allow its destruction for being a 'lump of wickedness', its residents having beaten those opposed to war), the next being sure it would survive. 'The awful stillness and suspense were unbearable.' But deep down he knew what the outcome must have been. His heart sank as he began to accept the reality. He had probably just seen his country lose the war.

But then, as the sun rose, he saw two things: firstly British soldiers sailing back, dejected, and then, at the fort, the storm flag coming down and another one being raised. It was limp at first, but it unfurled in the wind as it was pulled higher. And Key saw it wasn't British. It was those fifteen red and white stripes. Those fifteen stars. And the blood rushed to his head, his despair replaced with an elation the heights of which he'd never experience again.

In fact, as Key later learned, in spite of the firepower deployed by the British, hardly any damage had been done to the fort. Some wood had been splintered and a roof had caved in, but just four soldiers had been killed and one cannon knocked over. The bombs had turned out to be more an embarrassment to the British than a threat to the Americans.

Key began desperately rummaging through his pockets, searching for an envelope, his orders, any scrap of paper he could write on. He'd been writing poems and songs all his life, for friends and family, and he couldn't calm the impulse to record what he'd witnessed. 'If it'd been a hanging matter to make a song, [I'd still have] made it,' he later said of that moment. But this song wasn't going to be like any of his others, he knew. It wasn't going to be a 'To my Steed' or a 'To a Rose-bud'. He realised he already knew the perfect tune for the lyrics too: 'To Anacreon in Heaven'. He'd loved it for years and had even used it for songs before. Everyone knew its soaring melody. The fact it was originally a posh British drinking song – sung at meetings of a London gentlemen's club, the Anacreontic Society, with words about entwining 'the myrtle of Venus with Bacchus' vine' – apparently didn't cross his mind as making it a somewhat inappropriate choice.

*

Everyone knows the first verse of 'The Star-Spangled Banner', but few seem to realise that it's the description of a battle half fought. 'And the rockets' red glare, the bombs bursting in air, / Gave proof through the night that our flag was still there', it goes, but then it ends on a question:

> O say does that star-spangled banner yet wave,
> O'er the land of the free and the home of the brave?

Key is writing it as if still uncertain on the boat, praying for victory. It's only when people sing it now and remove that question mark that it becomes a triumph.

There are actually three more verses (like most anthems, only the first is sung now), and it's those that are most revealing about what Key went through that night. In the second, he finally sees the flag:

> Now it catches the gleam of the morning's first beam,
> In full glory reflected now shines in the stream.

But then look at the third. It's the words of a man spewing out his anger, his hatred and disgust at people he previously admired. 'Where is that band who so vauntingly swore [to destroy us?]', he writes, the British no better than a band of thugs. 'Their blood has washed out their foul footsteps' pollution,' he adds, revelling in their deaths. He goes on to call them 'hirelings' and 'slaves', saying they've fled in terror, because, ultimately, they're cowards, the lowest of the low. It's eight lines of the purest invective. Eight lines you wouldn't expect from a good Christian, a lawyer and a father of five. The final verse is always going to be a let-down after that. Key seems to check himself, realising that the British might come back after all and he should probably end on a few words to inspire in case they do. 'Then conquer we must, when our cause it is just,' he writes, 'And this be our motto: "In God is our trust."'

Key didn't set out to promote his song. He simply finished it off in a hotel when he got back to Baltimore then made his way home. But once in the city, he showed it to friends and one of them rushed it to a printer's. Within days, most of the city seemed to be singing it.

I ask Vince if he thinks the song's immediate popularity had anything to do with the third, violent verse. After all, he earlier told me that Baltimoreans were so angry after the battle, they'd tied dead British soldiers, victims of the land campaign, to fences so people could mutilate them. Any song that called the British thieves and cowards was bound to go down well. 'There was an anti-British sentiment he capitalised on, sure,' he says, his voice having calmed down slightly. 'But it was nationalism that made it popular. I mean, this was a war that didn't go as well as we hoped. There were so many American defeats. The Capitol was lost. The Treasury was all but bankrupt. All the invasions into Canada failed. So we needed something that made us feel good, something to latch on to and really play up the success. And this song was it.' From Baltimore, Key's song spread rapidly across America. Within six weeks, it was being sung in nine of the country's then eighteen states.

America didn't have an anthem at the time. It also wasn't apparently ready for one – most people in the country feeling they belonged more to their state than the nation. Instead it just became one of the handful of big patriotic songs you could never escape, alongside the likes of the comedic 'Yankee Doodle' (actually played at Fort McHenry after the flag rose) and 'Hail, Columbia' (an instantly forgettable march from the first days of independence). Key simply went back to his wife, though now a well-known songwriter as well as a lawyer. He had a few more children, wrote a few more poems. But he rarely spoke about the song. The one documented time he did in public, twenty years later, he simply thanked people for enjoying it then said any plaudits should go to 'the heroism of those who made me make it'.

*

After visiting Fort McHenry, I spent a couple of days in Baltimore talking to people about the anthem, trying to find out what it meant to them. Just like in Nashville, most of the teenagers I met saw it as a singing contest. Outside the Baltimore School for the Arts, the place that gave the world the rapper Tupac, a drama student, hoodie up, said, 'People say they're proud it came from here, like Phillies are proud of cheese steak. But that's it. Boasting. We don't *feel* it.' Then he asked me what the main difference between America and the UK was. We don't have guns, I said. 'How'd you do drive-bys without guns?' he asked.

But I also met plenty of people who actually did feel the song – people with real personal connections to it. Lisa Sherwood, Francis Scott Key's descendant, was the first. Her feelings for it had nothing to do with being his ancestor, she insisted; it was more memories of her father. When she was a child he worked in New York, 'but he'd be at our apartment at weekends and when he'd drink too much – or maybe he was just happy – he'd go out on our balcony, on the fourth floor of this building in the middle of Baltimore, and sing "The Star-Spangled Banner". He'd do the "Marseillaise" too. It was so cool.'

Then there was a former Navy Seal, Chanelle Johnson, whose young son was by her side dressed as an astronaut in a bright blue NASA suit. The boy couldn't stop smiling because his dad was coming home from Afghanistan that weekend. 'When I sing, I get choked up,' she said. 'Every time, I'm in tears. I had friends who died in Iraq, Afghanistan, all those places.'

There was a cop too. He was Greek, almost comically so. Fat and small with a bushy moustache, he looked as if he should be pushing handfuls of feta and olives into his mouth, not boredly walking a beat. He refused to tell me his name – 'Police regulations' – but said he moved to America aged six and felt it had given him a life he wouldn't otherwise have had. 'I can't explain it, but when I hear the anthem, I try to sit really still. I don't stand up. I just sit, silent, and try to think about what it means. I think maybe I have too much respect for it,' he added, with a laugh.

But the person I know I'll never forget is Stretch. I was walking past a project, the 'safest in Baltimore', I'd been told, and decided if I didn't speak to someone there I'd regret it. So I walked up to an old man with greying hair and a cracked face, sitting on the stoop outside his door. I introduced myself. 'Of course you can ask about the anthem,' he said languidly. Then he started to get up, and this small, cracked old man seemed to unfurl himself, becoming bigger and bigger until he was looming over me. He was six foot five at least. And he wasn't an old man at all: he was about thirty. He just had the yellow teeth and eyes, and the worn-out skin, of an addict. Crack or meth, I don't know, but he had a plastic cup between his legs filled with a bright purple liquid, probably sizzurp, a drug made by mixing codeine-filled cough medicines with Sprite.

'Yessir,' he said, 'I like the anthem. Now I tell you why. I tell you why. I was born Four July.' Independence Day, of course, a time where the flag is everywhere, the anthem too. 'You got me? FOUR JULY. IT'S MY SONG.'

He introduced himself. 'Yeah, Stretch, 'cause I'm so tall,' he said, his laugh giving way to a heavy cough. Then he put out his arm for a handshake and somehow managed to use it to swap our positions, blocking my only exit. Whether it was force of habit or preparation for mugging me, I couldn't tell, but there was nothing I could do about it, so I tried not to worry and simply asked him the question I'd wanted to ever since he'd said the anthem was his song: how on earth could he like 'The Star-Spangled Banner' when it celebrates a country that had given him nothing? 'I mean, I know this is rude, but you're obviously poor. I'm guessing you're an addict.'

He could have taken offence at that moment, used such a harsh question as an excuse to knock me over and steal my wallet. But he didn't. He gave me the most eloquent answer: 'What would I be if I was living somewhere else? India? Imagine me there, man. Wouldn't have this.' He pointed at his cup. 'Wouldn't be allowed to smoke. It's better to live in the place that causes the world's problems, than one that gets shot up by them.' He then elaborated for about fifteen minutes, expanding on his thoughts until they somehow involved Ronald Reagan, a potted history of the Beatles and several conspiracy theories about the international banking system, but I'd got his point.

He then started talking about the anthem again: when he'd first sung it and why it was important to him for reasons other than his birthday. I know he did. But I didn't pay attention as I could hear the flick of a lighter followed by a sucking sound coming from inside the house. I knew that was the noise of someone smoking something – heroin, probably – off silver foil. I'd heard it many times before on TV. I looked over Stretch's shoulder. The light from the lighter was making the wire mesh of the porch screen glow gold and behind it I could see an obese woman getting high. Her cheeks were sucked in and her breasts lifted up, as if she was pulling as much smoke into her lungs as she possibly could. There was enough light reflecting off the foil to see inside the house. The floor was bare wood. Some of the boards were missing. There was nothing.

As I looked, I realised that scene was exactly what I'd been hoping to witness ever since I approached Stretch in the first place, and I felt so guilty. I told him I'd come back the next day to finish our chat. When I walked past at 8 a.m., there were two chairs outside his home facing each other. I couldn't bring myself to knock.

Despite all those encounters, I didn't grasp the real importance of 'The Banner' for Americans today until I left Baltimore. I was going to meet a man called Babatunde Ogunnaike, sixty-odd miles away in Newark, Delaware. The trip was actually a detour – nothing to do with 'The Star-Spangled Banner'. Babatunde is one of the six men behind Nigeria's anthem, 'Arise, O Compatriots', and I'd decided I had to say hello to him since I was so close. I just wanted to shake his hand and take a picture, to add him to my anthem collection like an adventurer closing his net over a butterfly. But the final person I spoke to in Baltimore convinced me that the trip could be significant after all.

I got in a cab to head to the bus station and the driver – black, thirties – heard my English accent. 'You still drive on the left over there?' he asked. 'I used to have a leftie. A Volkswagen. Worst car I ever been in.'

'Where are you from?' I asked. He clearly wasn't from here.

'Nigeria!' he shouted proudly. I laughed and told him who I was heading to meet. There was a pause, a 'You serious?', a laugh just as big as mine had been, and then question after question about Babatunde started tumbling out of the man. 'What's he doing in America? . . . How old's he? . . . You sure he's not, like, two hundred? Anthems are *old* . . . Why hasn't the Nigerian government given him a job?' Then he just started shaking his head in disbelief and repeating, 'Wait until my wife hears this.'

I asked him if he knew the song. 'Of course I know it,' he said, and started singing as loud as he could, 'Arise, O compatriots, / Nigeria's call obey.' And once he'd finished that, he started on the country's old anthem, 'Nigeria, We Hail Thee'. He was still going after I got out and had slammed the door.

*

Babatunde Ogunnaike is the dean of engineering at the University of Delaware, and he looks almost comically suited to the job. He's tiny with grey hair, wire-rimmed glasses and pens falling out of his pockets – every bit the cartoon professor. But he's also a man with a permanent glint in his eye and cheeky smile never far from his lips. When I walk into his office, my eyes are immediately drawn to a grand eight-eenth-century painting of a scientist sitting at a desk. The desk is piled with test tubes, Bunsen burners and notes, but the scientist is ignoring them all to stare at a pretty woman by his side. 'He's got his priorities right, hasn't he?' Babatunde says, appearing behind me.

Over lunch, Babatunde talks about his memories of writing the Nigerian anthem. It's a song that raises itself above most of the other hymn-like anthems you find in Africa by virtue of, traditionally, having thunderous Afrobeat percussion beneath it, as if a troop of drummers has rudely interrupted a brass band rehearsal. Babatunde helped write it in 1977 when he was just twenty-one, a bright, optimistic and patriotic student. One day that year, he picked up a newspaper and saw early entries to a competition to be the new anthem. He was shocked at how bad they were. 'I thought: I'm not singing that. I'd better write something quick.' Nigeria was just coming out of a civil war and so he filled his entry with hopeful phrases, believing – genuinely – that his words might push Nigerians to fulfil their country's vast potential. About 1,500 other people thought their words could too, but Babatunde's entry was somehow picked out from the pile, along with five others. Bits of each were then cherry-picked and arranged together to make two verses. 'Do you know the expression "a camel looks like a horse stitched together by a comedian"?' Babatunde says. 'It was a bit like that.'

Babatunde had actually left Nigeria to study in the States before the competition winners were announced, and only found out he'd won because his dad sent him a newspaper clipping. A promised cheque for 50 naira ('A *lot* of money at the time') found its way to his parents' house, but never to him. Babatunde eventually went back to Nigeria with an American girlfriend, but decided to leave again in the late eighties after realising the only way he could make money there was by becoming a rice merchant; Nigeria apparently didn't need academics.

Babatunde starts talking about the problems Nigeria had in those days, and the fact that it still has most of them, and I get the feeling he could carry on doing so for hours. But given he is an immigrant to the US I realise it could be interesting to turn the conversation on to 'The Star-Spangled Banner', so ask if he's become an American citizen. 'Of course,' he says. 'I realised that if I was going to spend my life here, I wanted to vote, so I had to.'

'So how'd you feel about the anthem?' I ask. I'm expecting him to just say it's all right – 'It's got nothing to do with me really. I don't sing it' – but he doesn't. Instead he says, 'Oh boy,' and breathes out heavily, and for the first time since we met, he stumbles over his sentences, struggling to find the right words. 'It's actually really moving. To me. Okay, the start's not great. But then it builds. And when it gets to that line, "The land of the free and the home of the brave", that's the part that gets me. I feel it right in my throat. That line really says to me what America's about.'

I ask what he means exactly and he starts talking about the American Dream. 'I know it's a cliché – the worst cliché – but as a concept it's flawless. If you come in and you're willing to work hard and willing to keep your nose clean, then things will happen for you. You'll have heard stories of how immigrants come here with nothing in their pockets. Well, mine was worse. I owed my in-laws fifteen hundred dollars. I kid you not. I was living here in a room with my wife and our young son. I slept on the floor. We had a second son that year who slept in a pulled-out drawer. Seriously. That's where I started. From scratch. And within a year and a half I had a house, I had a car, I was about to buy a second. Okay, I wasn't living high on the hog, but in which other country can that happen?'

I ask if he's ever experienced racism, and he says of course and gives me a story about the time he was almost shot by a policeman after being pulled over for speeding. 'I said, "I'm very sorry, Officer, I'll happily pay the ticket." And nobody says that! But I was in my twenties, making an obscene amount of money as far as I was concerned, so it didn't matter. But that really put his nose up and he asked me questions for, like, an hour, and then when he finally asked for my papers, I reached for the glove compartment. The only reason I'm still alive is that I heard the safety click on the back of his gun.' Another time out driving, he was almost run off the road by a racist truck driver ('He leaned over from his cab, and said, "Get out of my way, you fucking nigger." He had a sawn-off shotgun. All that'). 'I could give you several more examples,' he says.

'How can you love the US so much given all that?' I reply. But he just smiles and points out that no one here's stopped him achieving.

So I ask the obvious final question: which anthem do you like more, your own or that of your adopted country? 'As poetry, what we wrote doesn't rise to "The Banner"'s level,' he says. 'In part that's because it was cleaved together. You get what you pay for. But the Nigerian anthem, that's also sad for me because when we wrote it, we were being aspirational: "Let's do something about this country to move it to where it should be." And ever since it's gone in the opposite direction. There's so much corruption. People don't want to serve Nigeria, they want to serve themselves, and that goes from the president all the way down. Sometimes I hear it today, and think: Oh come on, this shouldn't be our anthem. It's ridiculous how far the reality is from the words.

'But with "The Star-Spangled Banner", despite all America's problems, "the land of the free and the home of the brave" still rings true. There's the freedom to be yourself here and if you have something to contribute, people will welcome you. There's just *something* about that tune.'

He sees my sceptical eyes and laughs, instantly knowing I'm, shall we say, somewhat cynical about the idea of the American Dream, let alone the sentiment in Key's enigmatic line. From walking around America's second cities, your Baltimores, your Nashvilles, it seems clear to me they are just clichés with which people who've achieved can pat themselves on the back, and to which people who haven't can desperately cling in between drinks of sizzurp. The idea that America is the only country you can achieve in if you work hard is also something I've never been able to understand – something you could surely only believe in if you were using North Korea as the comparison.

But despite all that feeling, I have to admit that people's belief in it is genuine and not just Babatunde's – and it's partly Francis Scott Key's fault for summing it up so well in his anthem, in ways that people could still describe as 'ringing true' two hundred years after they were written.

If only Babatunde's own Nigerian anthem – 'living just and true, / Great lofty heights attain' – had had a similar impact in Nigeria.

*

'The Star-Spangled Banner' didn't actually become America's anthem until 117 years after it was written, in 1931. When Key wrote it, there were already plenty of 'national airs' – songs that people loved and sang on important dates, like the earlier-mentioned 'Yankee Doodle' ('Yankee Doodle went to town, / Riding on a pony, / He stuck a feather in his cap / And called it Macaroni'). But few politicians tried to get one song raised above the others.

Efforts to get a true national anthem largely came from far outside the political establishment. The legendary showman P. T. Barnum – who ran freak shows and circuses, where people could see monkeys sewn on to fish ('A 100% genuine mermaid') – held a contest to write an anthem in the 1850s, though he refused to hand out any prize money because all the entries were so bad. Then the Civil War came along, making the chances of the whole country adopting an anthem at all almost non-existent. In the South, whose supporters included all of Francis Scott Key's family, the minstrel tune 'Dixie' became the de facto anthem, perhaps unsurprising when you realise the song is sung from the point of view of a freed slave wishing he was back 'in the land of cotton'. They did play 'The Star-Spangled Banner' too, but as much to parody it as straight ('Oh say has the Star-Spangled Banner become, / The flag of the Tory and vile Northern scum?'). The North's brass bands, meanwhile, played dozens of tunes, but 'The Banner' was among the most loved. It was a song about the flag the soldiers were marching under, after all. Sometimes the bands even played it during battles as a way to keep the exhausted, scared men going. Whether many people were actually able to hear them amid the noise of a battlefield is anyone's guess.

It was not until a couple of decades after the Civil War, in 1889, that it became almost inevitable that 'The Banner' would become the American anthem. In that year, Benjamin Tracy, the dour, neat-bearded Secretary of the Navy, was having a standardisation drive and passed an order saying all bases must play the song when the flag was raised each morning. The following year, he ordered the Navy Band to play it – 'the national air of the United States' – at all concerts. Within a few years of that, the navy had ordered all its men to stand to attention whenever the song was played. The army, of course, quickly followed.

On a quick stop in Washington, I met Mike Bayes, senior chief musician at the Navy Band and its unofficial historian. He was cramped in a basement office in the city's naval yard surrounded by boxes of ancient papers, piles of photos and random memorabilia: an anchor here, a dusty saxophone there. 'I'm not sure what the catalyst was for the navy promoting it, but maybe the government wanted something to try to unify the states,' he said. 'You think of the period after the Civil War when reconstruction's happening. The union was very fragile; the whole thing could have come crumbling down. How could they keep people unified? Well, band music was popular, and this song was a rallying cry, telling people to look at the flag, remember who you were and that they were part of the union. It's the only song that did that. You could sing it in the south, west, north or east, so politically it made sense for some people in government to want the song out there, and the only way to do that was with the Navy Band because it travelled the country. It was really like a stadium rock band back then.'

The anthem eventually picked up momentum outside the navy too, being played more frequently at baseball games around the end of the First World War, in part to remind people of the troops off fighting in Europe. Some teams initially played it during the 'seventh innings stretch', the traditional rest break in games, but people complained that it was disrespectful to remember war dead while eating a hot dog or going to the toilet and so it was moved to the start of games.

However, the biggest push for the song came from a congressman, John Charles Linthicum. Linthicum was a Baltimore resident and a man who believed patriotism was 'the great bulwark of the Republic', so he was receptive when both his wife and local women's groups started harassing him to introduce bills into the House of Representatives for the song to be adopted as the official anthem. They also played on his home-town sentiments, as if he should 'do it for Maryland'. And he did. He tried five times over ten years without a hint of success.

It didn't help that the song still had legions of detractors. Countless newspaper and magazine editorials over the years said it was the wrong song to be America's anthem, particularly focusing on its difficulty. 'The American people have been trying in vain for nearly a century to sing it,' went a typical one. Another said the audience's response 'continues to be as pathetic as it has ever been desperate . . . Will not someone kindly present us with a new distinctively American hymn?' There were also campaigns against it, especially around Prohibition, with one group taking out full-page adverts in newspapers to slam the tune, pointing out it was a drinking song and an insult to British allies. How could the US ever consider giving such filth the highest status in the land? (Drinking connections don't seem to have ever put people off making songs anthems. The words to Slovenia's 'A Toast' were taken from a poem written so each verse looked like a wine glass.)

But 'The Star-Spangled Banner' had been gathering momentum regardless, and at Linthicum's sixth attempt, in 1929, the other congressmen finally listened to him and agreed

to hold hearings on the issue. It certainly helped that a veterans'
organisation turned up to those hearings with some 5 million
signatures backing the move. The committee let Linthicum's
bill go forward and it then slowly wound its way through the
two houses of Congress, until, in 1931, President Herbert Hoover
signed it into law.

*

A few days after meeting Mike Bayes, I'm in New York in Federal
Hall, a squat, pillar-clad building sitting amongst Wall Street's
skyscrapers. It's the place where George Washington became
America's first president and where the Bill of Rights was written,
guaranteeing freedom of speech. Today it's covered in red, white
and blue drapes, and there are guards in bright ceremonial
uniforms standing at each entrance, their guns shouldered, their
brass buttons gleaming. There are about a hundred people inside,
each waving a small American flag as high and fast as they can.
There's a Canadian Jew in a yarmulke, an Egyptian housewife
in a hijab, a seven-foot-tall former basketball player from Jamaica,
a Dutch banker in a fur coat, a Korean mother bouncing a baby,
and people from Argentina, Russia, Poland . . . All of them are
about to become US citizens, which explains why, right now,
they're reciting the strangest oath I've ever heard. 'I hereby declare
that I absolutely and entirely renounce and abjure all allegiance
and fidelity to any foreign prince, potentate, state or sovereignty,'
they each try to say, many unsurprisingly stumbling over the
word 'potentate'. They go on to promise, when required, 'to
bear arms on behalf of the United States', and to perform
'non-combatant service', and do 'work of national importance
under civilian direction'. And they say they'll do all of this 'freely,
without any mental reservation or purpose of evasion, so help
me God'. It lasts two whole minutes but for that entire time, no
one seems able to stop smiling.

Meeting Babatunde convinced me that in the US, the anthem is still of importance to at least two groups. There are those who serve, obviously – soldiers, sailors, pilots – who hear the song's message about standing until the end no matter how many bombs are flying your way, and remember why they signed up in the first place. It means a lot to many of their friends and families, too, and given that about 1 in 100 people in America is in the armed forces, that's a significant proportion of the population.

The other group – perhaps the more important – is immigrants. People who've just come to the country, or whose parents did. People who are striving to make it. Everyone in this hall. They hear the song's final line about 'the land of the free and the home of the brave' and it motivates them, pushes them to take on two jobs, or to study late into the night. These are people for whom the American Dream really matters; who, unlike me, are convinced of its truthfulness.

Perhaps then, Francis Scott Key shouldn't be recognised simply as the man who wrote the anthem, but as America's first great ad-man for helping create that dream in the first place, for giving this country its tagline, its slogan – 'the land of the free and the home of the brave'. That simple phrase has driven people to travel thousands of miles, to risk everything, just to be part of a country. It is the greatest boast a country has ever had.

But Key deserves the title for more than that. He also in effect named America's flag – the one thing this vast country of diverse states could unite around (although the phrase star-spangled had been around for some time before his song). And even his anthem's first few words, 'O say can you see', have been one of the greatest gifts ever handed to punning headline writers and advertising firms the world over.

'The Star-Spangled Banner' is sung at the naturalisation ceremony by Ryland Angel, a British opera singer who became a US citizen years ago. But like any proud professional, he gives it his own stamp, rushing some phrases and drawing out others. It's impossible for anyone to sing along with him, but there's a young woman from Cameroon in the front row who quietly tries to match his every word. The song clearly means so much to her and it's so touching to watch that I want the day to end right here. That's the image I need to leave America with, the proof of this song's continued importance and relevance.

But the ceremony doesn't end, and after some speeches and a message from Barack Obama ('With the privilege of citizenship comes great responsibilities') everyone is asked to watch an 'inspirational video'. Images start to fill the screen. There are farmers driving combine harvesters through cornfields, kids playing in the water from exploding fire hydrants, old couples standing outside rural post offices, marines in their white suits on shore leave, college football players, the Golden Gate Bridge, various Chinatowns. Every hackneyed image of American life is flicked up to tell people what they've let themselves in for. The music for this video isn't the anthem, it's 'God Bless the USA' by Lee Greenwood, a country musician who once travelled to Nashville in the hope of making it big. 'I'm proud to be an American,' the chorus goes,

> Where at least I know I'm free.
> And I won't forget the men who died,
> Who gave that right to me.

It's one of the schmaltziest, most emotionally manipulative pieces of music I've ever heard. A choir and an orchestra come soaring in halfway through to double up the melody, and there's a sudden key change where the song leaps higher, almost forcing everyone to stand up and pump their fists along. There's even a false ending. It is – as a music snob – one of the worst three minutes I'll ever stand through. But the audience loves it. They wave their flags and sing along, the words helpfully popping up karaoke-style on the screen, and they sway from side to side, Latvians next to Taiwanese, Dominicans with Indians. And I suddenly realise I'm swaying too. Against my will, and against all my sense of taste, I'm carried away on the happiness in this room. 'The Star-Spangled Banner', which has fought off so many competitors throughout its long life, may have another one to deal with.

Kimigayo

きみがよは
ちよにやちよに
さざれいしの
いわおとなりて
こけのむすまで

—

May your reign,
Last for a thousand, eight thousand
    generations,
Until the pebbles,
Grow into boulders,
Lush with moss

4

Japan

ANTHEMS AND CONFLICT

The town of Sera, a few hours' drive into the mountains east of Hiroshima, is so stereotypically Japanese it's almost as if it were designed by the country's tourist board. A couple of rivers run through it, each lined with cherry trees; children play among the fallen petals. There are fields right in the centre of town – next to the pachinko parlour, behind the hospital – plots that have been farmed by the same families for decades. And there's a bright red temple standing on the hill above everything, as if on guard. It's so peaceful, I'm not surprised when a young doctor tells me no one locks their doors here. 'Unless I want to . . . er, y'know . . . Unless my girlfriend's visiting.'

The only thing breaking the peace is the noise from the local high school: the call-and-response chants of baseball practice and the *slap-slap-slap* of pupils running laps around its track. There seem to be teenagers running that track continually, from first thing in the morning to last thing at night. It's as if their footsteps are powering Sera's generators and they're not allowed to stop. Such dedication has made the school famous for *ekiden* – the Japanese relay form of the marathon. It has won the national championship several times, and even Kenyan runners take scholarships here so they can train while studying. But that success is not the reason I'm visiting. I'm here because of a man called Toshihiro Ishikawa.

In 1999, Toshihiro was the school principal. There's a photo of him inside its main office. He has thick black hair, swept back and side parted, huge square glasses, and he's wearing a dark suit with a patterned tie done up slightly too tight. Before becoming the principal he was a maths teacher, and apparently loved by pupils for always trying to see the best in them, even when they were obvious disasters. He'd often pick up an exam paper, find the one question a pupil got right and then praise them to the heavens for it in the vain hope that this would encourage them to study a little harder. He would write letters to universities lauding students who would otherwise struggle to get in. He never shouted; never yelled. In two days in the town, I didn't hear one bad thing said about him.

He was about to retire when the photo of him was taken – to spend his days sitting in his garden listening to Tchaikovsky records, or Schubert if he fancied a change. He was obsessed with classical piano. He didn't play himself, but his son and daughter did, and he loved nothing more than to hear them practise or to drag them along to recitals. There were other plans he had for his retirement too – his wife, Masako, kept nudging him about skiing holidays, and he planned to rebuild their house from the ground up – but at the turn of the year, he got a call from Hiroshima's school board. At that year's graduation ceremony, they said, he had to do something differently: he had to play Japan's national anthem, 'Kimigayo', and he had to make sure every teacher stood for it.

That sounds simple enough, but the school had never made teachers stand for the anthem before, knowing almost all would object. One of the sports teachers used to rush out of the hall whenever it was played, as if allergic to it, only to apologetically creep back in fifty-five seconds later as its final note died away. Others also ducked out, or stayed sitting while it was played, or simply refused to attend the ceremonies at all. If students asked them why they objected, the teachers would say the anthem was militaristic, a remnant of Japan's troubled past, and they couldn't see how anyone could respect it. Some would break down in tears as they tried to explain. But the school board had had enough.

Toshihiro spent days, then weeks, trying to convince his teachers to stand for the anthem, worrying what would happen to him, to the school and to the students if he failed. The issue took over his life. He couldn't sleep. He couldn't even escape into his children's piano playing any more. On 27 February, a Saturday, he stayed up all night talking with Masako about what else he could do to change the teachers' minds. She helped him practise speeches and rehearse arguments, telling him not to worry and that soon it would all be over. The ceremony was only a couple of days away, after all.

The next morning, he got up and went into the garden to visit the family grave, just as he did every Sunday. He didn't come back. Masako found him hanging from a rafter in their storehouse.

The school's website lists him as retired.

*

All anthems seem to stir up controversy at some point. Musicians cover them and cause uproar – just think of Jimi Hendrix's feedback-drenched 'Star-Spangled Banner'. Athletes refuse to sing them and get thrown out of teams. Women's rights campaigners call for them to be changed – in Canada they've campaigned for decades to get one line of 'O Canada' rewritten from 'in all thy sons command' to 'in all of us command' – while staunch nationalists have been known to beat people up for not standing for them. Then there are the rows that emerge when businesses try to make money out of them (Bangladeshi mobile ringtone companies, especially) and find themselves hauled into the courts.

You also only have to glance at news footage of any revolution to know how controversial anthems can get, people singing them continually at each other in an effort to say, 'We're the ones who really represent this country.' In Ukraine in 2013, when protestors at Independence Square in Kiev were trying to overthrow the pro-Russian presidency, they sang 'Ukraine's Not Dead Yet' on the hour, every hour. I imagine the line 'We'll lay down our souls and bodies for our freedom' was shouted particularly loudly. Pro-Russian rebels sang the Russian anthem right back, and when the Ukrainian city of Donetsk tried to break away from the reborn country, its 'People's Republic' put out a call for a new anthem in the middle of the fighting – an anthem apparently being just as important as soldiers.

There are anthem controversies in all the places you would expect. Israel, for example. There, 'Hatikvah' – 'The Hope' – is regularly the subject of complaints, not least because a quarter of the population is Arab and few are keen on singing a song about how their 'Jewish soul still yearns / . . . To be a free people . . . / In the land of Zion'. In India, meanwhile, lawsuits are regularly served against politicians and movie stars deemed to have shown insufficient respect to 'Jana Gana Mana' ('Thou Art the Ruler of the Minds of All People').

But no matter how heated such controversies get, none comes close to that around 'Kimigayo'. It's a conflict that's been going on in Japan's schools for over seventy years. Teachers have lost jobs because of it. They've received death threats because of it. Parents have been left dazed by it, worrying about their children's future. And yes, Toshihiro Ishikawa committed suicide because of it.

*

'Kimigayo' is really the last anthem you would expect to cause any controversy. It's simple and solemn, without a hint of boisterousness or boastfulness – just forty-seven notes that move slowly and steadily up and down a traditional *gagaku* scale, like an old man patiently negotiating a flight of stairs. It's a beautiful piece of music, which to the Japanese sounds like something played in their imperial court, but to Western ears feels sad, almost elegiac, more suited to a wake than to being sung at baseball stadiums by children in Hello Kitty costumes.

The words are also among the most poetic found in anthems. 'May your reign / Last for a thousand, eight thousand generations,' it goes – the 'your' interpreted by most as meaning Japan's emperor –

> Until the pebbles
> Grow into boulders,
> Lush with moss.

That's it. Nineteen words. A single beautiful image, something that could easily be part of a wedding vow – 'May our love last until the pebbles grow into boulders . . .' – and nothing more.

It's also surprising that the anthem is such a contentious issue when Japan is a country where people seem to strive to avoid confrontation. You would think everyone here would be too embarrassed to get worked up about a song. I got a perfect illustration of that attitude on my very first day in the country. I visited Tokyo's Yasukuni Shrine, one of the world's most controversial religious buildings. It's where the spirits of Japan's war dead are enshrined, over 2.4 million of them. That number happens to include multiple war criminals: generals who were responsible for massacres in China and for forcing thousands of Koreans to act as 'comfort women' (a very euphemistic term for sex slave) before and during the Second World War. There's a museum attached to the shrine that tries its best to claim such things never happened. Whenever a politician visits Yasukuni, the Chinese, South Korean, North Korean and Taiwanese governments protest until they're hoarse. But it's also a place that tourists flock to, largely to take photos of a cherry tree that sits opposite its entrance. That tree is warped, propped up by sticks and wrapped in weeping bandages, but it's the most famous in Japan because it's used to announce when spring comes to Tokyo. Once it blossoms, the world's largest city can celebrate.

While I was there, a right-wing group turned up in a fleet of sound trucks, blasting patriotic slogans at passers-by (there are dozens of these groups, known as *uyoku dantai*, in Japan, many with links to the Yakuza). There were about twenty men, all in blue boiler suits. They got out and marched to the front of the shrine waving a huge Japanese flag in front of them, the red sun at its centre. In any other country, someone would have shouted at them to clear off, to stop politicising the shrine and spoiling everyone's Sunday. But no one said a word. No one even tutted. They just acted as if the men weren't there, stepping out of their way, then carrying on snapping photos of the cherry tree – a perfect demonstration of the Japanese attitude that it's best not to say anything if at all possible.

I tried speaking to some of the right-wingers afterwards, but even they did not want to draw more attention to themselves than they already had. 'We're just a club,' one pleaded. 'We meet once a month, come here with the flag and then go for a drink. It's a hobby. Please don't ask me anything more.' Then they drove off, five black trucks with their speakers ready to go, followed by a white one painted with the message: 'Sorry for any inconvenience caused.'

The same attitude surrounds 'Kimigayo'. Everyone here knows it's controversial, and they just don't want to be seen as stirring things up by talking about it. Half the people I tried to meet would only talk to me on the condition 'no politics'; the other half would agree to talk, only to then go out of their way to avoid giving an opinion.

'What do you think of "Kimigayo"?' I'd ask.

'Ahhhh . . .' they'd sigh, then spend ten minutes talking me blandly through its history in the hope I'd forget I ever asked their view. In fact, the only people who did not seem affected by this embarrassment were the teachers who hate it.

★

Kimiko Nezu clasps my hands between hers when she walks into the cafe in Suidōbashi – a part of Tokyo filled with flashing games arcades that give everyone's skin a fluorescent glow – then she apologises for not speaking English and bows, apologises again and bows some more. It's such a warm greeting it almost makes me forget why I've arranged to meet her. Kimiko, sixty-five with greying hair and a slight hunch, is the godmother of anthem protest here; a teacher who has been disciplined more than anyone else in the country. She's been fined, suspended, moved to schools three hours' commute from her home in the hope she'd quit, and made to attend endless 're-education' classes. She's been protested against and sent a small knife blade in the post – a traditional death threat. And her story illustrates better than anyone else's why 'Kimigayo' is such a problem here.

Kimiko grew up in the mountain town of Yamakita, an hour or two's drive west of Tokyo. Her parents were tangerine farmers and, like many rural girls in the 1950s, she had no desire in life apart from to become a good wife and mother to an exception-ally large family. Unusually, she sang 'Kimigayo' at school ('Every time I heard it, I felt so aroused – is that the right word? – because I felt proud to be Japanese. People always told me we were richer than other Asian countries. Luckier, happier'). I say 'unusually' because hardly any schools sang the anthem back then due to its controversial past.

'Kimigayo' goes back as far as the seventh century, a poem used throughout Japan not only to toast the emperor, but to show respect to others. People would recite it at the end of meals to thank the host, or sing it to express their gratitude after signing a business deal. It only got its current nationalist associations when it was set to music in 1869 by John William Fenton, a British bandleader who was in Yokohama teaching soldiers to play brass instruments. One day he asked his pupils if Japan had a national anthem he could learn. They looked at him confused, so he explained what one was, then offered to compose Japan one if they could find him suitable words. They picked 'Kimigayo' and Fenton set it to music based on a traditional tune he'd heard one of the soldiers playing on the biwa, a Japanese lute. One of its first airings was before the emperor and thanks to the positions Fenton's pupils later obtained, his song apparently soon took on the status of the anthem in the army and navy, the two places that mattered most.

Fenton's effort was overhauled in 1880 because it turned out to be completely unsingable if you were Japanese – 'Japanese is not a tonal language, but it has its highs and lows, and he got it completely wrong,' Professor Kazuo Fukushima, the director of Japan's Music Historiography Research Institute, told me – but after the rework it grew in prominence, especially as Japan's ruling elite tried to create a modern country headed first by the bearded, stern Emperor Meiji, and later by his grandson, the diminutive, bespectacled Emperor Hirohito. Those rulers wanted Japan to become a superpower to rival the US or UK and that meant having a song like them too, one that could be played at all official functions and taught to its children.

By the 1930s, the anthem was everywhere. When the country's troops were fighting abroad, they'd turn and face Japan to sing it, and when they colonised somewhere like Korea they'd force everyone there to sing it too. But its use was heaviest in Japan's schools, where teachers were encouraged to make pupils think that dying for the emperor was the most honourable act someone could do. They'd sing 'Kimigayo' to praise him almost every day, leaping to their feet whenever its first note was struck to avoid a beating.

During the Second World War, over 2 million Japanese soldiers died, many, as one historian wrote, almost 'devouring themselves' by undertaking suicide missions. They had fought without question, partly because 'Kimigayo' had burrowed its way into them when they were younger and made them believe in total duty to the emperor. When the war ended, many teachers felt so culpable for having sent so many boys to their deaths that they formed a union with the slogan: 'Never send our children to the battlefield again'. One of its founding aims was to oppose the anthem. It was almost as big an issue for them as pay. After that union was formed, 'Kimigayo' simply disappeared from schools. When Kimiko was a child, most would not have dared sing it for fear of the union members. I can only think her school was so rural, the union didn't bother recruiting there.

*

Despite the opposition, Japan's government never considered changing the country's anthem, unlike the Second World War's other defeated powers. In 1945, Germany had quickly realised it was no longer a good idea to sing the first verse of the 'Deutschlandlied' as its anthem, especially given its opening:

> *Deutschland, Deutschland über alles,*
> *Über alles in der Welt.*

Few foreigners were going to understand that wasn't actually a call for world domination, but had been written in 1841 to encourage German states like Prussia to unite under one flag.

West Germany's politicians tried out several other songs until
deciding it would be simplest to use another verse of the
'Deutschlandlied' instead. They picked the third, calling on
Germany to 'Bloom in the glow of happiness'. I rather wish
they'd picked the second, which praises 'German women' and
'German wine', but that was understandably deemed too sexist
for the world stage.

Italy similarly overhauled its anthem after the war, dumping
the sprightly, instrumental 'Royal March' after it voted to become
a republic. They replaced it with 'Il Canto degli Italiani', a tune
so rambunctious it should have been the country's anthem all
along – as full of emotion as a group of Milanese arguing over
football.

Both Italy and Germany also made sure their respective fascist
anthems were never played again – a decision that could have
been made on grounds of taste as much as politics, since both
feature some of the worst words ever put to song (the Italian
Fascist Party's 'Giovinezza' spends half its time telling 'the youth'
to 'shout hoorays' for Mussolini).

But Japan kept 'Kimigayo'. Even the Americans, who occupied
the country for seven years after the war, did not attempt to
force a change, the ruling General MacArthur believing they
needed Emperor Hirohito's personality cult to help them push
through reforms. So after Hirohito renounced his divinity, the
US played down his role in the war then sent him out on tour,
his song in tow.

Kimiko's views on the anthem did not change until she got
to university, but the change was sudden. It was the seventies
and Japan's teenagers were as idealistic as those anywhere else,
and on one of her first days on campus she looked at a bulletin
board and saw posters complaining about the treatment of
Korean and Chinese people in the country. She spoke to some
friends about it, and discovered that Japan had once colonised
both countries. She was so embarrassed she had known nothing

about such events that she started reading book after book on Japan's wartime history. 'I read what we did and it was just such terrible things,' she says. 'I was horrified. I started thinking: My dad went to China in the war. Did he massacre people? Did he use comfort women?' She went home as soon as she could to question him, and ended up doing so for three days and nights, her face sometimes inches from his. She remembers grabbing him by the neck at one point, shaking him, frustrated, exhausted with his answers.

'He insisted he hadn't actually been at the front line, that he had just been preparing food for people. He told me that over and over again. But I was eighteen. I didn't believe him. I was certain he'd done something. Killed people. I kept thinking that I was only born because he'd survived the war, but there were thousands of people in China who weren't born because of us. They could have had a life like mine.' She decided she could never respect the anthem after that, the flag too (it had the same associations). 'It was already twenty-seven years after the war and people were talking about it like it was the past. But to me, those issues were right now. It was my father. It was me.'

*

Kimiko became a teacher and every once in a while would give her students a lesson on Japan's past, telling them about the 'real meaning' of the flag and anthem. That didn't actually cause her any problems until 1989, when Japan's education board issued guidelines saying 'Kimigayo' 'must be played' and the flag 'must be raised' at entrance and graduation ceremonies, the two moments that are meant to be the most memorable of a child's life – for their parents at least. The change had been coming for a while – politicians had long argued the country's economic success was dependent on its children being proud to be Japanese, dedicated to working for its growth – but its immediate cause was the fit of patriotism that followed Emperor Hirohito's death that January. Why wouldn't children want to remember him with the anthem? What better way to welcome the new emperor – Hirohito's ever-smiling son, Akihito – than with song?

Hardly any schools actually complied with the guidance at first. In fact, things just got silly. There were reports of principals playing the anthem on Walkmen and singing along alone, so they could tick the box saying it had been played. Others played it the moment the school's gates opened so that no one was in the hall to hear it. Some complied with the flag rule by flying one at the bottom of their playing fields, behind the trees where no one could see it. One school even flew a set of 'carp streamers' – fish-shaped windsocks – instead. They put a baby red carp in the middle of several adult white ones, mimicking the risen sun flag almost perfectly.

Kimiko's school did not even bother making those concessions. It only started flying the flag five years after the rule came in, and the first time it did, Kimiko ripped it down, apparently with the full backing of students and parents ('My students were about to do it – they were protesting at the principal – and I had to act first. They couldn't get in trouble'). Her school would never have dared play the anthem, she says. Forcing teachers to put up with the sight of the flag was one thing; making them open their mouths and sing another entirely. But then two events changed everything.

*

Tokorozawa is a commuter town an hour's train ride north of Tokyo. It's a place where you can't imagine anything exciting happening. I visited for a day and the most exciting thing I saw was a 'doggy styling' salon. I walked in expecting to find a poodle mid-shampoo or Labradors in curlers, but there was just a bored middle-aged man desperate for custom. But Tokorozawa's always been known as a liberal town, particularly because of its local high school. That school's slogan is *'Jiyū, jishu, jiritsu'* ('Freedom, autonomy and independence') and children there do not have to wear uniform – a rarity in Japan. They can even style their hair how they want. Most dye it orange, making it one of the few schools in the world where ginger people are celebrated rather than mocked.

In 1997, it was the only school in Saitama Prefecture that wasn't even making a cursory effort to follow the anthem rules, almost a decade after their introduction, and so the region's government decided things had to change. It installed a new principal, Uchida Tatsuo, who, only a week after arriving, announced the anthem would be played at the following day's entrance ceremony. The news sparked a mini-crisis, teachers saying he couldn't just walk in and do this, and the school's pianist refusing to attend. The next morning, the teachers called a meeting to convince him to change his mind, but Tatsuo simply walked out halfway through, marching off to the hall where parents and students were already waiting, giving one child a ghetto blaster and telling him to follow. Tatsuo got up on the stage and was about to introduce the anthem when someone cut the school's PA system. He then tried to play the anthem out of his ghetto blaster, only to discover someone had stolen the tape. Flustered, he stood on the stage and apparently started singing by himself. Students, teachers and parents streamed out in protest. Tatsuo, to his credit I suppose, carried on going to the end.

A few months later, the student council polled all final-year students about whether they wanted the anthem at their graduation. Over two-thirds responded, 93 per cent saying they did not. The council decided to hold its own graduation festival and ignore Tatsuo's. In March 1998, only eighteen students attended the official event and sang 'Kimigayo'.

This display of student power was almost unheard of in Japan and the way people reacted to it, you'd think it was the Japanese equivalent of the American civil rights campus fights. It was news across the country for weeks. TV crews parked outside to report on developments, while newspapers ran editorials asking, 'Is this school a problem or are these students just what Japan needs?' One of the country's most famous manga artists even drew a comic strip about it, featuring cross-dressing students raping each other while shouting, 'Sex is my human right' – the idea being, if you let children refuse the anthem, this is what's next.

Today, Tokorozawa's students do sing 'Kimigayo' – 'They don't care about history any more,' one teacher told me, 'and all the teachers stand because they want to keep their jobs' – but people still worry about the school. Its image is still tarnished.

It was a year after the Tokorozawa incident that Toshihiro Ishikawa hanged himself. The two events were so close together and so dramatic that the government couldn't ignore them, and within months it had passed a law making 'Kimigayo' Japan's official anthem, and *Hinomaru* – the 'circle of the sun' – its official flag. They had never been officially recognised before. The government hoped that by passing the law, fewer people would argue against them. The country's foreign office must have breathed the biggest sigh of relief: its civil servants would no longer have to spend time calling Olympic committees to tell them that 'Kimigayo' was the anthem 'for Japan' rather than the anthem 'of Japan', begging them to use the correct wording if a Japanese athlete won gold.

*

Kimiko says the law had an immediate effect. Every school she taught at from then on played the anthem. However, every time they did so, she stayed sitting. She was not standing for that song.

Never. No one actually said anything about her small act of defiance until 2003, when Tokyo's governor, a man called Shintaro Ishihara, announced that any teacher who refused to stand would be punished. The decision was not out of character for him. Ishihara is an intellectual – a prize-winning novelist who made his name writing a book about a high school boxing team who spend their days getting drunk and chasing girls – but he's also nationalistic, to an almost ludicrous degree; the sort of person who says the Nanjing Massacre never happened and who once tried to buy the Senkaku Islands – a few tiny rocks in the Pacific – to end China's claims on them.

At the next entrance ceremonies, hundreds of Tokyo's teachers ignored Ishihara and refused to stand, and over 300 of them were disciplined, including Kimiko. A lot of them could not take being punished and so fell into line, but Kimiko didn't. She had her salary cut for one month, then six; she was suspended for one month, then three. By 2007, she was being suspended without pay for six months every year. She only once capitulated, standing for the anthem after a principal spent a year begging her to do so. He appeared to have lost weight every time she saw him, becoming sicker and sicker, and so she agreed to stand, fearing he would kill himself if she didn't. The moment she stood, every student in the hall turned to face her, gawping in amazement. She started hallucinating, picturing a soldier ordering her to kill. It was as though her body was breaking down under the stress. She made it through ten seconds before collapsing into her chair.

About this time, Kimiko also became the face of a 500-strong lawsuit against Ishihara's rules, arguing they breached teachers' freedom of thought. Tokyo's highest court agreed with her, but Japan's Supreme Court didn't, its judges admitting the anthem requirements were 'an indirect limitation' on freedom, but ruling they were still constitutional. Rules are rules: stand up or face the consequences.

In the middle of all this, even Emperor Akihito had a say. He bumped into a member of Tokyo's education board at a garden party and asked what the man did.

'It's my job to get all schools to sing the anthem,' the man proudly said.

'It's desirable no one's forced,' the emperor snapped back. No one seemed to listen.

*

For the next fifteen minutes or so, Kimiko carries on talking about everything she's had to go through because of her resistance to the anthem. She explains exactly how it's possible to live on only six months' salary if you grow enough vegetables, and what it's like being followed everywhere by right-wing protestors who shout at you through megaphones to 'go back to North Korea' ('Did they ever play the anthem at you?' I ask. 'Of course!' she laughs). She talks about the emotional reconciliation she had with her father after he'd been diagnosed as terminally ill, when he showed her his war records proving he had not killed anyone (he had in fact spent most of the war refusing orders). And she says she would not change her views even if Japan got an entirely new anthem. 'I can't agree with using symbols to make people look in the same direction,' she says.

But then I get to a rather difficult point: I ask if she feels like all her objecting has been worthwhile. I mean, she's retired now, spending her days helping the handful of Tokyo teachers who still refuse to stand. There's only two or three left. Most young teachers either cannot see any problem with the song, or simply do not want to destroy their career prospects by sitting down. 'Haven't you lost?' I say. 'Do you ever worry that it was all pointless?'

'Of course there are times when I can't find any meaning in

what I do, when I feel weak and want to give up,' she says. 'But just when I think they've won, someone else – someone new – pops up and refuses to stand, and that gives me the energy to carry on.' She starts listing other cities where people are protesting: Hiroshima, Okinawa, Nagasaki. For a minute, it feels like she's going to list every city devastated during the Second World War. But then she asks if I've been to Osaka.

*

Osaka is Japan's second metropolis – a place everyone in the country ridicules for being envious of Tokyo. Osakans, of course, deny it, but they'll then spend ten minutes telling you exactly how their city is *nothing* like the capital. 'Tokyo people are stuck up. They can't laugh at themselves,' one man said to me at a baseball game. 'Osakan people . . .' He drifted off to a proud smile, the difference clearly not needing to be spelled out.

Osaka is a far smaller city than Tokyo – only 2.6 million people compared to Tokyo's 13.5 million – and it feels friendlier, the breeze coming in from the sea seeming to make everyone more relaxed. But you can't help feeling a little sorry for it. Tokyo's not the only city to overshadow it; the old imperial centres of Kyoto and Nara do too, and they're virtually next door. People go to those cities to wander awestruck through temples and to drown in imperial opulence. The only people who really visit Osaka are food tourists: budding restaurateurs who want to see the home of *okonomiyaki* (stuffed pancakes slathered in barbeque sauce) and *takoyaki* (octopus balls). You can usually tell if a place is selling the latter by the ten-foot-tall plastic octopus suckered to its entrance.

Osaka is the home of one other thing right now, although it's not something that's likely to draw in many more tourists: anthem rows. Where Tokyo once led, Osaka is now dominant. In 2011, its regional government passed a law saying teachers *had* to stand for 'Kimigayo'. It also introduced a 'three strikes and you're out' rule, meaning teachers could only sit three times before they were sacked. Oh, and there's the small matter of the lip-syncing scandal.

In 2012, a school principal, Toru Nakahara, caused outcry when he spent a graduation ceremony checking whether his teachers' lips were moving while they stood for the anthem. It's not quite as bad as it sounds. He did it from afar; he didn't walk up to them and place an ear to their mouths. But anyone whose lips weren't moving was hauled into his office and asked why. The Japanese press ridiculed him for it, but somehow mocking headlines didn't affect Nakahara one bit. In fact, he was promoted to become Osaka Prefecture's education chief and almost immediately issued a directive ordering principals to follow his lead and undertake a 'visual inspection' of lips at ceremonies. The rule was supposed to come into force in 2014, but was mysteriously dropped – perhaps because someone realised it was unlikely to help Osaka lose its role as Japan's punchbag.

When Kimiko suggested I go to Osaka to look into these issues, I was actually one step ahead of her, having somehow talked its government into letting me attend one of that year's entrance ceremonies. They had been reluctant to let me anywhere near them at first, but in the end relented as long as it was one school: Tamatsukuri Elementary, one of the best in the city. I knew instantly there would be no chance of any teachers protesting the anthem there. Every one of them had been marked to become a principal; they wouldn't risk that. But I had to see one of these ceremonies for myself, to try to get some insight into what happens and to understand just why this anthem is so controversial, so, of course, I said yes.

★

It was a beautiful April morning when I arrived at Tamatsukuri's hall and right on 9 a.m., dozens of six-year-olds rushed into the school's hall in dark blue outfits and prim hats, most of them smiling, excited about their first day; a few nervously looking around for their parents, hoping they could go home soon. Some of the mothers were in kimonos, while most of the fathers were wearing suits. Grandparents had come along too and everyone had cameras, desperate to capture the moment. Then the headmistress walked in and with barely a hello, asked everyone to stand for the anthem. The pianist immediately started playing the gentle, solemn melody of 'Kimigayo' before most people had had a chance to stand, and I found myself fumbling through my pockets trying to find my phone to film it, then started running my eyes up and down the rows of teachers to see if any were sitting – none were – then back across the hall to see what the children and parents were doing too. Most of the children looked as though they didn't know the tune, but some were shouting it out, as if they'd been coached by their parents beforehand. Most of the parents themselves were just beaming at their children, oblivious to the song. And then before anything had really even got going, the music stopped and everyone rushed to sit back down. I don't know why I'd been expecting more: there's not much that can happen in fifty-five seconds.

A couple of hours later, I left wondering what all the fuss was about. How could anyone get worked up over something so simple in such a harmless context? But equally, how could anyone get angry about people sitting down during it? A lot of the other songs played during the ceremony were far more offensive than 'Kimigayo', especially a cover of the Pet Shop Boys' 'Go West', which had been reimagined to teach English. During that, all the children tried to open their eyes as wide as possible as if imitating Westerners, proving racism is alive and well in schoolchildren the world over. Outside, I asked a parent how they would have felt if some teachers had stayed sitting during 'Kimigayo'. 'I'd probably have thought they were tired,' he said.

*

It doesn't take much effort to find teachers who are refusing to comply with the anthem laws in Osaka. I made one call to a teachers' union and was soon in a room with five of them. There was a Christian who refused to sing a song that worships the emperor ('Only Jesus is God'), a peace activist, and a communist who kept telling me that all anthems and all nation states had to be abolished. But the two most interesting had more personal and emotional reasons for refusing to stand.

There was Toshimichi Masuda, in his fifties, whose father barely survived the atomic bombing of Hiroshima and was long ill due to it, and who saw Japan's militarism as ultimately responsible for that tragedy. 'That was my motivation to become a teacher,' he said, 'to tell children what really happened because of the war – so obviously I could never stand for the anthem.'

And then there was a sixty-something woman, Hiroko Tsujitani, whose mother had gone to school during the war and become so wrapped up in emperor worship that she wrote her brother letters telling him, 'Please die for this country. It would be an honour for us all.' After the war ended, horrified she'd ever done such a thing, she warned Hiroko that education and politics must never mix. 'I had to make sure nothing like that ever happened again,' Hiroko said, explaining why she became a teacher.

As I heard their stories, I became convinced these teachers were right not to stand. If they believed the anthem was really tied in with militarism and family tragedies, how could they? And why would anyone force them? But I also realised I was talking to the wrong people. I needed to meet the men behind these laws to find out why on earth they were passing them – and I needed to find out why the Japanese public were seemingly happy for them to be in place.

*

Tōru Hashimoto is the Mayor of Osaka. He's a huge figure in the city, admired by many for being a straight-talking antidote to traditional Japanese politics, hated by others for the inappropriate comments he seems to make at every opportunity (on the day I arrived he told a group of businessmen to take mistresses, then buy them flats downtown in order to revitalise the city's economy). If you talk to people about him here, they either adopt a look of awe or stick two fingers down their throat and pretend to vomit.

In political circles, he's respected nationwide for overcoming an appalling background – involving the early death of a Yakuza-connected father – to forge a successful career. But in right-wing circles, he's more respected for being an ardent nationalist. He once set up a political party called the Japan Restoration Association, named after the Meiji Restoration of the 1860s, the time when Japan tried to become a superpower. That choice of name should tell you all you need to know about his character, but he's also made a habit of denying Japan's wartime problems – 'When soldiers are risking their lives by running through storms of bullets and you want to give these emotionally charged soldiers a rest . . . it's clear you need [comfort women],' he once said – and he's also the main reason for Osaka's anthem rules. Hashimoto has defended those rules many times to Japanese journalists, jabbing his fingers at them, shouting at them, telling them that they do not understand the real issues and that civil servants have to do as they are told if they want to keep their jobs.

But for some reason he does not want to defend them to me. I requested an interview with him months ago, but was told he didn't do one-on-one meetings with writers. I was then told I could attend one of his daily press briefings instead, but when I turned up his press secretary looked so shocked it was as if he had never been expecting me to actually do so.

'Can you come back tomorrow?' he said. 'And please, no political questions.'

'But he's a politician,' I replied.

'I know, but just ask him personal things.' There was a pause. 'Please.' The man looked so desperate I said the condition was fine. And it was, really, because what I most wanted to ask Hashimoto was personal: why does this anthem mean so much to you that you push these rules? Was there one time you heard it that was so emotional you can never forget it?

I returned to his press briefing the next day genuinely excited. This was going to be my breakthrough moment in understanding the 'Kimigayo' rows, I thought, as I joined three dozen reporters on the fifth floor of a bland government office. That excitement veered slightly towards confusion when Hashimoto walked into the room in a white jogging outfit, looking more like he was ready for a game of squash than to meet the press, two bodyguards flanking his sides. But I introduced myself, and my interpreter Miki asked him the three questions I'd prepared. Hashimoto stared back at her intently as he answered slowly and assuredly; the three dozen reporters started typing out his every word as if what he was saying couldn't have been more important. I stood there expectantly, thinking I'd got a scoop. Why else would everyone be typing so furiously? Then he finished, smiled and moved on to someone else. Miki leaned over to me. 'He didn't really answer you,' she whispered. 'He said he can't speak personally, only as the Mayor of Osaka or the head of the Japan Restoration Association.'

'He said that for *every* question?'

'Well, he changed his wording each time, but basically...' Miki smiled in the way Japanese sometimes do to hide embarrassment.

It's at this point I'd like to say I simply laughed at Hashimoto's skill – a politician who knows how to avoid a difficult question when he comes across one – and then listened politely to what he said next, maybe then congratulated his press secretary for warning him in advance about what was coming. But I didn't. Instead I rudely interrupted the next journalist and asked a rather long, somewhat angry question that could neatly be summed up as: 'Why would anyone vote for you if you won't answer straight-forward questions?'

Hashimoto didn't take it well. 'First of all, I would like foreign journalists to only do news-gathering activities after they have accurately grasped the facts,' he said. 'We are not ordering people to sing. We're just ordering teachers, who are public employees, to stand up when they play the national anthem at important occasions.

'If teachers do not comply with rules for a reason of their thought or conscience, education cannot hold. What would happen if students, for the same reason, claimed the right to not do homework? Or to not go to school? Or to do violence to others? Order could not be maintained. Government officials make an oath to comply with laws when they are hired and they must follow them regardless of their conscience.

'I am proud of the anthem with its long history and tradition. I am ashamed of the situation we have in Japan where we have to set up these kind of rules while other nations' teachers stand up spontaneously. That isn't normal behaviour, I think.'

*

Over the next few days I met other people who I thought might be able to shine a light on why the anthem laws are so needed. I spoke with Seiya Numamori, an official at the city's education board, who, with a broad smile and slicked-back hair, told me children had to be exposed to the anthem so they could engage with the world. Children cannot understand other cultures if they don't understand their own, he said. 'We want to try to motivate children to sing by teaching them the meaning and importance of the song. So if teachers are expressing their personal view to children by not standing, that is intolerable.'

I also met Mitsuhiro Kimura, the head of the ultra-nationalist organisation Issuikai, the sort of group that spends its weekends shouting at strangers to have more samurai spirit and greater respect for the emperor. His office was filled with pictures of Yukio Mishima, the brilliant novelist who in 1970 committed ritual suicide after failing to wrest power from meddling politicians in a coup (he wanted the emperor to have political control over Japan once more). Mitsuhiro insisted he had never protested against the teachers as he respected their views, but at the same time he couldn't understand why anyone wouldn't stand. 'The teachers who go against "Kimigayo" don't admit the historical fact that the Japanese people want this song. It's deep in our soul. After the war, left-wingers set up a committee to find a new anthem, but they couldn't come up with a good enough one. I always tell these people, "If you deny 'Kimigayo', you need a replacement. And what happens if the Japanese people refuse to accept yours?"'

I asked how often he sang the anthem. 'I suffer from stress, so I sing it in the bath, just to relax.' I decided it would be impolite to ask him how often he bathed.

I also spoke to people in the street, just asking them why teachers should stand and sing this song. A girl near Osaka's castle got out her phone and played around with a translation program for a while. 'Common sense!' she shouted triumphantly after finding the right words. 'It's common sense.' All her friends agreed.

But I didn't feel as if I really understood why the public had such a casual attitude to the issue until I met Michael Cucek. Michael's an American political consultant who has lived in Tokyo for more than twenty years. He speaks Japanese and is married to a Japanese woman. He is the closest a foreigner will ever get to being an insider in this country, but thankfully he does not have to watch his tongue or worry about causing a fuss like an actual Japanese would. We met for lunch in a place called Sugamo, a Tokyo suburb that's known as the 'old person's Harajuku'– a fashion destination for people over sixty, featuring shops that sell nothing but walking canes or sunhats in fifty-seven shades of grey. Walking around it on a weekday is like being attacked by a horde of grandmothers, especially if you are over six foot and they keep on bumping into your waist.

'Most people here feel that the anthem debate was captured by the ultra-left – the communists – decades ago,' he said, 'and the arguments that teachers make against it just don't stand up. I mean, "Kimigayo" is based on a poem, written ostensibly to the emperor, and was associated with the emergence of Japan as a political and military power in the world. But it doesn't talk, like America's does, of "bombs bursting in air" or anything remotely militaristic. So the association is not with the words, but with the people who used to sing it.

'So if you protest against "Kimigayo", you're protesting against people who don't exist any more! That's basically it!'

He gave me a whole list of other reasons why the public doesn't care about the anthem laws: Japan's strong group mentality; the charisma of politicians like Hashimoto who blame teachers for the 'spiritual dilution' of Japanese society; the rise of China making people fearful of a new war; the popularity of the imperial family following the Fukushima disaster (they travelled everywhere trying to bring hope to victims of the tsunami). But ultimately, he said, people accept the laws because they just can't see why people are complaining about a short, poetic song sung in ancient Japanese.

'You should really be talking to geologists,' he added as we finished eating. 'If anyone should have a problem with the song it's them. I mean, stones gathering together to become rocks? That's not how it works, is it?'

*

A few days later, I decided to visit Yokohama, the place where the anthem was written back in 1869. Today it's one of the world's largest ports and wherever you look there are cranes taller than any of the city's skyscrapers, unloading shipping containers. It's supposedly its own city of several million people, but it's only a short train ride from Tokyo, and if you look out of the window on your way there, you would be hard pressed to guess where Tokyo ends and Yokohama begins.

In 1853, American ships arrived just south of here, pointing cannons at the coast and firing a few warning shots to show what they could do, before ordering the long-isolated Japanese to open up to foreign trade. Japan reluctantly accepted a trade treaty the next year and Yokohama had the shock of being turned from a sleepy fishing village into a port and foreigners' encampment. The wealthy whites put themselves up in the Yamate district, a hilly area overlooking the city, renaming it the Bluff. There's a museum there today, next to a foreigners' cemetery, which gives you an idea of what life was like back then. There are photos of English-style churches, tennis and rowing clubs, of Japan's first brewery and its first ice manufacturer too. All the women are in bonnets or pinafores, and there isn't a man without a hat. It looks like Victorian England, in other words, and life for the original composer of 'Kimigayo', the British bandleader John William Fenton, must have been that of an English gentleman, full of promenading and concerts in the park. To be honest, you don't have to visit the museum to realise that. The Bluff today is a museum piece in itself. There are rows of clapboard houses each with their own neat rose garden, private sports clubs with pretentious names (the school's football pitch is called the Lawn) and quaint cafes that sell old-fashioned sundaes and cream teas. The Japanese come here to paint watercolours and imagine they are in imperial England, turning their noses up at the vulgar city below.

Fenton does not seem to have been the type to turn his nose up at anybody, and enjoyed nothing more than trying to teach his Japanese students to play their new instruments. He used to meet them at the Myōkōji Temple, just off the Bluff, and gave them lessons four times a day. They would stand there looking every bit the Japanese soldiers – even wearing swords – while he would be in an immaculate three-piece suit, long sideburns and bushy moustache. He had only taught them for a few months before writing the anthem, and some say that's the reason 'Kimigayo' is so simple: it was written for beginners.

Myōkōji Temple today is different to any other temple you'll find in Japan, with dark purple sashes draped across its entrance and an art deco logo – a deformed 'M' – stencilled everywhere, making it seem more like a place for worshipping 1930s design than the gods. Inside, an ornate altar rises up towards gold lights, although it's really the pair of drums at the front of the room that dominates the space, reminding you that sutras are chanted – and banged – out daily. While I was there, I got talking with the temple's guard, a thirty-one-year-old in a dark blue robe called Masa Ikeda. He spoke perfect English, and turned out to be a former Japanese ballroom dancing champion – he waltzed across the car park in case I didn't understand – who had once moved to London to try and make it as a professional ('It was a lot harder than in Japan,' he said, explaining why he was back). He told me he loved 'Kimigayo', and couldn't be prouder to work at the song's home. Hearing the anthem reminded him of the days when he won contests, 'and it's about Japan – our family, our relatives – and that community's very important. It says Japan should last for thousands of years and I'd like that to happen.'

He sounded like everyone else I'd met – quietly nationalist

and far prouder of being Japanese than, say, a British person is of being British. Whether that is because of how people are taught here, or how newspapers report, or just because people genuinely love being Japanese with the distinct culture that entails, I don't know. So I asked for his view on the teachers and expected him to say, like almost everyone else here, that they should stand without question, but instead he said this: 'I'm sure they have their reasons for sitting. They are different to me, I'm different to you and I'm also different to the next Japanese. No one can do anything about that. That's just the way the world is.'

To hear a man in a temple basically say 'Why can't everybody get along?' should have felt like the most clichéd moment of my trip, but in a country where no one seems to want to compromise, or put the individual before the group, I found it instantly refreshing. I wanted to immediately call Osaka's mayor, Hashimoto, and insist he met this man. I wanted to get all the teachers down here so maybe they wouldn't feel so strongly about the anthem either. And I wanted to call the girl who told me it was common sense for teachers to stand and tell her that this sounded far more like common sense to me.

As I strolled back to the Bluff I found myself wondering if Japan's anthem rows – and those of other countries too – say more about the importance of national anthems or the absurdity of them; whether the fact politicians (typically of the right) manipulate and use them for their own purposes means they can never really be enjoyed or respected by the majority of people (that'd certainly explain why so many people I met in France and the US seemed turned off by them). 'Kimigayo' is a beautiful song that's been compromised by politics and it's sad that people like Hashimoto, who claim to be its defenders, either don't seem to realise or don't seem to care.

★

A few weeks later an email arrives from my interpreter Miki. She seems to have become an anthem buff since we met, scanning the internet for information about 'Kimigayo' that I might find useful. She's sent me a copy of a magazine interview with Shintaro Ishihara, the former governor of Tokyo – the man who was responsible for the city's anthem crackdown in 2003 that made Kimiko Nezu's life so hard. In the piece he is asked about Japan's imperial family, to which he gives a short three-sentence answer that says everything about the absurdity of what's happened in Japan. 'I'm not interested in the [royals] very much,' he says. 'I don't sing the national anthem and when I have to, I change the words so I sing to "My Japan" rather than [to the emperor]. When I sing like this everybody looks at me.'

My Kazakhstan

Алтын күн аспаны,
Алтын дән даласы,
Ерліктің дастаны,
Еліме қарашы!
Ежелден ер деген,
Даңқымыз шықты ғой.
Намысын бермеген,
Қазағым мықты ғой!

Қайырмасы:
Менің елім, менің елім,
Гүлің болып егілемін,
Жырың болып төгілемін, елім!
Туған жерім менің – Қазақстаным!

—

Sky of golden sun,
Steppe of golden seed,
Legend of courage,
Take a look at my country!
From antiquity,
Our heroic glory emerged.
They did not give up their pride,
My people are strong!

Chorus:
My country, my country,
As your flower I will be planted,
As your song I will stream, my country!
My native land – my Kazakhstan!

5

Kazakhstan

ANTHEMS IN DICTATORSHIPS

Everything about Kazakhstan's capital, Astana, feels wrong. It's a city literally in the middle of nowhere – surrounded by steppe, nothing but yellowing grass to its east or west, giving central Asia's winds a thousand-mile run-up before they clatter into it. (The winds are so strong, in fact, the government had to grow a ring of trees around the city to help deflect them.)

It also feels less a city than two that have been badly stuck together. On the northern side of the Ishim river is the old town. It was once known as Akmola, 'the white graveyard', a name that tells you exactly how its Russian founders felt about it (it comes from the colour of the soil), and it still looks and feels very much a Soviet city, with rows of colourless apartment blocks and endless bus queues. But on the southern side, there's . . . well . . . how can I put this? There's a 77-metre-tall pyramid with stained-glass doves flying to its peak; there's the world's largest tent, which throbs pink, green and yellow through the night like an alien giving birth; there's a gross replica of the White House; a building that looks like an egg hatching; another that looks like a bike helmet; a Romanesque theatre; and a Dutch windmill. There's even one of the world's largest mosques, its sparkling turquoise prayer hall empty because there are so few devout Muslims to fill it. The place is absurd. You bus around it desperately guessing at what you'll see next, struggling to take everything in. It's like someone told a group of architects to build a capital from scratch, adding, 'Don't worry about money, or taste, or practicality. Just blow people away.'

That is, in a way, exactly what has happened here. Astana is the creation of one man: Nursultan Nazarbayev, who has ruled Kazakhstan since 1989, shepherding the country through the collapse of Communism to become the oil giant it is now. He's the father of the nation and its eternal hero, and no one can say otherwise. Well, not here, at least: insulting him or his honour is punishable by up to five years in prison.

Astana is Nazarbayev's pride and joy. In 1994 he announced that it was to replace the wind-free southern city of Almaty as Kazakhstan's capital, and just three years later forced all his politicians and bureaucrats to make the 600-mile move. He allegedly designed all its major buildings himself, sketching ideas and even picking colour schemes before handing them over to architects for realisation. Almost all these buildings have plaques screwed to them saying, 'Built at the initiative of the leader of the nation, Nursultan Nazarbayev.' Even the ice hockey stadium has one, making you wonder if the city's team used to smack pucks around an icy car park until the president turned up and said, 'What you guys need is a stadium.'

But the reason I'm here isn't to gawp at the almost overwhelming number of architectural wonders; it's to see one in particular. It's called Bayterek and it is Astana's centrepiece: a 110-metre-tall tower that's meant to look like a golden egg sitting in a poplar tree, as if the legendary 'bird of happiness' has laid its young in the equally legendary 'tree of life'. Inside, you can take a lift to the egg and stare out at the steppe while being bathed in golden light, or you can ignore the view and join a queue of excited Kazakhs waiting to do something else: to have their photo taken while putting their right hand in a cast of Nazarbayev's. A golden cast, naturally, which sits on top of an ornate plinth in the middle of the room.

On my first day in Astana, I headed straight for Bayterek and spent a good half-hour watching Kazakhs laying hands on that cast, some closing their eyes to make a wish as they did so. There were glamorous women in thigh-slit dresses, podgy men in cardigans and dozens of others, all stern and unsmiling, this clearly being 'a serious moment'. I even saw two parents lift up their newborn to do it. I stayed watching for a long time, partly out of fascination and partly in the hope that some dignitary or other would appear – the President of Eritrea, perhaps – because I'd heard what happens when someone important places their palm on that cast. Drums roll, cymbals crash and massed choirs, hundreds strong, starts singing, '*Meniñ elim, meniñ elim, / Güliñ bolıp, egilemin*' – 'My country, my country, / As your flower I will be planted.' The noise is apparently so loud that people jump back, and the attendants have to stifle laughs. The song? Yes, of course it's the country's national anthem, 'My Kazakhstan', a tune that sounds every bit the post-Soviet march you'd expect. But why have I travelled all this way to hear it? Because its words were written by one Nursultan Nazarbayev, the only serving world leader to have written his own anthem.

No one important arrived, unfortunately, so in the end I had a go myself. I put my hand into Nazarbayev's surprisingly large palm. The music didn't start. It clearly knows a dignitary when it feels one.

*

If you were to guess who writes the world's anthems, chances are you would soon name some of history's more infamous leaders: the vain and egotistical men – it's always men – who, once they've achieved power, seem to force their way into every aspect of a country's life. Such men wouldn't blink at requiring schoolchildren to sing their praises each morning, would they? And surely they'd never let simple musicians take credit for having written something as important as their anthem, even if the idea that they could have written it themselves is scarcely believable. So it is surprising just how few dictators, demagogues and autocrats have felt able to toy with anthems, or force their names into them. It's as if these songs are untouchable; as if altering them would be a step too far, like changing a country's name or replacing its very soil.

There's no mention of Kim Il-sung – the Great Wise President-for-Life Dearly Beloved and Sagacious Leader – in North Korea's 'Aegukka', for example, and there's no mention of his pop-culture-loving son, Kim Jong-il, either. Instead you get a soaring tune in which North Korea is transformed into a country 'Limitlessly rich and strong'. That might be because even the Kims knew there were limits to their personality cults, but experts on North Korean music think it's more likely because they had so many other songs written about them, they didn't need the anthem as well. The most famous song in North Korea is not the anthem, but the 'Song of General Kim Il-sung', written by a farmer, Kim Wôn'gyun. 'Tell, blizzards that rage in the wild Manchurian plains / . . . Who is the partisan whose deeds are unsurpassed?' it goes. 'Who is the patriot whose fame shall ever last?' The chorus gives the inevitable answer. That song's lyrics are pasted alongside mountain pathways to inspire walkers who pass, as if the views alone are insufficient. Wôn'gyun wrote it in 1945 and Kim Il-sung asked him to write the anthem a year later, almost as if it were a prize.

China did for a while have an anthem praising Chairman Mao – from the start of the Cultural Revolution in 1966 until Mao's death ten years later – but that seems more forced on the country by accident than as a result of Mao's egotism. From the start of Communist rule, China's anthem was the 'March of the Volunteers', that chirpy melody you'll have heard at so many Olympic medal ceremonies. It was originally written to entertain cinemagoers in the 1930s, the musical centrepiece of a film about the resistance to Japan's invasion of Manchuria, which may explain why the lyrics are so dramatic: 'Arise, all you who refuse to be slaves, / With our flesh and blood let's build a new Great Wall!' it starts.

In Mao's early rule, that song's lyricist, Tian Han, was lionised as one of China's greatest writers. His plays and operas, which took characters from Chinese history and used them to push Communist ideas, were almost compulsory viewing. But then Mao launched his Cultural Revolution, which included getting rid of the old intelligentsia who he saw as endangering Communism, and overnight Han's plays were reinterpreted as 'great poisonous weeds' undermining the nation. He was thrown in prison, and in 1967 was tortured to death. The Communist Party really had no choice but to ban the 'March of the Volunteers' after that, its role as the anthem soon taken by 'The East is Red'. As one historian has pointed out, this is an anthem that almost deifies Mao. It's 'a creation myth, a historical vision, a belief system and a moral landscape' all in one. 'The east is red, the sun is rising,' it goes:

> China has brought forth a Mao Zedong.
> He works for the people's happiness,
> Hu erg hai ya.

Those last four words are nonsense, taken from the original folk song it was based on, but that nonsense became the Chinese people's alarm clock and their kiss goodnight for a decade. China's first satellite was even called East is Red. It played the song to prove it was working.

*

But if you look hard enough it is possible to find dictators who have actually turned anthem writers. There's Pol Pot, for a start, who many believe was involved in writing the anthem used in Cambodia during the Khmer Rouge years. It's called 'The Glorious Seventeenth of April', a reference to the date his regime took control, and has so many references to blood in its first verse it reads like a horrific premonition of the Killing Fields. 'The bright red blood flooded over the towns and plains of our motherland,' it begins,

> The blood of our good workers and farmers,
> The blood of our revolutionary fighters, men and
> women.

Pol Pot's signature isn't on the song's score, but writing it is the sort of thing he would have done, and there are apparently hints in the song's grammar. Ieng Sary, the Khmer Rouge's third in command, also once remarked that Pol Pot thought of himself as an 'incomparable songwriting genius' as much as a political one.

There's also Turkmenbashi, the broad-shouldered, thick-necked former leader of Turkmenistan, who ruled there for sixteen years until he died of a heart attack in 2006. He was as much of a lunatic as Pol Pot. While in charge, he closed all hospitals outside the capital Ashgabat and renamed April after his mother (it became Gurbansoltan); he banned lip-syncing and wrote an autobiography called the *Ruhnama*, which was meant to be almost as much of a spiritual guide to the people as the Qur'an. It opens with his anthem, the uninspiringly named 'National Anthem of Independent Neutral Turkmenistan'. Musically, he did a great job, picking a tune by the composer Weli Muhadow which sounds like a symphonic orchestra riding across endless deserts. Unfortunately Turkmenbashi's words didn't quite match up to the promise of the melody. 'The great creation of Turkmenbashi / . . . Long live and prosper, Turkmenistan,' goes the chorus. Learning the anthem was compulsory; you could be asked about it during your driving test (as you could anything in the *Ruhnama*). The anthem's reference to Turkmenbashi was not removed until two years after his death.

So, you have Turkmenbashi and you have Pol Pot. And then you have Nursultan Nazarbayev. I doubt he appreciates the company.

*

In the middle of Astana's old city is the Museum of the First President – three storeys dedicated to Nazarbayev's life. It's the only museum I've ever been to where they make you wear fluorescent blue shoe-covers to avoid staining the carpets. Inside you can see every one of Nazarbayev's citizenship cards, watching him change from a bouffant-haired teen in the 1950s, not unlike a Communist James Dean, to the perma-tanned, ever-smiling ruler of today. You can also see hundreds of the gifts he's been given by other world leaders and wonder why on earth Queen Elizabeth II gave him such a cheap-looking carriage clock, and then why on earth Nazarbayev would want it on display.

But the first exhibit you come to isn't about Nazarbayev's life at all, it's about Kazakhstan's symbols: its eye-popping blue and yellow flag, its golden emblem filled with winged horses, and, of course, its anthem, adopted in 2006. On a screen, there's a copy of the words to the original 'My Kazakhstan', a march written back in the 1950s, the music by a composer called Shamshi Kaldayakov and the words by songwriter Jumeken Najimedenov. But Najimedenov's words are covered with pen marks: some blue, some black, annotations and crossings out everywhere. It turns out to be Nazarbayev's handwriting and it shows him rewriting practically the whole song, turning it from a historic relic into a ballad for his reimagined country. 'From antiquity / Our heroic glory emerged,' he scribbles over the first verse,

> They [the Kazakhs] did not give up their pride.
> My people are strong.

He ends the second verse with the simple, if rather presumptive, 'Our country is happy, / Such is our country.' It is signed 'P', for President.

It's easy to jump to conclusions about why Nazarbayev decided he should write this anthem. After you've spent a few days here, bumping into photos of him on street corners and in subway stations – 'Oh look, there's a ten-foot-tall Nazarbayev stroking some flowers' – you get the feeling it's probably because he feels he has to leave his mark on everything in the country, so that when his time ends, his legacy won't. No one would have the guts to tell him it was a bad idea either: this is a country, after all, where politicians once proposed renaming the capital Nurstana in tribute to him.

However, he would say that explanation could not be further from the truth, that he wrote the anthem simply because he loves his people and wanted to give them a song that would 'have a strong emotional charge, raise their morale and bring them together to achieve a higher purpose'. Those are his exact words, in fact, taken from an email his office sent me after I'd harassed them for the best part of a year. The email goes on to say he started writing poems as a boy, carried off by a 'romantic perception of the world', and has never let that passion go. 'Reflections on the past, worries for the future of our people, the feeling of love for my native land, all inspire me to write,' he says. The anthem is just another example of that inspiration hitting. He picked 'My Kazakhstan' to rewrite because it was a song that had 'already achieved wide acceptance and love, played in every home, on every holiday, prompting high patriotic feeling'. It just needed 'some refinement', a touch-up here and there, since the words were written so long ago.

When Nazarbayev's office sent me that email, I think they

assumed it would end my desire to learn anything else about the song and certainly be enough to stop me visiting ('You're here?' were the first words I heard when I called his office from the capital). But Nazarbayev's comments, interesting as they are, don't seem an entirely believable explanation of why he wrote the song, if I'm honest. And they also leave a lot of questions unanswered. What was wrong with the old anthem in the first place? Did Nazarbayev really do the rewrite? And, most importantly, does Nazarbayev's authorship affect people's feelings towards this anthem? Does it turn something that's meant to be apolitical into just another tool for his rule?

Nazarbayev was born in 1940 and grew up in a village called Chemolgan in the south of the country. His parents worked on the local collective farm (in spite of having a withered arm, in his father's case) and Nazarbayev had to help: moving cows, watering crops, or helping protect flocks in the mountains in summer (wolves apparently always a danger). The only entertainment was hearing his mother sing folk songs at night, his father occasionally accompanying her on the *dombra*, the Kazakh two-string guitar. He was apparently the best student at his school – everyone here tells you that, while museums have his glittering report cards on show. What is less discussed is that he was also the sort of boy who stood in front of the mirror at night practising speeches for the next day's class – something that says more about how he got to become president than a few good grades ever could. It was at school that his 'serious passion for music began', he says. 'My friends and I sang folk and pop songs, played music together. I started to play the accordion, mandolin and *dombra*. As the Kazakh proverb goes, the real Kazakh is not Kazakh, the real Kazakh is *dombra*.' Like most proverbs, it loses something in translation.

Aged eighteen, Nazarbayev had just graduated from school when he saw an advert for Young Communist League members to go and train to be metallurgists at a steel plant in Temirtau,

300 miles away in the north of the country. 'A metallurgist has a noble and proud profession,' the advert said. 'It's a job for real men who will earn the highest wages.' It didn't mention that the steel plant had yet to be built, that the town's nightlife consisted of watching people fight or that he'd have to live in a dormitory where there was no space even to dry clothes ('We left our work clothes outside at night because it was easier to put them on when they were frozen than when they were wet,' he once said). Those omissions may explain why he so enthusiastically signed up. By the age of twenty, Nazarbayev was working eight-hour shifts at a blast furnace, working with molten metal at temperatures above 40°C, feeling the weight drop off him, and drinking half a bucket of water every day in a futile effort to keep it on. He barely stopped working when his shifts were over, either, spending his time organising events for friends and colleagues, everything from weddings to fishing trips. The Communist Party soon took notice of this drive and organisational ability and offered him a job as the second secretary of the committee in charge of the heavy industry department of the Temirtau City Communist Party Committee, his first step on to a very long ladder of even longer job titles.

By 1989, Nazarbayev had done so much climbing of that ladder, he'd become First Secretary of the Communist Party of the Soviet Republic of Kazakhstan, a surprisingly succinct name for the highest position in the country. He'd got there through skill, greasing the right palms (being a politician in the Soviet Union was as much about knowing who to bribe to fix production figures as anything else) and a fair dose of luck (he survived a KGB investigation). So, as Russian Communism wheezed its last, he suddenly found himself leader of the world's ninth-largest country, albeit one with more problems than almost any other former Soviet state. Kazakhstan had been Russia's dumping ground for over 100 years: the place where the tsars exiled their supposed opponents (including Dostoyevsky) and where Stalin tried to deport whole populations, such as the Chechens. Russia tested its nuclear weapons there too, and had left over 1,200 warheads sitting in silos in case Nazarbayev wanted some explosions to welcome in independence. The country was also ridden with anxiety: the then majority Russian population worried what Kazakh nationalists would do next; the Kazakhs worried the Russians would either leave or revolt. And on top of all that, the economy had collapsed.

*

Zhadyra Daribayeva, a beautiful sixty-six-year-old poet whose dimples get deeper with each smile, is sitting in a cafe explaining what life was like immediately after that independence. 'It was very difficult,' she says with slight understatement. 'I was travelling a lot then, and I saw people crying everywhere. When they spoke about the future they'd break down. Everyone's clothes were rags. No one had food. We had no water, no light in the cities. People had to do whatever they could to earn money . . .' She trails off. 'I saw so many horrible things, but I had hope because our president was honest with us. He said, "Right now, everything is difficult, we just have to be strong."' She waves her hand around the cafe, filled with chattering women eating dainty sandwiches and pouring out pots of herbal tea, as if to say, 'Look, he was right.' 'Don't misunderstand me,' she adds. 'I was filled with happiness because we had independence. We felt free! It was just difficult.'

The reason I've arranged to meet Zhadyra is that she is one of the authors of Kazakhstan's first anthem, the one Nazarbayev replaced when he wrote 'My Kazakhstan'. Actually, she's more important than that: she's one of only a handful of women to have ever written an anthem – a fact that seems to say as much about how wrapped up patriotism is with testosterone, as it does about historical inequality.

At independence, Kazakhstan actually had two anthems. The

first was the Soviet Union's, which people could no longer sing without laughing or crying ('Long live the creation of the will of the people, / The united, mighty Soviet Union', it went). The second was the anthem of the Kazakh Soviet Socialist Republic, which people might have been tempted to carry on with if it hadn't been full of lines like 'To the great Russian people we say: "Thank you!"' and 'Victorious path of Lenin never be tarnished'. At one point it even talked of Kazakhstan being covered in fog, 'But Lenin went forth as the morning, and it was morning!'

Unsurprisingly given those two choices, Nazarbayev soon launched a competition for a new anthem, asking for new words to the Kazakh SSR tune. Zhadyra decided to enter after having a dream in which she was a bird struggling to find a roost – as if someone was trying to tell her she wouldn't find peace until she'd had a go. So she left her husband and three boisterous children in Almaty and headed for a rural library where she could study other countries' anthems – France's, Turkey's – and conjure some suitable words. 'Out of three hundred and sixty entries, I came last,' she laughs, 'but they couldn't decide on a winner so the president said they'd have to try again. A lot of people then said to me, "Maybe your words are actually good, but you're not famous; you're a woman. Try joining up with others."' Zhadyra, showing admirable restraint, somehow didn't tell any of these people to shove their chauvinism somewhere unpleasant. Instead she found some men willing to work with her – famous men at that – and the group spent the next three months sending letters back and forth, toiling to put all of Kazakhstan's history and its people's emotions into just three verses and a chorus. 'We are a valiant people, sons of honour,' their final song opened,

> And all we've sacrificed to gain our freedom,
> Emerging from the malicious grip of fate, from hell
>   of fire,
> We've scored a victory.

It's a mouthful, but something in there obviously touched Nazarbayev since he chose it above 780 other entries. Maybe it was the references to the past. Kazakhstan was not long ago home to three nomadic tribes, who traced their heritage to such great horseback-riding warlords as Genghis Khan and Tamerlane, and who could point to monuments like the ruins of Sauran – a vast, walled city in the desert – as evidence of their power. That heritage was all disrupted when the Kazakhs were forced on to collective farms and had to sit back as the Soviet Union did its best to ruin them – the 'hell of fire' referred to in Zhadyra's song. 'People always want to forget history, but they have to use it to build a new future,' Zhadyra says.

Over the next few years, Zhadyra heard her new anthem (blandly called 'National Anthem') wherever she went – schoolchildren had to sing it daily; public events opened with it. But in 2000 Nazarbayev started saying it needed changing, Zhadyra's words especially. Zhadyra, somehow, wasn't surprised, or even the remotest bit disappointed. 'I used to see children try to sing it and it was really difficult for them, because it's words for adults really. You have to understand them; you have to feel them. And everything had changed by then. Life wasn't a struggle any more. Everything was new. I'm of another century really and so's my anthem.'

She starts wistfully telling me about Nazarbayev and the many meetings she's had with him. He'd of course have been the best person to write the new anthem, she says. 'He knows everything that's happened in our country, and he's always thinking about what will be and how we can get there. And he's a poet too. Did you know that? He used to read me his poems and they were very good.' I clearly make a face of disbelief. 'I'm not just saying that!'

*

It took me all of about thirty seconds to realise I wouldn't be asking Mukhtar Kaldayakov any difficult questions about Nazarbayev. I had gone to Mukhtar's home – a modest three-room flat in Almaty littered with children's toys – to learn about his father, Shamshi, the man who wrote the music for the original 'My Kazakhstan', which Nazarbayev then took for his anthem. Mukhtar welcomed me inside, then introduced me to his children. 'And this is my youngest, Nursultan,' he said, lifting up a wide-eyed boy barely past his first birthday. 'Name just like president's! Sort of gift to him. He's done so much for my family.' He then showed me his gun collection. 'This can kill from three and a half kilometres,' he said, passing me a rifle so heavy I could barely lift it.

Mukhtar is easily one of the most hospitable people you could hope to meet in Kazakhstan. Round-faced, with hair rapidly receding, he spent the best part of the next three days showing me anything he could think of connected with the anthem, as well as plenty of things that weren't. He's a conductor himself, having inherited his father's passion for music, and he took me to Almaty's opera house, where he got his alto and tenor colleagues to sing 'My Kazakhstan' for me, their voices so powerful they shook my rib cage. Later, he took me out to the countryside to eat horse sausage, drink camel's milk and see the mountains that inspired Nazarbayev to write poetry, even if Mukhtar's father didn't feel quite so warmly towards them ('He always said to me, "Why'd you go out there? For someone to kill you?"'). He even took me to see his mother, a decision he appeared immediately to regret when she started telling me that Shamshi used to get so wrapped up in music he forgot they needed money to eat, and that he once went through a phase of drinking so heavily it turned her hair white with worry ('Musicians!' she said dismissively). Mukhtar only seemed to calm down when she pulled a ream of photos out of a bag. There was Shamshi, in dozens of pictures, from his teens to old age, always with a gentle smile on his lips and a faint moustache above them, so handsome I'm not surprised she forgave all his vices.

Shamshi was destined to be a composer, it seems. He was born Shamshi Donbaiev, but ran away from school and, wanted by the police, had to change his surname. He decided on Kaldayakov, meaning 'he has a mole on his foot', because his own father did indeed have one. 'He was the first person in the world to be called that,' Mukhtar cries out when telling this story. 'That's how much of a born composer he was. He even composed his name!' Shamshi didn't start playing music, though, until he was about seventeen and joined the army, taking up the mandolin to entertain new friends. He went on to have a long career writing Kazakh pop songs – most in a waltz style – but 'My Kazakhstan' was one of his first compositions and his only march. Shamshi wrote it in the early 1950s, when Nikita Khrushchev – then leader of the Soviet Union – had just launched his 'virgin lands campaign' with the hope of turning northern Kazakhstan into Russia's corn belt. The fact he labelled it 'virgin land' tells you exactly how much contempt he had for the Kazakhs living there, and to make matters worse he also proposed carving a new regional area out of their country to be put directly under Russia's control.

'Imagine if someone came and tried to break up London,' Mukhtar says, hitting a table in disgust. 'It's just like that. My father composed the song to stop them doing this. "Don't do it. This is our land"' (Mukhtar insists his father basically wrote the words too, telling Jumeken Najimedenov what to write). The song became popular, even with the Soviet authorities, but unfortunately not popular enough to stop Khrushchev; the cold, dry north of Kazakhstan was soon dedicated to growing crops it was completely unsuited for.

I ask Mukhtar why he thinks the song's appeal lasted so long that almost sixty years later Nazarbayev picked it, and he says it's all down to his father's melody. 'He used to know three hundred songs – every Kazakh song, every Russian song. And he'd always say, "You have to know all songs if you're to find your own style. It's like rain and you're trying to run through the water. If you know everyone else's, you get through. If you don't, you get wet." That's why the anthem's so good – it's unique music.' However, it doesn't take more than a cursory listen to 'My Kazakhstan' – sprightly, but like many other marches – to realise Mukhtar's judgement's been clouded by family ties. The real reason the song stayed so popular is, I'm sure, down to how it was used after it was written, long before becoming the anthem. And in particular, what happened on three days in December 1986.

On the 16th of that month, Mikhail Gorbachev appointed an unknown Russian as Kazakhstan's new leader, overlooking the local candidates (Nazarbayev was next in line). The next day, thousands of people, mainly students, gathered in Almaty's main square to protest, finally so fed up of Russia's contempt for their identity they were willing to take the risk of confronting its police. The police reports of that day say most of the protestors were drunk and rowdy, throwing rocks at anyone who tried to reason with them. But what most people actually spent the day doing, according to Mukhtar and many others I spoke to, was singing, and singing 'My Kazakhstan' in particular. The authorities clearly thought even that minor show of dissent was going too far, as by the end of the day they had ordered the army to clear the square with batons and dogs. At least two people died and apparently thousands were arrested, many of those then beaten in custody.

Showing immense courage, most people then came back for two more days of singing – this time with a lot of genuine rioting thrown in. 'My father was out of Almaty at the time,' Mukhtar says, 'but my brother and I stood on our balcony and watched what was happening. I saw it myself. People came and crushed everything. I was shocked. I didn't understand what was happening, especially when they started singing. I understood: This is my father's song. The whole street's singing it. They're coming together. But that's it. Looking back now, it was like watching history. The French Revolution! With music! But then I had no idea what was going on.'

Mukhtar couldn't really have joined in if he'd wanted to as it'd have just meant going to prison. 'I was a student and we got a telephone call from the deacon: "Please stay at home. Don't go out to study." We had to stay in for three days. Every two hours someone called asking, "Are you still there?"'

Shamshi himself seemed to realise just how important his song had become. He was in hospital in 1992 when Nazarbayev announced the competition for a new anthem (the one Zhadyra eventually won). 'Some of his composer friends came to see him and they were all talking about it,' Mukhtar says. '"Maybe we'll compose a new anthem, what do you think?" But my father said nothing. When they left, my mother asked him why, and he said, "What could I say? They'll never compose the anthem." It was like he knew that he'd already written it, that one day his would be chosen.' Shamshi died a few weeks later; Nazarbayev rewrote his song fourteen years after that.

I ask if any of the family are annoyed by Nazarbayev changing the words when he did make it the anthem, but it gets the response you'd expect from someone who lives in an autocracy and whose father is now known as the composer of his country's most important song: 'What a stupid question!' I barely ask Mukhtar anything else about the president after that, but the question clearly sticks in his mind. On our final day together, driving through the countryside, he suddenly asks me to 'be nice' when writing about the president. 'Write about him like he's your grandfather,' he says, 'because to us, he's like ours. He's made Kazakhstan safe. We're not Georgia or Uzbekistan or Tajikistan, with civil wars and things.' He looks at me, and clearly unconvinced I'm going to do as he asks, tries another tack: 'You know we have a saying here: "Write nice things about president and nice things will happen to you."'

*

If most people I met in Kazakhstan were nervous talking about Nazarbayev, there was one topic no one held back on: *Borat*, the film about a Kazakh journalist who goes to America and shows up the small-mindedness of the people he encounters by acting as preposterously as possible. As soon as I told people I was writing about the anthem, most assumed it was because of that film, since it features a very funny fake one ('Kazakhstan, greatest country in the world, / All other countries are run by little girls,' go two typical lines). If you search for Kazakhstan's anthem online, it's that *Borat* one that comes up first, which probably explains why in 2012 a Kazakh athlete, Maria Dmitrienko, was accidentally played it after winning gold at a shooting competition in Kuwait. She didn't appear to notice the error, even when the words 'Kazakhstan's prostitutes cleanest in the region, / Except of course for Turkmenistan's' echoed around the stadium. At another sports ceremony the same year, officials accidentally played Ricky Martin's 'Livin' la Vida Loca' instead, an incident that's far harder to explain especially as it occurred in Kazakhstan. Nazarbayev's government reacted to both mix-ups by passing a law saying that anyone who disrespects state symbols faces a year in prison. Another law quickly followed forcing athletes to know the anthem by heart or lose funding.

Now, all of that sounds very interesting to ask people about. And it would be, if Kazakhs didn't appear to believe that *Borat* had committed more historical damage to their country than any of the empires that have traipsed across their land. On my very first day in the country, I got chatting with a student, Dauren Joldybenov. Intelligent, interesting and funny, he told me a lot about Nazarbayev, about how Kazakhstan was changing and even about the state of Islam in the country (it's growing among the young, who see it as linked to their heritage). He was great company, in other words, until he suddenly asked if I'd seen *Borat*. 'Is it true it was financed by oil companies angry that Nazarbayev renegotiated the terms of their contracts?' he asked. 'You do realise none of it's true? It wasn't even filmed here!'

After a week in Kazakhstan, it wasn't just conversations about *Borat* making me uncomfortable; I was starting to feel somewhat overwhelmed by all the love for Nazarbayev – especially the repeated meetings I'd have with people who'd talk about him dewy-eyed while sitting yards from a billboard of him smiling down on us. The reason it made me uncomfortable was that I knew all the, shall we say, less-than-favourable things about him and his government: the accusations he siphoned money from oil deals in the 1990s and asked energy firms to buy him private jets and tennis courts in contract negotiations (none of them proven, admittedly); the fact newspapers are closed for little reason; the difficulties of politically opposing him (several prominent activists have gone to jail); his government's response to the Zhanaozen massacre, when fourteen striking oil workers were killed by police, which seemed to focus more on putting protestors on trial than finding out the truth of what had happened (there was no independent investigation); and the fact that in presidential elections, the leaders of the opposing parties that are allowed to run always seem to be pro-government (in April 2015, he won his fifth five-year term with 97.7 per cent of the vote). Most human rights organisations you can name put out annual reports about the country, all of which make claims such as that torture occurs in the country's prisons and that some of the country's laws contain clauses so vague they can be used to crack down on any activity the leadership dislikes.

There was once even a scandal around Nazarbayev involving the anthem. Back in 2000, a few days after he started saying Zhadyra's anthem needed replacing, politicians proposed adopting a song called 'My People'. Nazarbayev had written the words to it and it does indeed sound like a great anthem for a country bursting into life. 'The dawns have become clear, / the mountains are soaring high / . . . the day of our dreams has come true,' it starts. But there was a problem: Nazarbayev's lyrics appeared to be remarkably similar to those of a poem by a man called Tumanbay Moldagaliev, one that had been published two years before the president had put pen to paper. The two only differed in their titles, according to reports in opposition newspapers.

Serikbolsyn Abdildin, the Communist Party's leader at the time and a long-term thorn in Nazarbayev's side, wrote a long article highlighting this 'sheer plagiarism' just before parliament was due to vote on whether to adopt it. A few days later, Nazarbayev wrote to the parliament thanking the politicians for their kind thoughts about his song, but asking them to drop their plan. He'd not written 'My People' to be an anthem, he said, merely to inspire the youth.

Abdildin devotes a few pages to the incident in his memoirs. 'I do not find any pleasure in discussing this situation, when a leader abuses his position to add his name to the creative heritage,' he writes. I asked Jonathan Aitken, a former British politician who once went to prison for perjury and who is Nazarbayev's English biographer, about this incident. He hadn't heard of it, and insisted Nazarbayev was a good enough songwriter to not need to copy others, but he did joke that 'plagiarism isn't the same in Kazakhstan as it is here, especially if you're the president'. (Nazarbayev's office unsurprisingly denied the accusation, sending me a letter headed 'Dear Mr Marshall!' – the exclamation mark, I assume, highlighting my impertinence – stressing that the president is the 'only author of the poem' and 'all the information . . . regarding accusations of plagiarism is unfounded and incorrect'.)

With all this in mind, I started actively searching for people who might be opposed to Nazarbayev, to try to get their take on him and his song. The problem was, their views turned out to be pretty much the same as anyone else's. One afternoon, I went and saw Saule Suleimenova, an artist who made her name in the late eighties holding anti-Communist exhibitions, although her recent output is far less confrontational, consisting of still lifes made from plastic bags, a comment on the number you find dropped in the countryside. Her flat was filled with a few of these beautiful canvases as well as numerous piles of fag ends and stacks of paint. I told her my predicament and said several people had recommended I speak with her. 'Of course,' she laughed. 'I'm an artist. I'm free.'

But that freedom only seemed to stretch to criticising corrupt mid-level bureaucrats; she wouldn't touch Nazarbayev himself. 'Why would I?' she said without a hint of sarcasm. 'I like him, especially his foreign policy.' And as for the anthem: 'To be honest, I didn't know it was his text until now,' she said. 'He's done a pretty good job. It's much better than the last one.'

Another day, I got talking with an ethnic German, Alex (not his real name, which he asked me not to use). I'd stopped him in Almaty to ask for directions to Panfilov Park, a place where couples have wedding photos taken against brutalist war memorials and old men gather to play chess. He offered to walk me there and after a lot of small talk about what I was doing said conspiratorially, 'Remember to tell the truth about Kazakhstan. Tell it like it is.' He seemed a bit melodramatic, but I suggested we went for a drink and, over a beer, he told me numerous unprintable allegations about Nazarbayev, his senior officials and his family, repeatedly saying things like, 'Everybody says we're successful, that we have all this oil and gas, but look around – most people are poor. Where's the money going?'

But then he spent just as much time praising Nazarbayev, especially for keeping peace in this multi-ethnic country, telling me that no other politician would have managed it. And he also couldn't stop telling me about Nazarbayev's forays into music

outside the anthem. 'Have you heard "Ush Konyr"? It's this song
by MuzArt, our most famous boy band,' he said at one point. I
had heard it and it's pretty fantastic for a Kazakh boy band.
'Nazarbayev wrote the words to that too. He did it in a few
minutes at a party one night, writing on the wrapping from a
chocolate box. He's really talented.

   'Don't forget to tell the truth,' he reminded me as we finished
up. I wanted to reply that I wasn't sure what the truth was any
more.

*

At the end of my time in Kazakhstan, I spent three days in Astana,
trying to find a politician who would talk to me about the anthem.
I thought perhaps they might be able to give me insights into
Nazarbayev that no one had so far, assuming they would have
had more dealings with him than members of the public. But
none of them would talk. One initially said yes ('Sounds fun!'),
only to phone back the next morning to say he'd had a think
and decided it really wasn't his place. I was starting to worry it
was a futile chase until I tracked down Bekbolat Tleuhan.
Bekbolat turned out not to be a politician any more – Nazarbayev
had made him step down from politics for being a Kazakh nationalist ('I'm not. That's an awful word. I'm a patriot!') and annoying
many of the country's Russians – but he is a famous traditional
musician and, even better, wrote music to accompany one of
Nazarbayev's poems, the very one that got caught up in the
plagiarism scandal.

   He suggested we meet at the bottom of Bayterek, that tower
that's meant to look like a bird's egg stuck in a tree, and houses
the cast of Nazarbayev's hand. He was easy to spot. Bearded, in
a turtleneck jumper and wearing mirror shades, he looked more
like an Iranian secret agent than a musician, an impression which
only increased when I realised he had four minders with him, all

bursting out of their suits, and all incongruously licking children's ice creams, comically small in their huge fists. We walked and talked, occasionally interrupted by star-struck Kazakhs coming up to shake his hand.

I started by asking why no one here seemed surprised Nazarbayev had written the anthem, pointing out that he was the only leader alive to have done so and in the West it'd be seen as somewhat odd (I didn't say dictatorial, but the implication was clear). The question didn't cause Bekbolat any pause for thought. 'We cannot understand each other,' he shrugged, meaning the West and Central Asian countries. 'Our mentalities are different.' But why didn't Nazarbayev ask anyone for help, like you? I said. 'Because he's fine by himself. If he wasn't president, he could be a poet or musician easily. His voice isn't good, so not a singer, but a normal musician? Yes. He's a relative of Zhambyl Zhabaev – one of our great poets who was unfortunately used by the Soviets – so he has a poetic soul. It's in his blood.' Bekbolat was just as positive when talking about Nazarbayev more generally. 'I don't think there's another person who can compare with him here,' he said. 'He's seen everything. He went to Kazakh school and Russian school. He was fighting, riding horses, working at the steel factories. He's very intelligent. He can forgive any person, but at the same time he can punish. It's very rare to find such a strong man.'

'He doesn't like me much,' Bekbolat added. I tried to see if there was any emotion behind that statement, but could only see my own reflection in his glasses.

Bekbolat was charming and indulgent no matter what I asked him, but I don't think he actually warmed to the interview until I mentioned that I had been listening to a lot of his dombra music lately – ten-minute pieces over which he sings epic poems about nature and love. His music feels timeless, as if you could have come to Kazakhstan hundreds of years ago and found herdsmen singing songs just like it. I told him I was surprised how sad it all sounded. He smiled for the first time and nodded agreement. 'It's a reflection of our nation,' he said. 'The Kazakhs, we're a country who've suffered. In the 1930s, a lot of us died because of famine. In the 1950s, the Soviets tried to break us up and destroyed all our elite. All this unconsciously comes through in my melodies. You can write poems that hide your emotions, but music is always a reflection of your soul, of things that come through your heart. Confucius said you can tell a lot about a country from its music. When the nation's music is sad, she has a future. When its music is glorious, she'll terrorise everyone around her. And when it has no soul, she won't last. The Soviet anthems had no soul.'

We were running out of time, so I decided to ask him a final blunt question. Well, as blunt as is possible in Kazakhstan. 'Why are there so many photos of Nazarbayev everywhere?' I said. 'I'm half expecting to see him half naked soon, advertising under-wear.' 'We're in a period where we need very strong political power to guide us,' he said. 'And you cannot change a horse between two points. We have to close our eyes and follow our leader. And to follow him, we need to believe in him, and to believe in him, we must love him, and to love him, we have to see him everywhere.' And hear his songs too, no doubt.

*

After talking to Bekbolat, I found myself starting to think that maybe Nazarbayev had done a good thing by changing the anthem, by going from a song few cared about – a Soviet relic, essentially – to one most people seem to like, many have deep connections with, and some are even inspired by. Maybe a profes-sional songwriter would have done a better job, but then maybe they'd have made the words too complicated, or tried to be too clever, filling the song with metaphor and allusion that nobody would understand. Clearly autocrats and dictators don't just get to the position they are in solely through force – to some extent they have to know what their people want – and Nazarbayev has proven he does know Kazakhs with this song, even if he wrote it more out of ego than anything else (the fact his name's always first whenever the anthem's on display tells you that). It's a worrying realisation to come to: that a dictator can produce an anthem that resonates more than most of those chosen through the most democratic of processes (just look at Kosovo's). It makes me feel a little sick, to be honest, especially as it means the people I should compare Nazarbayev to aren't Pol Pot and Turkmenbashi, it's the handful of world leaders who weren't dictators but also wrote their anthems; presidents and prime ministers who never had such stains on them.

There's Léopold Sédar Senghor, the poet and first president of Senegal, who wrote 'Strum Your Koras, Strike the Balafons', an anthem named after the traditional instruments it should be played on. That song's not only filled with good poetry ('The red lion has roared. / The tamer of the savannah / Has leapt forward') but is drenched in so much optimism it's inspiring ('Sunlight on our terrors, sunlight on our hope. / Stand up brothers, here is Africa'). It's no surprise Senghor was the first African leader to step down voluntarily.

Then there's Barthélemy Boganda, the first president of the Central African Republic, who wrote his anthem also to be a focus of hope, but didn't manage to express it quite as well ('To work!' orders his song's chorus). Or there's Thomas Sankara, 'Africa's Che Guevara', who wrote Burkina Faso's uplifting 'Une Seule Nuit' ('One Single Night'), in the short time he was in power in the 1980s before being deposed in a coup by the middle classes his Marxist ideals annoyed (it's the only anthem to feature an academic reference to neocolonialism). And, looking much further back, there's Charles Rogier, the permed, liberalising prime minister of Belgium who in 1860 completely rewrote his country's anthem, 'La Brabançonne', partly so it stopped being rude about the Dutch but also so he could get everyone to shout 'Le Roi, la Loi, la Liberté' at its end, hoping to give them a catchphrase to hold on to (looking at the state of Belgium, with many people identifying as Walloons or Flemish rather than Belgian, he did not succeed).

There's even Pedro I, the Emperor of Brazil, who wrote the gently operatic music to his country's first anthem, 'Hino da Independência', in 1822 – although I expect he did that less out of patriotism than for his own entertainment. He used to spend a lot of his spare time making up songs with his wives and, after his death, 'some bawdy verses, illustrated with pornographic doodles' were found in his papers.

Maybe those men actually wrote their anthems because they were even bigger egotists than Nazarbayev, determined to brand their names into their countries, but it just doesn't feel anywhere near as awkward praising their songs as it does praising his.

*

It's my final morning in Kazakhstan, and I decide to make a quick return to the top of Bayterek to beg the staff to turn on Nazarbayev's golden palm so it plays the anthem when I touch it. Their English isn't great and my Russian is non-existent, but I manage to get them to understand what I want after a lot of pointing and awkward singing. 'Wait for electrician!' one of them shouts. I assume there's a problem with the hand that needs fixing but when he arrives ten minutes later it turns out that he's simply the person with the remote control. He hits play before I even have a chance to put my hand in the cast and the music suddenly bursts out at us from every angle, shockingly loud – a cacophony of women's voices, distorted by the volume. All the tourists adopt a shocked look of 'What the hell is that?' And I do too, not because of the noise, but because what's playing isn't Nazarbayev's anthem. It's not Zhadyra's old one either. Or even the USSR's. It's 'My People' – the poem Nazarbayev allegedly stole. 'The day of our dreams has come true,' the women sing, their voices flying so high it's like they're trying to shatter the glass of the golden egg. So, he's made sure it's the anthem somewhere, I think, until deciding I shouldn't leap to judgements like that. If you're building a capital, you can't be expected to keep tabs on everything, can you?

Oben am Jungen Rhein

Oben am jungen Rhein,
Lehnet sich Liechtenstein,
An Alpenhöh'n.
Dies liebe Heimatland,
Das teure Vaterland,
Hat Gottes weise Hand,
Für uns erseh'n.

Hoch lebe Liechtenstein,
Blühend am jungen Rhein,
Glücklich und treu!
Hoch leb' der Fürst vom Land,
Hoch unser Vaterland,
Durch Bruderliebe Band,
Vereint und frei!

—

Up above the young Rhine,
Liechtenstein is resting,
On Alpine heights.
This beloved homeland,
This dear fatherland,
Was chosen for us,
By God's wise hand.

Long live Liechtenstein,
Blossoming on the young Rhine,
Fortunate and faithful!
Long live the Prince of the Land,
Long live our fatherland,
Through bonds of brotherly love,
United and free!

6

Liechtenstein and the UK

ONE SONG TO THE TUNE OF ANOTHER

Ever since starting this book, there's been one chapter I've been dreading. This one. The one telling the story of my own anthem, 'God Save the Queen'. It's because I know what's expected – a personal journey in which I'm converted to the joys of the world's most important anthem. It's meant to be the turning point in the book.

This chapter should, of course, start with me looking back at my first moments with the song: half-remembered Cub Scout jamborees where I'm told we sang it around a pile of damp logs, none of us having been able to rub two sticks together vigorously enough to turn them into a campfire. It would then move on to more vivid memories of the Italia '90 World Cup, of being glued to the TV and seeing fans belting the anthem out at stadiums in Naples and Turin, full of blind optimism (they were usually drunk, something my nine-year-old self couldn't really identify with, but definitely wanted to). Back then I was probably a little in awe of the song, if I'm being honest, as I was of the Queen herself. She was the woman on my pocket money, after all.

From there, I would have to stumble through a few sentences about my awkward teenage years, a time when I read too much and suddenly thought I knew everything. I was the kind of teenager who formed a Communist Party to run in the school election, and it should be no surprise that once I learned about colonialism I decided I couldn't be proud of a song that had been imposed on half the world, translated into Sanskrit for Indian schoolchildren and sung by British officers as they shot Zulus. I would probably also feel the need to mention that I grew up on the rim of east London, not far from the then homeland of the British National Party, and that once you have seen such flamboyant, racist nationalism, it tends to put you off songs like 'God Save the Queen' for life. Having said all that, I actually played the anthem a lot as a teenager. I was a member of my local symphonic wind band, and on memorial days we would sit in wet bandstands and run through it for a handful of pensioners. I played the euphonium – a mini-tuba, basically – which doesn't so much glide its way through songs as stomp over them like a frightened elephant, so my playing was never going to make me feel 'happy and glorious' about the anthem. God knows what it did to the people listening.

After that, I would have to move on to how I feel about 'God Save the Queen' today, as a belligerent music fan who makes far-too-snap judgements about every song he hears. And I would feel the need to explain that I can't stand the way that first word – that 'God' – thuds into the melody like a boot into mud, sticking the song into its plodding rhythm. I'd also need to ask, is this really the best poetry the United Kingdom has to offer? I mean, it rhymes the word 'queen' with, well, 'queen' three times in the first verse alone ('God save our gracious Queen! / Long live our noble Queen! / God save the Queen!'). By the third, it seems to have given up on rhyme altogether ('May she defend our laws, / And ever give us cause, / To sing with heart and voice'). I might even decide I'd have to talk about the fact this song means nothing to me; how it doesn't say anything, really, about the UK or the people who live here.

But once I had put all those feelings out there, I would still be expected to – somehow – undergo a conversion. Maybe I'd dig through my great-grandfather's diaries. He was a sergeant major, a well-liked one at that ('I have never met anyone who could be more sarcastic,' wrote one of his men), and he fought all over Africa – against the Boers in the 1890s, in Egypt during the First World War. He was also stationed in Palestine, India and Ireland. Surely it isn't beyond the realms of possibility that he wrote about locals singing 'God Save the Queen' to him, as if he were their saviour, coming to bring them railways, milky tea and the gentlemen's game of cricket? Okay, it is, and not just for reasons of colonialism – my mum says he didn't keep a diary, but I could always forge one, dipping the pages in tea to make them look old, burning the edges with a lighter. And after I'd had my stirring encounter with those forged words, I could sit down with my trusty euphonium and play the anthem once more. It would feel like I was hearing it for the first time again. Fresh. New. Until someone banged on my door and told me to stop that bloody parping.

The problem is, when I started this book, I couldn't envisage that journey. I still can't. When you dislike a song, you dislike it. There's no going back, especially when you are talking about one you have heard hundreds, maybe thousands, of times. If it's not for you, it doesn't matter how other people have experienced it or how their lives have been changed by it. I couldn't go on any such journey and be genuine.

Which is all a rather long way of telling you why I couldn't have been happier the day I realised I could tell the story of 'God Save the Queen' without going on any sort of personal journey at all. I just needed to go to the world's seventh-smallest country and get an audience with a prince.

*

It's almost midday on 15 August, and I'm standing halfway up a mountain in Liechtenstein. The sun is glaring off the river below and the snow above, but I can still make out the entirety of the one-valley country beneath me. It's a surprisingly unkempt mix of industrial estates and wheat fields, Alpine villas and office blocks with more nameplates on their front doors than strictly seems legitimate (some 46,000 businesses are registered here due to the country's relaxed tax regime), but it's bewitching all the same. It's National Day and surrounding me in this meadow are a good 3,000 Liechtensteiners. Some are in traditional dress – women in maids' outfits with intricately stitched halos for hats, men in thick multicoloured tunics straight out of the age of empires – while others look as if they've stumbled here by accident, greasy hair plastered to their faces and last night's drink sweating out of them. But everyone is singing. Even the man right at the front: Hans-Adam II, a silver-haired, ever-grinning billionaire and the fifteenth reigning prince from and of Liechtenstein.

'*Oben am jungen Rhein / Lehnet sich Liechtenstein, / An Alpenhöh'n,*' they sing. Up above the young Rhine, Liechtenstein is resting, on Alpine heights. '*Dies liebe Heimatland, / Das teure Vaterland / Hat Gottes weise Hand / Für uns erseh'n,*' they go on, praising this beloved homeland and this dear fatherland, that's been chosen for them by God's wise hand. And as each word comes out, my smile gets wider, because here, some 700 miles from home, I'm hearing a tune that could not be more familiar. The melody is unmistakable. Maybe slightly quicker than I am used to, but there is not one note's difference. We rush into a second verse and some in the crowd start doing hand actions to accompany the words. When they hit the word 'prince', they shoot their right arm out straight, before drawing it back just as quickly, a look of embarrassment on their faces. They do it again for the word 'fatherland', like the most apologetic Nazi salute you could ever witness. It is without doubt the best version of 'God Save the Queen' I have ever heard.

Five minutes after the final words – '*Vereint und frei*', united and free – die out, I find myself talking to Baron Eduard von Falz-Fein, a 102-year-old who I've been reliably informed is the soul of Liechtenstein. He was born in tsarist Russia, but had to flee due to the Revolution. After a period stateless, travelling on a Nansen passport, he ended up representing Liechtenstein at the Olympics and later even redesigned the country's flag when he realised it was the same as Haiti's (he added a crown). He's also the main reason anyone has ever visited this country, having almost single-handedly developed its tourist industry by convincing bus companies they could make a six-country tour of Europe into a seven-country one just by driving an extra twenty minutes across the Austrian border. He asked them to stop at his tourist shop and soon became extremely wealthy. I tell him what I've just witnessed.

'What do you mean, it's your anthem?' he says, prodding a finger in my direction from his perch on a windowsill where he now spends his days (he hasn't been able to walk for two years). 'I have looked it up on the internet and it says that in 1757 Joseph Haydn composed the melody for Austria. Then it went to Germany. Then to here. And then to you. One hundred per cent what I am telling you is true! And you say that's wrong; that it's your anthem. Don't English people know their history? Incredible!'

I try telling him you shouldn't believe everything you read on the internet, but after another bout of finger-pointing it seems like a good idea to move the conversation on to safer ground, so I ask how a Russian émigré came to live here. He runs through his entire life story, focusing more on his days reporting as a cycling journalist in France and his past as a Casanova than on his escape from Russia ('I had a lot of girls in my life. Now it's gone – since years – finished!'). But the simple answer turns out to be that when he visited here for the first time and saw the mountains and the flowers spilling out of the fields, he realised he didn't need anything else. I ask if he found it hard to adjust to life in such a small country given that he was such a ladies' man. 'I never touched a girl from Liechtenstein!' he says, offended by the idea. 'This country is too small! Girls are very jealous! It would have been impossible! All my *conquêtes* have been abroad.'

But talking about girls does seem to put him in a better mood, so I decide it's safe to move back to the anthem. He tells me about the time he went to the 1936 Olympics in Berlin, watched a British medal ceremony and heard his new home's anthem suddenly playing. 'It was the same as ours. I did not understand what was happening!' he shouts. A couple of decades after that, he says, he went to a bobsleigh world championships and the organisers played a novelty pop song he had helped write called the 'Liechtenstein Polka' because they thought the real anthem couldn't have the same tune as 'God Save the Queen'. And about twenty years after that, he appeared on American TV after a Liechtenstein skier, Hanni Wenzel, won gold at the Olympics. He was asked what Liechtenstein's anthem sounded like. 'I told them it was the same as Britain's and everyone found it so funny. I became a hit just for saying it!'

The more the baron talks about the anthem, the more it seems to dawn on him that maybe it is strange that Liechtenstein has the same tune as the United Kingdom after all, that perhaps they should have changed the music by now. 'People say Liechtenstein has no composers, but we had one: Rheinberger,' he says at one point, referring to an organist who died back in 1901. 'We should have asked him to write something.' But even that realisation doesn't seem to make him think I'm right about the song's origins. 'Are you sure we didn't have it before you?' he asks as I'm about to leave. 'Have you looked at the internet?'

Liechtenstein is, despite what the baron says, the only country outside the United Kingdom's influence that still uses the melody to 'God Save the Queen' for its anthem. That melody once meant 'anthem' to the world, with everyone from Russia to Denmark using it. But all those countries soon realised they might actually be able to conjure a tune for themselves; that perhaps a Russian or Danish song might mean more to the people than a British hymn, that one might even help turn those people into Russians and Danes by making them feel an attachment to something bigger than their village or feudal lord. Some countries dragged their feet, of course. Switzerland did not replace its 'God Save the Queen'-stealing 'When You Call, My Fatherland' until 1961, while Australia did not drop it until 1984 and a referendum on the issue (the equally lethargic 'Advance Australia Fair' was chosen after winning 43 per cent of the vote, 'God Save the Queen' dropping in status to the royal anthem as it had long been for most of the Commonwealth). But no matter how many other countries have got rid of that melody, Liechtenstein has clung to it so tightly it makes you start to wonder if it actually has any musicians to write a tune of its own, Rheinberger or not.

Liechtensteiners would say it's unfair to criticise them for the lack of originality. For example, Cyprus and Greece share the same anthem, 'Hymn to Liberty', even if Turkish Cypriots refuse to recognise it (more for political than musical reasons, obviously). Estonia, meanwhile, stole the tune of its anthem from Finland's 'Maamme' ('Our Land'), and Fredrik Pacius, the composer of both, had in turn apparently just ripped off a German drinking song. The music for Poland's sprightly if worryingly named 'Poland is Not Yet Lost' (Poles know it instead as 'Dąbrowski's Mazurka') was 'borrowed' by both Yugoslavia and later Serbia and Montenegro before they fell apart. There's also South Korea and the Maldives, both of which originally used the music to 'Auld Lang Syne' for their anthems until, I assume, one of their diplomats went to Edinburgh for a New Year's Eve and decided perhaps it wasn't the best idea.

There are also an almost endless number of composers who have 'taken inspiration' from 'La Marseillaise' when writing anthems. The worst offender is perhaps Enric Bons, a priest who wrote Andorra's anthem, 'El Gran Carlemany'. He came up with a melody so similar to 'La Marseillaise' you can only assume he was actually trying to remix it rather than write his own composition, although perhaps he can be slightly forgiven since his country sits right next to France. Less forgivable is James Frederick Mills, a British naval bandleader who wrote Oman's anthem in the 1930s. For thirty seconds, his tune is an original work, a gentle military fanfare any sultan would be pleased to have as his anthem. But then, out of nowhere, he jumps straight into the opening phrase of 'La Marseillaise'. There's no denying the similarity. He tweaks a note or two, of course, but it's too little to hide the resemblance – the compositional equivalent of an incompetent burglar shutting the door of the house he's just robbed in the hope no one will notice.

But as bad as all those examples are, none of them come close to Liechtenstein's aping of the world's most important anthem with 'Oben am Jungen Rhein'. It's not like size is an excuse. The six countries smaller than Liechtenstein all have their own anthems (Monaco's even makes a virtue of its size, containing the lines, 'There are not very many of us, / But we strive to defend our traditions'). So too do many of the world's dependencies. Even the Pitcairn Islands – where the mutineers of the *Bounty* landed and whose population totals a staggering fifty – have managed several unofficial 'anthems' over the years, although most of them do sound like they were dreamed up by a cruise ship's marketing department. 'We from Pitcairn Island, we welcome you today,' goes one. 'We're glad you come to see us, but soon you'll sail away.'

*

If there's one person who can explain why Liechtenstein's never changed its anthem's melody, it's the man sitting before me, Josef Frommelt. Rapidly approaching eighty, he looks as if he should be spending his days painting watercolours in his garden or ruffling the hair of smiling grandchildren, but he's still hard at work; he is both Liechtenstein's main cultural historian and its 'princely music director', a grand title that means he's given occasional tasks such as producing an official arrangement of 'Oben am Jungen Rhein' so that people sing it at the same speed and in the same key (apparently once a huge problem). I've arranged to meet him at a cafe in the centre of Vaduz, Liechtenstein's miniature capital, to talk through the song's history, although right now it's proving somewhat hard to get him to do anything except reminisce about his childhood. 'There were punches and kicks, bloody noses, black eyes and, er . . . How do you say when your skin goes purple? Yes, bruises! Everywhere!' he laughs, swinging his arms across the table, re-enacting the fight like a schoolboy boasting to his friends. 'And all because of the anthem! So you could say we fought to have your tune.'

I'm lost, I feel the need to admit, and he apologises for getting ahead of himself. 'Our anthem was actually first called "Oben am Deutschen Rhein" – "Up above the German Rhine",' he says, 'because we were part of the German Confederation when it was written. And in the 1930s we had a very strong group of Nazis here. I was a small boy then, of perhaps three or four years, but I remember every Saturday afternoon near my father's house, the *Hitlerjugend* would make the marching parades in the brown uniforms with the Nazi banners and the Nazi flag and so on, and they'd sing these Hitler songs. Then they would sing the anthem and shout every mention of the word "Germany" as if they wanted us to be part of the Third Reich. Then the Scouts would sing it back at them, but change the words so there was no mention of Germany. And then there'd be a big fight!' He starts swinging his arms again. 'It was very exciting for me. And in the end the Scouts won.' So when did Liechtenstein officially remove those German references? '1963,' he says. 'Change can be a bit slow here sometimes.'

I start to ask about why Liechtenstein has never changed the music if it felt happy to change some words, but he cuts me off. 'Before we talk about my anthem, you should really know the full story of "God Save the Queen". It's rather long. How many nights are you staying here?'

*

On 28 September 1745, Thomas Arne, the thirty-five-year-old Roman-nosed musical director of His Majesty's Company of Comedians in London and the famed composer of 'Rule, Britannia!', found himself urgently in need of a patriotic crowd-pleaser. His city was about to be ruined, everyone around him was saying. Charles Edward Stuart – Bonnie Prince Charlie, the Young Pretender to the British throne – had recently landed in Scotland and raised an army of Highlanders. There were only a few thousand of them, apparently, but they had managed to rout King George II's men near Edinburgh and had now entered England. The Jacobites were coming, determined to take back the crown they'd lost sixty years earlier.

Arne's colleagues in the company seemed to be among the most moved by the threat. That morning they had put an advert in the *General Advertiser* saying the company was 'to raise 200 men in defence of His Majesty's person and government . . . The whole company of players are willing to engage.' It's impossible to know if Thomas shared their enthusiasm. He was a staunch Catholic despite the problems admitting that caused at the time – he never wrote music for the Church of England – and his mother was even more of one (the only contemporary description of her says she was a 'bigoted Catholic'). He might, then, have been quite happy for a Catholic Stuart king to retake the throne. But he also knew his job: he'd suddenly found himself in 'the most pious, as well as the most loyal place in the three kingdoms' (of England and Wales, Scotland and Ireland), and his music that night needed to show that. There's no record of what he did that afternoon. I like to think he headed out of the Drury Lane Theatre and into Covent Garden's streets, hoping the air would help him think of a song – the perfect song – to end that night's performance and sum up the city's mood, swerving around hawkers and dodging carriages while humming to himself. But equally he could have just searched through his songbooks until he grabbed one called the *Thesaurus Musicus* that had been published the year before, and saw the perfect choice sitting there on page 22, a simple tune 'for two voices' that had somehow been forgotten.

That night, the company performed Ben Jonson's *The Alchemist* to a full house. As it finished, the audience 'were agreeably surprised' when three soloists and a male choir strode out to the front of the stage and launched into the song Arne had arranged that day. I'm not sure how much that song would have sounded like the 'God Save the Queen' we know now. The tune is in the style of a galliard, a dance that includes a leap into the air once a phrase, and the singers, accompanied by harpsichord, might have felt obliged to perform it as one. Back then soloists also liked showing off. A lot. What was the point in having one note for each word when you can have ten? Why sing straight when you can trill? The 'God Save the King' heard that night, then, was probably drawn out and ornamented as richly as possible, first sung by the soloists, then by the choir booming in to repeat it all.

But however it sounded, it worked. There was 'universal Applause' and 'repeated Huzzas', the *General Advertiser* wrote, making use of a system of capitalisation that was old-fashioned even then. The song 'denoted in how just an Abhorrence [people] hold the arbitrary schemes of our invidious Enemies and detest the despotick Attempts of Papal Power,' it added. It went down so well, in fact, that they started to sing it at the end of every show, and rival theatres felt obliged to copy the idea. Shortly afterwards, the song was printed in the popular *Gentleman's Magazine*, alongside articles like 'Can England be otherwise than miserable under a Popish King?'

The magazine printed all three verses, including the occasionally controversial second:

> O Lord our God arise,
> Scatter his enemies
> And make them fall.
> Confound their politics,
> Frustrate their knavish tricks,
> On him our hopes we fix,
> O save us all.

That verse brilliantly summed up people's feelings towards Bonnie Prince Charlie in 1745. It seems less appropriate today, probably explaining why the royal family pretends it doesn't exist when it hands out versions of the lyrics. (It's not the most infamous verse. That goes to one penned in tribute to Marshal Wade, who led the king's initial forces in 1745. 'May he sedition hush, / And like a torrent rush, / Rebellious Scots to crush, / God save the King,' it goes, although it was only occasionally sung and not documented until 1822.) Not everyone was happy with the original song, though. Just two months after it was printed, the *Gentleman's Magazine* published an anonymous 'attempt to improve the song "God Save the King", the former words having no merit but their loyalty'. 'Tell Rome and France and Spain, / Britannia scorns their chain,' it started. It didn't catch on.

'God Save the King' didn't, of course, become what we'd call 'the national anthem' immediately, even though it kept being sung long after Bonnie Prince Charlie had fled the country in 1746, with parodies of it even being used to sell fish ('Nature's best treat / . . . May turbot eat'). People didn't really think of themselves as Britons back then, for a start, and the government was only in the early stages of trying to create a unified identity (even if some Scots called themselves North Britons in a desperate attempt to prove it existed). But by the late 1780s, there was apparently no other patriotic song to rival it.

That seems to have happened partly due to the madness of King George III. Throughout his reign, he suffered bouts of mental illness that, at worst, caused him to become deranged, talk gibberish for hours and foam at the mouth. Many feared he would have to be replaced by his extravagant and debt-ridden son, George, Prince of Wales. 'God Save the King' seems to become a rallying cry against that change, a prayer almost, begging for the king's recovery. In 1789, George III recovered from his first major bout of 'madness' (most likely the kidney disease porphyria) and went on a trip to the south coast to convalesce. His party stopped at the village of Lyndhurst on the way and decided to go for a walk. 'The moment they stepped out of the house, the people, with one voice, struck up "God Save the King!"' writes Fanny Burney, one of the queen's assistants, in her diary. 'I assure you I cried like a child twenty times in the day at the honest and rapturous effusions of such artless and disinterested loyalty . . . These good villagers continued singing . . . during the whole walk . . . 'Twas well the King [decided] he could walk no longer . . . they would have died singing around him.'

There were other factors at work, of course, pushing people to want patriotic songs, like the loss of America and the Seven Years War with France. But perhaps the real reason for the song's rise was the fact it mentions nothing apart from the monarch and God – the only two things people could agree on, and see themselves as belonging to, back then. There are no references to any country – even a landscape – for people to get angry over or feel left out from. There's not even a reference to 'Great Britain', a phrase the monarchs started pushing in the 1700s. People in England and Wales, Scotland or Ireland could all sing it without having to feel part of an imagined community or even dropping their hatred of each other. Its lack of specificity is probably its greatest asset in that respect. The irony that the first real national anthem wasn't a national anything is one that hasn't been missed by many historians.

If you want more proof that the tune was becoming more an anthem than a song, you only have to look at its reception abroad. In 1790, the tune appeared in Denmark as 'Heil dir im Siegerkranz' ('Hail to Thee in Victor's Crown') and was used to praise that country's king. By 1793, a similar song had appeared in Germany and 'almost at once was officially adopted by Prussia, Saxony, Hanover, Brunswick and Weimar' to praise their rulers (it was still the Kaiser's anthem during the First World War). In 1816, the music was being used for 'The Prayer of the Russians'. It soon spread further afield too, by 1861 even turning up representing the Kingdom of Hawaii.

The world's greatest musicians were also swept up by its charms. During the 1790s, Joseph Haydn stayed in London twice and heard 'God Save the King' practically every time he went to the theatre. Somehow, he didn't leave the country fed up with it, instead envious that Britain had 'a song through which it can show in full measure its respect, love and devotion to its ruler'. Back in Vienna, he wrote his own tune for Francis II, the Holy Roman Emperor. He composed a melody far more graceful and stirring than the one that inspired it. It's now known as the 'Deutschlandlied' and is Germany's national anthem.

Beethoven was likewise smitten with the anthem, writing seven majestic and fun piano variations on it in 1803, then, a few years later, featuring it in his Battle Symphony – easily the worst piece of music he ever composed, a fourteen-minute musical fight between Britain and France that's meant to involve real cannon fire and drummers pretending to march to their deaths. 'I must show the English a little what a blessing they have in their "God Save the King",' he wrote in his diary while preparing that piece. One critic dared rubbish it and Beethoven scrawled alongside a copy of their review, 'What I shit is better than anything you have ever thought.'

*

However, the most interesting aspect of the story of 'God Save the Queen' is not its travels but its origins, or, to be precise, the fact that no one has the faintest idea what those origins were before it suddenly appeared in the *Thesaurus Musicus*, with no composer or lyricist named.

We do have some ideas about the lyrics. They may, ironically, have been written during the reign of James II, England's last Catholic king, when he was about to be overthrown. The clue to that is in the song's final verse, where it pleads for the king to 'defend our laws' like a list of terms and conditions for his 'saving'. James was seen as a notorious autocrat, repeatedly ignoring the wishes of Parliament in order to get his way and make life easier for Catholics and Protestant Dissenters. The belief is that whoever wrote the words wanted him to survive, just not to keep acting a fool if he did. A similar song has also been found in Latin, which some have argued is further evidence it could originally have been written to support a Catholic monarch. But having said all that, the words equally could have been written far earlier, since its main phrases were common even in the 1500s. In Henry VIII's time, for instance, the newly formed Royal Navy used 'God save the King' as a password, 'Long to reign over us' being the required answer.

As for the music, there's just as little certainty about who wrote it. Thomas Arne, the man who brought the song to London's stage, was once asked if he knew and said he 'didn't have the least knowledge, nor could guess', and with that admission he opened the floodgates to a tide of chancers desperate to write their name into history. It's hard to decide which of the claims to authorship is the most ludicrous.

In the 1790s, a man called George Carey insisted his father, Henry, had written it. It wasn't beyond the realms of possibility: Henry had been a famous satirist and songwriter in the 1700s, a go-to man for London theatres. The only problem was that George claimed his father wrote it in 1745 specifically for Arne's performance, which couldn't have happened as he'd killed himself two years earlier, hanging himself with a cord. George probably didn't do his claim any favours by asking the king for a £200 yearly pension ('Some *little* relief', as he called it) in recognition of his father's service to the country. He was shouted out of the palace.

There are also those who claim Jean-Baptiste Lully wrote it. Lully was a French composer most famous for dying of gangrene after accidentally stabbing himself with his own conducting baton. That story first appeared in the memoirs of a French noblewoman, the Marquise de Créquy. Renowned for her artistic friends, she insisted that Lully composed the tune for some nuns in 1688 so they could welcome Louis XIV, who was planning a visit to their convent. She even knew the words they sang:

> Grand Dieu sauvez le Roy,
> Grand Dieu vengez le Roy,
> Vive le Roy!

A few decades later, she wrote, the dastardly composer Handel sweet-talked the same nuns into letting him see that music, then copied it down and sailed back to London with, I assume, the copy hidden in his bouffant wig, so the English could proclaim it their own. It's such a good story it's almost a shame to learn the marquise's memoirs are fake.

There have been dozens of other claims, each one pushing the bounds of credulity further than the last. There is one, however, that does not seem quite so far-fetched. It is made on behalf of John Bull, who was one of the most famous musicians in the 1600s, a man whose baroque organ pieces caused rapture in churches all over Europe. If you find a portrait of him from the time, Bull couldn't look more enigmatic (or less like his namesake, the portly, top-hat-and-waistcoat-wearing personification of Britain). He has a sharply chiselled face and greased moustache, and he always seems to be looking over your shoulder, as if eyeing up a young woman who's walked into the room behind you. The portraitists may well have captured his character perfectly, as he seems to have been something of a womaniser, and was forced to flee Britain having been found guilty of 'fornication, adultery and other grievous crimes' (he died in Antwerp).

Bull was linked to the anthem largely through the efforts of an amateur historian, Richard Clark, who in the 1800s went on a one-man crusade to prove his authorship. Clark first made the claim on Bull's behalf after seeing a collection of the composer's work that included a piece called 'God Save the King'. He even claimed to know the exact date for the tune's unveiling: 16 July 1607. That night Bull had entertained royalty on a 'very rich pair of organs' and, Clark argued, must surely have played it. The one problem with this story was that Clark hadn't actually checked the music, and when someone did, they found it 'no more like the anthem than a frog is like an ox'.

Clark tried to ignore the criticism and carried on insisting Bull was the author, but he became a laughing stock, to the point that forgers one day targeted him with fake Bull sheet music they claimed to have found being used to wrap food in a cheesemonger's. Undeterred, Clark kept searching for evidence and one day bought Bull's music collection to have a look at the supposed 'God Save the King' for himself. His critics were right – the song was nothing like the anthem – but sitting thirty pages further on there was another tune that was. It's not exactly the same, certainly not enough to name Bull the composer, but it is close enough to seem like a premonition, the melody 'God Save the King' might have been based on. Clark should have published his discovery at once, but for some reason he didn't. Instead he got a quill and altered the music, adding the title 'God Save the King', writing '2 more verses' at the end, changing the song's key and even adding a few sharps here and there to improve the resemblance. He then varnished it and tried to sell a book telling all about this miraculous discovery. It didn't take long for his deception to be uncovered – Clark went back to being a laughing stock.

*

Sitting in Vaduz, Josef Frommelt rubs his hands together, happily relieved to learn he doesn't have to tell me about 'God Save the Queen' and he can just go straight into explaining how this song became Liechtenstein's anthem and why, unlike seemingly everywhere else, it wasn't dropped soon afterwards. 'It's because of a man called Jakob Jauch,' he says. 'His life was a tragedy. Really a catastrophe.' He suggests getting some wine to make his tale more cheerful. 'Have you tried ours? It's made by the prince.'

Jakob was a priest, or at least he wanted to be one. In 1852, aged fifty, he was living in Switzerland, studying at a priest college and effectively unemployed. The problem was that no bishop in the country wanted anything to do with him, all remembering his father, Xaver, a priest too and a man even God would have struggled to love. 'Jakob's father offended all the Catholics [in

Switzerland], then he changed his religion and became a Protestant and offended all of the Protestants too,' Josef says. 'I think he didn't have a brain.'

Xaver so annoyed the Swiss, in fact, that he had to move to a Russian agricultural colony because it was the only place that would have him. It was looking like Jakob himself might suffer a similar fate until he wrote a begging letter to a local bishop, saying he would take any posting, 'even the quietest place with the poorest flock, where no one else wants to go'. They took him at his word and sent him to Liechtenstein.

Back then, Liechtenstein was little more than a few isolated villages hemmed in by the Rhine on one side and Austria's mountains on the other. About 8,000 poor people lived there tending to a few thousand even poorer cattle. It was a sovereign state and part of the German Confederation, but it shouldn't really have existed. When Napoleon swept across Europe in the early 1800s, he had got rid of most small principalities like it, only sparing Liechtenstein because he liked its prince, Johann I. Johann was a commander in Austria's army, and a leader of numerous successful cavalry campaigns. He met Napoleon while negotiating peace between the two empires, and did such a bad job protecting Austria's interests that he was forced to resign, although he did at least manage to save his own country. Liechtenstein's survival, of course, also had much to do with the more simple fact that it wasn't really worth invading. It had no gold, no cities, no strategic value; nothing. It was so easy to ignore that even its princes didn't seem to give it much thought, preferring to stay in Vienna (the Liechtenstein family bought the land in 1712, but no reigning prince set eyes on it for 130 years).

Jakob Jauch didn't care that he was headed to such a dismal place. It was a final opportunity to prove himself, and he took one look at its people and decided he would do everything he could to improve their lives. Realising they needed education, he built a boys' school; realising their agricultural methods were out of date, he brought in experts from Hungary to teach modern farming techniques. Jakob sounds like a godsend, but unfortunately he did all this in much the same manner as his father would have done. Jakob had a 'choleric' personality, Josef says, a polite way of saying he was hot-tempered and irritable. He came across as condescending, going around telling everyone they were living the wrong way. And he also seemed to favour just a few families, awarding them contracts to build his school and ignoring everyone else's bids.

Thanks to all of this, he had soon made enough enemies in the country for there to be an active campaign to get rid of him. Villagers started to write letters to the bishop containing every slur and accusation they could think of. Jakob misspent funds, they said. He ignored his priestly duties. He insulted them. 'After four years, the bishop decided he had to shoo him away,' Josef says. 'He was made to leave Liechtenstein with a day's notice and was sent to Sicily. He spent the rest of his life writing letters asking to come back.'

The love Jakob had for Liechtenstein can be seen all through the five-verse song he wrote for the country (whether he wrote it while living there, or while lamenting in exile, is unknown). 'From green rocky heights / It's lovely to gaze at: / How the Rhine's silver band / Hems the beautiful land / . . . Of silent bliss,' it goes at one point;

> Where the chamois leaps freely,
> The eagle soars boldly,
> The herdsmen sing the Ave
> For home.

Okay, it's a bit syrupy, but it comes from the right place. Why did he set those words to the tune of 'God Save the Queen'? It's probably not because he was trying to write an anthem, Josef says. He would have known the tune well, having lived in London earlier in his life while working as a priest for German expatriates, and he probably just picked it because he liked it, because it was a tune so easy even an amateur musician like himself could fit words to it.

No one would actually have ever known Jakob wrote 'Oben am Jungen Rhein' if he hadn't mentioned it in one of the many letters he sent to Liechtensteiners from exile, all in a secret code to stop his old enemies reading them. In one of these he talks of playing songs on his harp: 'But when I started to sing [my song], my voice failed me, choked by tears for the poor folk of Liechtenstein.' Jakob died in 1869 after having two 'very, very explosive' aneurysms, according to Josef. Thirty years later, there were reports in a local newspaper of huge crowds singing his song as if it was the most natural thing to do. The lack of records before then means no one has the remotest idea how it got this anthem status.

*

'But why's the music never been changed?' I ask Josef.

He gives an unknowing shrug. 'When it was written, the English melody was the mark of all anthems so it was normal, I suppose, for some people to want to adopt it,' he says. 'And in the 1930s, when there were the Nazis, the song became so important to us because it was part of the fight against Germany. That's when this country was born really.' He goes on to say, somewhat pointedly, that it's only foreigners who have really called for the music to be changed. Some have even written their own suggestions. 'I once organised a concert, "The Twenty-five Nicest Anthems of Liechtenstein", where we sang a lot of them,' he says, chuckling at the memory. He reaches down to a bag filled with papers and finds a letter an American composer once sent to Franz Joseph II, Liechtenstein's prince in the 1980s. 'I have written you a new anthem,' the American's written. 'The words are in English so may not be completely satisfactory, but my music is far more powerful and inspiring than "God Save the Queen". I doubt if you will find better.'

'He included a tape with it,' Josef says, 'and we put it on and there's this long chord, then a cracked whisky voice came in: "Ohhhhhhhhhhhhhhhhh, Liechtenstein!" It really is the funniest thing.'

I'm about to thank Josef for his time when I remember he's a musician too. Haven't you ever tried writing one? I ask. 'I thought about it,' he says, 'but then I remembered that sentence of Beethoven saying what a wonderful melody it is and I thought: So I have to be better than him? That's hopeless! A pipe dream! We're better off keeping what we have.'

*

Over the next few days, I speak to what feels like Liechtenstein's entire population about the anthem and it seems Josef is right: no one has the slightest problem having the music of 'God Save the Queen' for their anthem. If anything they take pride in it. It's another thing that puts the country on the map – like their prince, or the fact they have no army. It helps make the country interesting and plays into the national idea of Liechtensteiners as being unusual. If they had their own music, their anthem would just be unheard and unremarkable, like those of their neighbours Austria and Switzerland.

I meet Mario Frick, Liechtenstein's greatest ever footballer, a striker once good enough to play in Italy (even if his international career statistics read 117 appearances and 16 goals). He happens to be wearing an England football shirt, which he insists is by accident, and starts reminiscing about all the 'times we played Wales or Northern Ireland or Scotland, and there'd be our anthem and it'd be incredible, just all these whistles.

Always whistles.' He puts his fingers in his mouth and blows, in case I couldn't guess what 40,000 angry Scots drowning out an anthem sounds like. 'But we know the history, and we grew up with it, so why would we change? It's too late now anyway.' The only thing he says he'd change is how many people sing it. 'We're a proud people for sure, but we're not like the Italians or Spanish, loud and emotional. The first time I heard the anthem as a footballer was here and I had goose bumps. But it might as well have been an empty stadium; there were only about four people singing.'

I also go and meet one of the country's most respected politicians, a cross-dressing car mechanic named Herbert Elkuch, who bluntly says, 'It's our hymn, not yours – just look at the words,' and then spends a long time telling me that the country's taxes are too high and asking me to get that message out.

I even stalk the country's musicians in the hope one will say that they want to write a new tune themselves, but the closest I get is a composer called Marco Schädler. 'In general, we have low self-esteem,' he says. 'It's understandable because of our size, but it means we don't have much faith in our own knowledge and capabilities. Sometimes we act like kids who always need the help of our big brother – that's Switzerland – or our father, the prince. We have to work on that self-esteem first. Once it's reached a high enough level, the right anthem will come like the baby to the Virgin.' I ask him how long that might take. 'It took us about sixty years to change two words about Germany,' he says. 'So maybe another sixty.'

There is one complaint I hear a lot though. 'The text. I don't like it,' says Jasmine Spalt, a young teacher in Ray-Bans, with a jewelled stud stuck to one of her canine teeth. 'It's too "I love the *Fürst*",' she adds, using the German word for prince. 'It puts him above everyone. I'm not against him personally, I think he should be here, but I think he has too much power.'

The reason for such views is the prince's right of veto.

Liechtenstein is meant to have the most developed democracy in the world; it's a country where anyone can propose a law to parliament if they get 1,000 signatures, and if the parliament turns it down, there's an immediate referendum. The only disappointing feature of the system is that the prince can step in and veto any law he wants, even if the entire country backs it. Hans-Adam II claims this 'protects against initiatives that are too populist at the cost of the general good' but the only recent time he's threatened to use it was in 2011 when there was a referendum to legalise abortion.

'We shouldn't have one person with so much power,' Jasmine says, 'and he has a lot of strange conservative beliefs I don't really support.' She isn't alone in complaining. I heard the same comments almost to the letter from other young women. 'His family doesn't even speak our dialect,' said one, who asked not to be named. 'Yet everyone's so afraid of offending them.' She then spent ten minutes trying to explain to me the difference between Austrian German and Liechtenstein German, a conversation I really wouldn't recommend anyone enters into.

*

Prince Hans-Adam II – or Johannes Adam Ferdinand Alois Josef Maria Marco d'Aviano Pius Fürst von und zu Liechtenstein, to give him his full title – is standing in the rose garden of Vaduz Castle, the shadow of its turret the only thing stopping him from getting sunburnt. It's the afternoon of Liechtenstein's National Day and the silver-haired monarch is about to meet his people. He's put on free beer and finger food for everyone in his grounds and he'll soon be walking around, talking to anyone who fancies a word while presumably trying to cross the great Liechtenstein German/Austrian German language divide. Once he's finished here, he'll head down to the town centre where one of the biggest parties in the world is meant to happen: all 36,000 of the country's population drinking and dancing to every sort of music you can think of. For now, though, he's trapped in media obligations, having to tell Liechtenstein's two newspapers about the country's '*cashflow-probleme*' and what he's going to do about it.

As I wait my turn, I should perhaps be thinking of intelligent questions to ask him about nationalism. This is a prince, after all, who once wrote a book called *The State in the Third Millennium* about how the only way countries can survive is if they become 'like service companies' and stop relying on national sentiment to bind people together (those services companies would be run by princes, obviously). But it's rather hard to think as all I can see in front of me is the prince, who seems to be knocking back cup after cup of lager. It reminds me of watching a groom on a stag weekend, with every cup he finishes being immediately refilled by an aide. I'm still struggling to take in the sight when I'm ushered over to meet him. 'Are you taking photos?' he says. 'No? Great! I can drink my beer,' and another cup is ushered straight into his hand.

We talk a bit about what makes Liechtenstein what it is today, and he laughs about how there are so few people here that of course everyone feels special. Then he talks more seriously about how the fact Liechtenstein has survived independent for so long is what's really key to that feeling. But then I get round to explaining what I'm actually doing in his country and he immediately slams his mouth shut, desperately trying to hold in a laugh. A snigger slips out of the side of his lips and he manfully tries to hold on for a moment more. But then he realises it's so obvious he might as well let the whole laugh out. He's not being rude, he has just never been asked about something as strange as his anthem before. I ask him how it feels to have a song about himself, as that's in part what the anthem is about, with everyone saluting his name. 'Well of course it is a little bit strange. But it [became the anthem] to a certain degree when there was the Third Reich and the Führer was across the border, so we wanted to stress that the prince was our own Führer – you have yours, but we don't want him.'

'So why do you sing it?' I ask. 'Doesn't that mean you're effectively praising yourself?'

'*Ja*, my wife was teasing me about it earlier!' he laughs. 'But of course it's natural. I had to learn it in school. I've sung it for so long now I've got used to it. It's everyday.' The prince's aide puts a finger up to show I've got one more question left, and so I ask about that music. 'It's been so popular here there's never been an idea to change it,' he says. 'Well, maybe once or twice, but we saw what happened in those countries that did change – Switzerland – and their new anthem was not very well received, so here we said, "No, no, no, we won't." And we're in good company with the UK. Great company, I would say.' And with that, he's pulled away to meet his people.

Later that night, I walk around the party hoping to bump into the prince again to ask him a few more questions, but he's not at the 'hip-hop und pole dance' show, and he's not twirling his wife around at the 'salsa und reggaeton' stage either. I don't even see him at the fireworks display, which lasts half an hour and involves bangs echoing down the valley so loudly they turn Liechtenstein temporarily into a war zone. It climaxes with rockets exploding to the anthem's soaring strains and the words '*Für Fürst, Gott und Vaterland*' – 'For Prince, God and Fatherland' – beamed on to the side of the castle. The prince is probably fast asleep after all that lager, but I like to imagine he was actually sitting somewhere with a guitar having thought about my earlier question and decided that perhaps Liechtenstein does need a new melody after all.

*

The next morning, somewhat worse for wear, trying to keep down the apple concoction the landlady has made for my breakfast, I'm hit by the thought that perhaps I shouldn't have gone to Liechtenstein after all; that I should have stayed in London. Not so I could have had that dreaded personal journey, but because the country that's actually most likely to give up the melody of 'God Save the Queen' first isn't Liechtenstein, but the United Kingdom.

There have always been people in the UK who have hated the song, even in England. In 1902, a barrister called Stringer Bateman went to the trouble of surveying the great and the good of British society to see if they thought any improvements could be made to this 'illiterate anthem'. George Bernard Shaw told him the song was 'absurd from the literary point of view', while William Gilbert, of Gilbert and Sullivan fame, called it 'contemptible doggerel', adding, in case his views weren't clear enough, 'I don't think it could be effectively patched [up]. There isn't a convincing line in it.'

It's the second verse that has normally got people worked up – the one about frustrating enemies' 'knavish tricks' and 'confound[ing] their politics'. Newspapers used to regularly run competitions for new words to it, their letters pages filled with debate about such aggression's suitability outside the 1800s. Queen Victoria was once, allegedly, even presented with an alternative verse for approval about 'Bless[ing] England's enemies / And mak[ing] them good.' She's meant to have replied, 'I wish to confound their politics, thank you very much.' (Her love for the song was well known – she was once presented with a dress that played it every time she sat down.)

Today so few people know the second verse of 'God Save the Queen' that there are no longer concerns about those words. In fact, most people in Britain, including myself, seem to see the anthem as so unrelated to their lives it's not worth their time at all, just like people in most other European countries feel about theirs when external 'threats' are no longer immediate enough to push people towards nationalism. But despite that, the anthem still seems to have plenty of detractors. You don't have to look hard to find a newspaper commentator or politician pointing out that the Welsh have their own anthem – the wrenching 'Land of My Fathers' – while the Scots have several they could pick from, with 'Flower of Scotland' being the people's choice. 'Why isn't there an English anthem for English people to sing proudly at sports events too?' They say that without perhaps realising that adopting an English anthem would effectively turn 'God Save the Queen' overnight into simply a royal anthem, one only heard at royal weddings and on state visits – one even further away from the public than it is now. But it's not hard to envisage a scenario when those calls grow stronger and wider. Just think of when Elizabeth II's reign ends and Prince Charles is crowned king. He's a man who hasn't exactly received unanimous love from the British public, and when people go to the next England football match, and the anthem is played, are they going to bellow out 'God Save the King'? I think they'll more likely keep on singing 'Queen' as the final word, part in tribute, part as protest. Even if they do happily move on, everyone will find the experience of changing that one word bizarre, just as I found it bizarre to hear Liechtensteiners singing it with German words. It will feel like hearing their anthem for the first time again. Fresh. New. And it might make some wonder if they want to keep it much longer.

What could take its place? The usual suggestion is William Blake's poem 'Jerusalem', set to music by Sir Hubert Parry in 1916 for an ultra-patriotic campaign (he preferred it when the suffragettes adopted it as theirs a year later). It's a song that evokes the legend of Jesus walking across England's 'green and pleasant land' and is an undeniably beautiful hymn. But the first verse is also a series of four questions, the answer to all of which is 'No'. ('And did those feet in ancient time / Walk upon England's mountains green? / And was the holy Lamb of God, / On England's pleasant pastures seen?') The second verse goes some way to clarify them – 'I shall not cease . . . / Till we have built Jerusalem, / In England's green and pleasant land' – but does England really want to dump 'God Save the Queen' for a song that's so easy to make jokes about? Surely there's a better option. I mean, if there really is no problem taking someone else's tune – as Liechtenstein shows, and Finland, Estonia, Greece and Cyprus do as well, for that matter – then why doesn't England just steal the tune from another, better anthem and change the words? What could possibly go wrong with that? Germany wouldn't mind, surely?

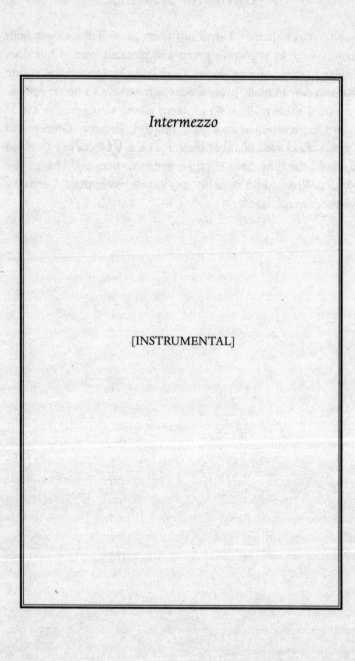

Intermezzo

[INSTRUMENTAL]

7

Bosnia and Herzegovina

AN ANTHEM IN NEED OF WORDS

I should have realised that Dušan Šestić, the composer of Bosnia and Herzegovina's anthem, wouldn't exactly have a joy-filled story to tell. The clues were there. Bosnia's history, for a start: the war that started just weeks after it declared independence from Yugoslavia and which no one – Bosniak, Croat or Serb, Muslim, Catholic or Orthodox – got out of untouched. Then there was the phone call from Bosnia's embassy in London after they tried finding him for me. 'The good news is I've found his wife,' one of the secretaries said happily. 'The bad news is she doesn't know where he is and never wants to hear from him again. Why didn't you tell me this would be so much fun?' But somehow I didn't realise; not until the moment I saw him.

I was waiting outside a sleek bar in Banja Luka, the capital of Republika Srpska – the Serb-dominated country-within-a-country that makes up almost half of Bosnia's territory, and even has its own postal service. Banja Luka's one of the few cities in Bosnia that doesn't show any signs of the war: its buildings aren't splattered with shrapnel holes like Sarajevo's; its historical monuments aren't cheap reconstructions like Mostar's. It was a bright October day and the bar's patio was filled with people smoking and throwing back coffee, basking in the last sunshine of the year. But there was one person who I couldn't take my eyes off, a man in his sixties wandering between the tables as though he was lost.

He was wearing a baseball cap pulled down so tightly it looked as if he was trying to crawl into it, and his gaze was fixed on the ground, apparently in the hope that no one would be able to see him if he didn't look up. He pulled out a phone, dialled a number and my phone immediately rung. This was Dušan.

I offered him a seat, but he preferred one in the bar's empty inside, as far away from everyone as possible.

Dušan wrote Bosnia's anthem, known as 'Intermezzo', just three years after the war, when the fighting was still, unsurprisingly, weighing heavily on everyone's minds. The war had begun in April 1992 when Bosniaks and Croats voted for independence and the Serbs reacted by taking control of much of the country (helped by soldiers from Serbia itself). It soon descended into one of the most vicious and confusing of conflicts, at some point Bosniaks bizarrely fighting alongside Serbs, at other points factions descending into in-fighting. It was the war that introduced the idea of ethnic cleansing to the world, when Serbs forced all Croats or Bosniaks out of villages so they could claim the territory as their own, murdering many of those who refused to go (Croats and Bosniaks eventually did the same). It was also the war of atrocities like the Srebrenica Massacre (where Serbs executed some 8,000 men and boys who were meant to be in a UN safe haven) and the Siege of Sarajevo (where they surrounded, bombed and sniped at the city for over three years, killing thousands) – events it's hard to believe occurred in 1990s Europe. The war ended only once NATO stopped trying to negotiate a peace and instead bombed Serb positions, but the years immediately afterwards didn't prove much better for anyone who had been hoping a unified country could still emerge. Bosnia was now effectively split into two parts (Republika Srpska on one side; a Croat and Bosniak federation on the other) all governed by Byzantine political processes meant to ensure no one was undermined. Unfortunately, most politicians quickly realised they could use those processes to carry on stoking ethnic tension and block anything useful from happening.

That political inertia even ran to choosing an anthem. In 1998, the country's internationally appointed High Representative launched a contest for a new one because he'd become so fed up with politicians failing to do so themselves. Dušan, then a violin teacher and film composer, didn't pay any attention to the competition at first – he didn't feel Bosnian, more a Yugoslav living 'in the ruins of a once great country'. But then he went to the seaside with his children for their first summer holiday in almost a decade and realised he was desperately short of money. The competition offered 2,000 marks to each of the top three entries. That was only about £700, not much even then, but it was better than nothing. 'So I thought: Why not? Why shouldn't I try composing something? There was no other motivation except money,' he said, between drags on a cigarette once we'd finally got seated. 'Money, money, money,' he added loudly in English, rubbing his fingers together in the internationally recognised sign, in case my interpreter wasn't getting the message across. 'I just wanted to write a composition good enough to get in the top three. I wanted to be anonymous, put the notes in my wallet and move on, but it turned out to be different.'

The song Dušan won with is odd for an anthem: it's graceful and understated rather than boisterous and proud, and it carries an air of nostalgia, as if meant to soundtrack Bosnians abroad tearfully reminiscing about their country. It's well written and beautiful, certainly, but it's not what you'd think of as traditionally anthemic and you can tell why Dušan didn't really expect to win with it and certainly why he was surprised by the trouble it brought him once he did. 'Immediately I was no longer good enough for my people – the Serbian side,' he said wearily. 'There were many insults, lots of name-calling from those who were opposed to the existence of Bosnia. "You're a collaborator." "Traitor!" All that. Then there was a big opposition from the Muslims, because here was a Serbian writing their anthem. The Croats didn't like that either. So I was no longer welcome anywhere. Getting any kind of serious work after that was impossible.' Dušan wasn't even invited to the anthem's unveiling. I decided to ask, somewhat rudely, if the anthem was the reason his marriage had ended. He sat back in the plump leather chair, propped his hand under his nose and thought. His silence lasted an unnaturally long time (eighteen seconds, I discovered when I checked the recording later). 'No, I don't think so,' he said, finally. 'But of course when there's no money, love escapes through the window.'

Even when the public's appetite for ethnic strife seemed to drop, Dušan's problems did not. About ten years after he wrote the anthem, someone discovered its melody was almost exactly the same as the theme tune to *National Lampoon's Animal House*, a 1978 film about an American university more notable for its jokes about underage sex than its music. Newspapers ran articles calling him a thief and demanding he give his winnings back; one even went so far as to contact the original composer's family and encourage them to sue. There were calls for his anthem to be dropped.

Dušan insisted there was no plagiarism – 'If I was a thief I'd be a politician and doing far better in life,' he laughed – but admitted the resemblance, saying that 'perhaps as a young man I'd seen the movie or heard the theme and it stuck in my brain somehow'. At the time, he pointed out to anyone who'd listen that there were some differences between the tunes. Legally, it couldn't be classed as plagiarism, he said. But after that, any vestiges of his career as a musician were gone. I asked why he doesn't leave the country; he'd studied music in Belgrade when he was young and lived in Croatia too while he was a military musician – he could always try his luck in those places. He'd also told me that he was in love with the sea. Move to the coast somewhere and retire, I said – take your violin and enjoy the sun. 'I've thought about it, but I can bear this,' he said, his whole demeanour – body slumped in his seat, cigarette butts screwed into the ashtray in front of him – suggesting otherwise.

I asked if there's any way this situation could have turned out differently and Dušan looked at me as if I hadn't understood anything he'd said about how crippled Bosnia is by ethnic politics. His look wasn't what I had wanted. I'd been hoping he was going to say, 'Well, giving my anthem words might have helped.'

*

There are two things that you would think every national anthem needs: a tune, obviously, and some words to accompany it. It's the words, though, that at first glance seem most important. It's the words, after all, that tell a person what their country is about: how its hills roll and its leaders govern; the ordeals its people have been through and the dreams they hold. And it's the words that are meant to make people's hearts swell with pride or at least make them nod 'How true'. Anthems also need words for a more simple reason: so that people can sing along when they're played; so they can look around at everyone else singing and feel part of the same community, and revel in the collective agreement. Only someone who believes in the lost art of humming would argue otherwise.

But despite that, Bosnia is far from alone in having a wordless anthem. The most famous, of course, is Spain's 'Marcha Real', its 'Royal March', a highly whistle-able thirty-five seconds (in its original form) but one that sounds more like the coda to an anthem than an anthem itself. Written by Manuel de Espinosa de los Monteros, it appeared in a book of military calls in 1761 and was originally meant to be a march for Spain's grenadiers (given it's just thirty-five seconds, you have to question their dedication to marching). However, the nation-building King Carlos III soon took it as his own and it started being played to welcome him wherever he went. Carlos would have known about Britain's 'God Save the King' at that time, so why he didn't ask for words to be added in praise of him is unknown. Perhaps he thought having a band soundtrack his every step was praise enough. It has been given words a couple of times since, most notably during Franco's dictatorship, when it gained a verse that sounded like it was written for a keep-fit class ('Raise your arms, sons / of Spain, / who are rising again'). But none were officially adopted and it's unlikely any could be now due to opposition from Basques, Catalans and other Spaniards who want their own states. (Catalans might be especially opposed. Their own anthem, 'The Reapers', is all about driving away the 'conceited and . . . contemptful' Castilians of Madrid, whose dialect any Spanish anthem would be sung in. 'Strike [them] with your sickle!' it says repeatedly over a tumbling, funereal melody.)

San Marino is the only other country that has a wordless anthem today, but the historical list is long. There's Italy's old monarchical anthem, the 'Marcia Reale d'Ordinanza', for a start, and Russia's in the 1990s, when Boris Yeltsin chose Mikhail Glinka's 'Patriotic Song' to help move on from the Soviet Union. Then there's the State of Somaliland, which for its five days of independence in 1960 had a song that was best played on bagpipes rather than any instrument Somalilanders had to hand (it was written by a bandmaster from Britain's Royal Highland Fusiliers); and the Ottoman Empire's many anthems, most of which sound unflatteringly as though they were written by someone trying to compose an opera about a sultan wobbling through his court (Donizetti wrote two of them). But the idea of doing without words has been most popular in the Middle East – a surprise perhaps, given poetry is considered the greatest of art forms in most of its countries. Kuwait's anthem, for instance, was initially just a fifteen-second brass flourish and so boring at that it could have done with being half the length. Iraq, Qatar, the United Arab Emirates, and North and South Yemen (the two countries that preceded the current one) also didn't feel the need to have words to their original anthems, although from the 1950s onwards they all seemed to cave in, one after the other, like embarrassed teenagers desperately trying not to look out of place at the school disco. Kuwait's anthem is now a word-packed two minutes (at one point it praises the country's emir for 'Fencing us all fairly'). It could still do with being cut in half.

But for all that history, the idea of Bosnia having a wordless anthem just doesn't feel right, given it's a country in need of anything that could create even a sliver of unity. In fact, it doesn't even feel sensible, especially if you've had the pleasure of watching one of the country's football matches.

*

It's tipping it down at the Bilino Polje stadium in Zenica, a depressed steel town an hour's drive north of Sarajevo. It hasn't rained here for four months, apparently, and after five minutes the drains don't appear able to cope. Everyone in the crowd is grabbing whatever they can for shelter – I turned down the offer of a plastic bag from the man next to me – and there's water rushing down the steps of the terraces. Bosnia plays its home games here rather than in the capital and it's easy to see why. The ground is tiny – it holds just 15,000 – and the crowd seem about to tumble on to the pitch, all of them looking as if they've come straight from the steel mills, broad-shouldered, shaven-headed, wrapped in the country's blue and yellow flag, intimidating for any opposition even with plastic bags on their heads. The ground is also surrounded by tower blocks, the residents leaning out of the windows seeming close enough to lob their microwaves on to the pitch if they get annoyed by a bad tackle.

Luxembourg's players certainly look terrified standing for their anthem, 'Ons Heemecht' ('Our Homeland'). There are only a few of the country's fans present, which is a shame as it means no one gets to hear the words praising the country's ability to produce a half-decent wine ('Where fragrant vineyards grow / On the Moselle's banks'). There's polite applause when it ends, to be instantly forgotten by everyone present. But now it's Bosnia's turn, and Dušan's graceful hymn begins crackling out of the stadium's speaker system. Most of the crowd stands quietly observing it, not even moving to sweep the rain off their faces, surprisingly solemn for a football crowd, but then from one corner, the stand housing the most fanatical fans, a song starts up. '*Zemljo tisućljetna, / Na vjernost ti se kunem,*' it begins, clear throughout the stadium thanks to everyone else's silence. 'My thousand-year-old land, I pledge my loyalty to you,' it means. '*Od mora so Save, / Od Drine do Une,*' the chant goes on, listing Bosnia's main rivers, laying out the country's borders for anyone who doesn't know. They're words that sound perfect for a national anthem, which is because that's exactly what they once were: taken from a song called '*Jedna si Jedina*' ('You Are the One and Only'). It was Bosnia's anthem during the war, written during the Siege of Sarajevo and loved by every resident of that city no matter their ethnicity or religion. The problem is, this anthem has nothing to do with Dušan's. It's to a completely different tune, and you couldn't make its words fit his melody no matter how hard you tried. As the fanatics carry on – '*Jedna si jedina / Bosna i Hercegovina*' – someone turns up the volume on Dušan's anthem in an attempt to drown out the singing. That only succeeds in making things worse, the fanatics increasing their volume too, turning what's meant to be a polite minute into a farce, one song to the tune of another. God knows what the Luxembourgers are thinking, but I doubt it's helping with their nerves.

The game kicks off, and Bosnia are quickly 2–0 up, but I'm not really paying attention as I'm trying to get my head around what I've just heard. In a country with such a history of ethnic strife, you wouldn't expect everyone to respect the anthem, of course. Some Bosnian Serbs would always say their anthem is really Serbia's 'God of Justice' (music written by a Slovenian) or perhaps even 'My Republic', Republika Srpska's official song ('Where the most beautiful sunrise awakens, / There live good people, honourable and proud'). Some Bosnian Croats would say their anthem is Croatia's 'Our Beautiful Homeland' (music by a Serb), or even that it's still 'Hey, Slavs', the old hymn of Yugoslavia. However, out of all the country's diverse groups, the one you would expect to respect Dušan's anthem is the Bosniaks. His anthem is the song of the only country they have – the place they fought for years for – and so it makes little sense to trash one of its main symbols. And yet the fans who started singing are all Bosniaks. It's a bizarre situation, and one that seems to please few people in the stadium with me, let alone in the country. It doesn't even please the person who wrote the song they're singing.

*

Dino Merlin, Bosnia's answer to Paul McCartney, is busy arranging items on a restaurant table. We're in Sarajevo and he's trying to recreate the first time he escaped from the city's siege. The table is meant to be Sarajevo's airport, a coffee cup is a United Nations jeep, and there's a handful of sugar sachets doing a very bad job of representing Serb snipers hiding in their base in the mountains. There's a Pepsi can too, which I think is meant to be Dino. Unless he's the spoon. I'm not sure exactly, the details having got rather lost amid Dino's enthusiasm. 'So,' he says, smiling broadly and clapping his hands together, 'I had to get out to go to Eurovision. It was in Cork. Ireland! I'd written Bosnia's first ever entry and I was needed for rehearsals. It was very important for us,' he adds, using a word not normally applied to Europe's high-camp songwriting contest. 'So I had no choice but to run across the runway. Did you hear about it? It was the only way to get out to safe territory back then, but it was really dangerous! There were United Nations soldiers patrolling all the time, and if they caught you they put you back in the city. And from this side' – he points at the sugar sachets – 'snipers were shooting. So you had to be very, very lucky and very, very brave. When I got there, I saw all the people were running this way.' He picks up the Pepsi can and moves it towards the sugar. 'And the snipers were shooting them.' He knocks the can over with a comic effect he perhaps wasn't intending. 'So I decided to go the other way, and I made it!'

'How did you get on at Eurovision?' I ask.

'Sixteenth!' he says proudly, before saying he was back in Sarajevo just weeks later.

Dino's real name is Edin Dervišhalidović. He's in his early fifties, bearded and silver-haired, and he's a star across Eastern Europe. As we sit drinking Turkish coffee outside this restaurant, passers-by do double takes when they notice him, a few managing to pluck up the courage to walk over and say hello.

Dino was already famous back in April 1992 when the siege began, so he wasn't the sort of person you'd have expected to find living in the city. In fact, he wasn't even *in* the city when the first bombs fell, launched by Serbian artillery dug into the mountains that surround Sarajevo and make it so picturesque. 'I was in Sweden when I heard,' he says, 'but I came back and tried to live a normal life like everybody else. I felt it was my duty to be here, to play music, you understand? Because you know when people hear one of my songs, something they can whistle, it makes them feel better. It gives them some respite.' I ask him about the siege and he talks about the bombs, the constant fear, the deaths of friends and band-mates, the lack of electricity, food and water. And he talks about it all completely emotionless, as if it's something he just wants to pretend never happened. However, his eyes light up as soon as we start talking about 'Jedna si Jedina'.

It was during the siege that he wrote it. He was in the Holiday Inn – a jaundiced yellow and brown block that still dominates downtown Sarajevo. It was the closest thing the city had to a safe haven, the place where all the foreign newspaper reporters stayed. 'It was a horrible day,' Dino recalls, 'hundreds of bombs fell. I was in the basement and one of my friends turned to me and said: "Hey, Dino, you know we're independent now. Why don't you write us an anthem?" He was laughing – he meant it as a joke – but I thought: What an excellent idea! And I ran home – as fast as I could, given the bombing – and wrote the lyric in one breath. I chose one of the best Bosnian folk songs for the melody. I had the whole thing finished in about an hour. I called my friend and said, "What do you think about this?" and he started crying, so I knew it was good.'

I ask how he managed to do it so quickly and Dino says, almost wistfully, 'It's difficult to explain, but when you're under siege and you think you might die any minute, in that situation you are able to do things you normally can't. Today, it'd be impossible.' He played the song for the first time a few days later at a party in the Hotel Belgrade (which had been hastily renamed the Hotel Bosnia). 'You can't believe it. I stood on this table and played it maybe ten times back to back. Everyone kept calling for it. It was like hitting the rewind button on a tape player again and again.' In November 1992, seven months into the siege, it was made the country's anthem. Dino's sure it was soon being sung everywhere in the country, even perhaps by the people bombing him, 'because my songs were never propaganda. I didn't talk about Serbs, Croats or Muslims. I was talking about freedom, about love. My song, it's not a hard anthem about the past or God or something like that. It's an ordinary story of a place between two rivers. That's it. Nothing special.'

After the war, there was never any question that Dino's song could stay the country's anthem. It was too closely associated with the war, and seen by too many people as a song for Bosniaks only. Dino didn't mind – 'If my anthem was collateral damage for a better life, then I don't have a problem with that' – and he seems genuinely angry that it's still sung as if nothing has changed. I mention the football game I saw the night before. 'They're crazy people,' he says. 'It's a cacophony! I'm a legalist – is that a word? – and I would like people to respect the new anthem because the law is the law, a new time is a new time, the past is the past.' In dozens of interviews he's asked the fans not to sing it, but they don't listen. It's only out of spite they keep singing, he says. He suggests that anthems are like toys, 'and children hate someone who steals their toy'. A moment later he tries to expand that point from a different angle. 'A national anthem is a kind of emotional pilgrimage. When you sing it, you are going towards the unreal – towards your dreams – and the politicians here cancelled people's dreams.' He means they've stopped Bosnia becoming what it was meant to be – united and prosperous, something that his song was meant to represent.

I ask if things would change if Dušan's anthem was given words, but Dino says it's a pointless question given that the country is 'still divided'. 'Nowadays, children in Republika Srpska, in the Croatian part of the country and here each learn completely different versions of history. That's how separate it is. And everything has to be changed and improved before we can expect an anthem that unites people.' His celebrity smile fades for the first time. 'I would like to live in a Bosnia where people don't know anything about governments, presidents, anthems. It'd be excellent. It'd mean humanity is the most important thing to everyone at last.'

*

There have been some efforts to give the anthem words. In 2008, ten years after Dušan wrote the music, there was an official contest, and an eleven-member committee of politicians, poets and musicologists trawled through all 336 entries – even the ones that didn't seem to be taking the endeavour entirely seriously. One entry focused on Our Lady of Medjugorje, an apparition of the Virgin Mary that's been appearing daily to a handful of women in the south of the country since 24 June 1981 (the Catholic Church is sceptical). Another was about Radovan Karadžić, the first president of Republika Srpska and one of the people responsible for the war's worst atrocities, including the Srebrenica Massacre (he was later indicted for war crimes along with the likes of the former Serbian president Slobodan Milošević and the paramilitary leader Arkan). At the time of the contest Karadžić was still on the run in Serbia, disguised as a practitioner of alternative medicine complete with voluminous beard and wild hair. The entry started, 'Come, Raso, come down from the mountain.' I'm unsure if it was sincerely praising him as a new messiah or simply an excellent piece of satire.

In the end the committee did manage to find one entry they thought was worthy of winning – by, of all people, Dušan Šestić. Dušan was due to get a staggering €30,000 for his words, but there were, inevitably, objections from Bosniak and Croat politicians. A Serb cannot write both the words and music to Bosnia's anthem, they said, and so Dušan was made to collaborate with a Bosniak poet, Benjamin Isović (they were allocated two verses each). The final lyrics were the result of eight months' discussion between the two men and seemingly Bosnia's whole political machinery. Politicians examined and questioned every word put forward. 'Delete this. Put this in. Change that. Move these verses around,' one would say, before the next would order it all reversed. I wouldn't be surprised if there were even arguments about how many words were written in Serbian, Croatian and Bosnian, despite all three languages being basically the same (they wrote in Bosnian, for the record). One politician, Slavko Jovičić, summed up the absurdity of the process in a newspaper interview: 'If we were singing about grass – "Our grass is the greenest" – Serbs would immediately reject it because green is a Muslim colour. "It's for the Bosniaks" [they'd say].' Jovičić is a Serb himself.

The final version of the words reads with the kind of emotional blandness you would expect given the process through which they were chosen. 'You're the light of the soul, / Eternal fire's flame,' they start, promisingly enough,

> Mother of ours, land of Bosnia.
> I belong to you.

But then it descends into a string of unimaginative phrases of the sort you find in so many anthems. 'In the heart are your / Rivers, mountains / And blue sea,' goes the second verse. 'Proud and famous / Land of ancestors, / You shall live in our hearts / Ever more,' reads the third. And as for the triumphal ending?

> Generations of yours
> Show as one:
> We go into the future,
> Together!

The words were announced to much fanfare but then went to Bosnia's parliament for approval and were immediately rejected – including by some of the very politicians who had chosen them in the first place. Dušan and Benjamin Isović are still owed €15,000 each.

After that farce, only a handful of people have dared raise the issue again, the most prominent being Nermina Ćemalović, a psychiatric doctor by training and once one of the few politicians in the country people actually liked (she lost her seat at the last election). 'I put forward an initiative to get words three times,' she says from her home in Cazin, a small town near the Croatian border. 'I told everyone that a country needs an anthem like a person needs a passport, that words would make people feel a little prouder of the country – but each time they said, "Today's not the time." So I'd ask, "When is then? It's been twenty years!" and they'd just shrug their shoulders and smile.' She lets out a sarcastic laugh. 'I was so embarrassed to be a politician at the end.'

Nermina made her final attempt to get words at the start of 2014, when Bosnia was getting ready for its first appearance in the football World Cup, sending a multi-ethnic squad that was tipped to do well. 'I told people we needed words for the simple human reason that there should be something to sing in the stadiums – for the players to sing! – but again, of course, no. This is how it is with all areas of life here. It's impossible to make something positive for the country.' I ask if that is because some Serb and Croat politicians just don't want this country to exist. Nermina seems to agree at first, starting to talk about Serb politicians as if they're to blame, saying one told her, 'We have our own anthem in Republika Srpska, we don't need yours as well,' but then she corrects herself, remembering that her own Bosniak party were against the anthem too, for reasons she can't fathom. The only way things are going to change, she says, is if Bosnia's entire political structure is ripped up and the country starts again. Or if there are riots so large politicians are forced to listen.

As if we've both realised that the conversation is getting rather heavy, we start joking about what words could be acceptable to everyone. It seems as though it would have to be an endless list of rivers, mountains and towns, naming every single one in the country so no one could possibly complain. It sounds dreadful, rather like one of those sections of the Bible where people endlessly 'beget' more people. If the lyrics have to be so exhaustive and anodyne in order to be acceptable, is there really any point in having them at all? 'It's okay if it's boring,' Nermina says. 'At least we'd have something.'

*

The strangest thing about Bosnia is that as much as it seems crippled by ethnic politics (which is blamed for everything from Bosnia's 60 per cent youth unemployment rate, to the difficulties people have getting medical care), it proves incredibly hard to meet anyone here who believes that questions of ethnic identity are remotely important. You can talk to people in coffee shops or over *ćevapi* (the national dish of meat fingers) and they'll all say they couldn't care less about such issues and just want a job, that they wish arguments around identity could just be left in the past, the politicians with them. The only time I came close to meeting a Serb nationalist in two visits to the country was when I went to Banja Luka and met Mladen Matović, the long-haired and gregarious composer of Republika Srpska's anthem, 'Moja Republika', who spent an excruciating amount of time trying to avoid saying he wanted Bosnia to break up. 'Let's be truthful and admit the majority of people in Republika Srpska wish to one day be an independent state,' he said at one point, before meekly adding, 'But this is a question for politicians not artists,' as if afraid to be quoted. No one else I met came remotely close to even saying that. In Banja Luka, Mirala Markovic, a Bosnian Croat and my interpreter Dragan's mother, told me she didn't know which ethnic group she was meant to belong to any more and she didn't care – she just wanted to meet a sheik who could take her on shopping sprees in Abu Dhabi. I asked her what words Bosnia's anthem should have and she suggested:

> Why are we still living here?
> We must be really stupid.

Admittedly pockets of ethnic nationalism may exist outside the cities. Also it is quite easy to meet Bosniaks who are proud of their country, given what it has been through. But even among them it's hard to find people you would class as bigoted nationalists; they don't rant about Serbs and Croats, or say the country would be better off if they left. Nidžara Helja, a student in Sarajevo, for instance, told me she couldn't feel happier whenever she hears Dušan's anthem. 'I'm like, "This is mine. This is MINE! Pay attention!"' She did little jumps up and down like a spoilt child while saying this, as if to prove her enthusiasm. But then she said she was happy for it to be wordless for the sake of unity.

'If it ever did get words, I'd probably be like, "Why? What have the politicians done now? It must be really bad if they've had to cover it up with this."'

The person I met who best seemed to sum up the way most people feel was Brano Jakubović, the ever-unshaven leader of the ska band Dubioza Kolektiv, who are well known across the former Yugoslavia for writing both heavily political songs and ones calling for people to smoke more marijuana. 'I actually like the anthem since I discovered it's a rip-off from a film,' he laughed, over a beer in the centre of Sarajevo. 'It fits perfectly with our situation here. Bosnians will always manage to survive. You can put these people anywhere and they'll find a way. They will cheat, steal, whatever, and that's why I like this – you have a composer making an anthem because he's short of money and taking the melody from someone else. And then the politicians pick that one! You see how fucked-up this country is?' It took him a while to stop laughing. 'We should keep with tradition and steal some words for it. Take them from Jamaica's anthem or something: "We have a very nice ocean and coconuts and we're all black."'

Brano has every reason to be a rampant nationalist. He grew up in Sarajevo during the siege, playing in death metal and hardcore bands as a way of 'escaping the madness' (bands used to steal electricity from the police and army so they could perform). He was about to be drafted right as it ended. But instead he couldn't be more of the opposite. 'Every year, I hate this word "patriotism" more and more,' he said at one point. 'I mean, who's ever moved by a national anthem actually? Why don't you listen to anthems in your car? Because they don't have any real feelings inside them. It's just a well-paid songwriter who only plays the white keys on the piano. They don't touch the black keys, the sad ones. If we really need a melody because the football rules say we have to play something before a game, why can't we choose our own? If you, me and ten thousand other people want to have "Smoke on the Water", why can't we do that? It'd be funny, and we should always make jokes about this kind of national pride – that's the only way to stop violence.' The closest thing he's ever had to an anthem, he said, was a football chant popular a few years ago that roughly translates as, 'I've had seven Jägermeisters and my dad's going to kill me' – a phrase a girl uttered one night on live TV when a camera crew asked her how she was celebrating Eid.

'There is a society here,' he added, worried I was getting the wrong impression of his country, 'but it's not built by the government. We had these floods, in 2014, and it was important to see Muslim villages helping Serb villages, to make people realise how silly this confrontation is, and remind everyone what it was like before the war.'

'So what'll it take to change the politics?' I asked.

'If you have any ideas, please tell us,' he laughed. 'Just don't say our anthem should get words. That's not going to solve it.'

He's right, of course: giving the anthem a few verses and a chorus would achieve little, but there's no doubt the current lack of them only leaves a gap both politicians and football fanatics can exploit to exacerbate ethnic tension. The United Nations seems to think otherwise, though, presumably assuming that no words means fewer opportunities for confrontation, to the point that wordless anthems appear to have become a typical part of its solution to conflicts. You only have to look at the fact Kosovo's anthem is wordless too (if you can remember back to this book's Prologue), or that in the early 2000s the UN put forward a plan to try to reunify Cyprus, split in the 1970s, which included a wordless anthem – the music ready to go and streaming online (it was quickly rejected by both the Turkish and Greek parts of the island, hopefully because the tune was so dismal).

But this approach isn't the only one available. Rwanda changed its anthem in 2002 as part of efforts to move on from its civil war, dropping a song called 'Our Rwanda' for the far-too-similarly named 'Beautiful Rwanda' and making sure it included lines about how 'Our common culture identifies us, / Our single language unifies us' as quickly as possible. Similarly, Nicaragua, back in the 1910s, decided to have a competition for new words to its anthem after repeated periods of civil war, the one condition being they could only mention 'peace and work'.

And then, of course, there's Iraq, where the US forced an anthem on the country after its second invasion. Actually, that might not be the case; it depends who you listen to. Under Saddam Hussein's rule, the country's anthem was 'The Land of the Two Rivers', named after the Tigris and Euphrates that meet in the south of the country. It's a song that at first glance seems standard anthem fare, filled with boasts about how the country's 'made of flame and splendour, / [with a] pride unmatched by the highest heaven'. But then it hits its third verse, and suddenly swerves into an ode to Saddam's Ba'ath Party. 'Oh company of al-Ba'ath, you pride of lions,' it goes. 'Advance like terror to a certain victory.' It was unsurprisingly discarded as soon as the first Saddam statue was pulled down, and replaced with a song called 'Mawtini', written by a Palestinian, Ibrahim Touqan, during his people's revolt against British rule in the 1930s. 'My homeland, . . . / The youth will not tire until your independence / Or they die,' goes its second verse, showing its suitability for Palestine, perhaps less so for Iraq. The question is, who made that change?

Most Iraqis believe it was Paul Bremer, the suave, heavily side-parted American who governed the country immediately after the invasion. He attended a 'culture evening' not long after taking charge, they say, where 'Mawtini' was played. Bremer enjoyed its jaunty rhythm and looked around at the audience to gauge their reactions. He saw a few Iraqis crying and so immediately decided, 'That'll do.' It became the anthem the very next day. It's a story that seems so believable, filled with the arrogance and insensitivity most Iraqis associate with America's rule of their country; and it's no surprise that it regularly pops up in newspapers there and is plastered across the internet. The one problem with it is that Bremer insists it's not true. 'I have no idea where the assertion comes from that I chose it,' he told me by email. 'From day one, I made clear to the Iraqis that the anthem was a matter for them to decide.' He does remember the culture evening, though – actually the first concert by Iraq's re-formed National Symphony Orchestra. 'There were many Iraqis in tears at hearing this song that had apparently long been banned under Saddam,' he says, 'and I was impressed and moved.' Around that time, he asked Iraq's governing council to set up a commission for a new anthem. They didn't do it, he says, like they didn't do much else, too busy carving out personal fiefdoms. But, a few months later, Bremer wrote to his wife saying 'Mawtini' 'seemed to be becoming like a national anthem' and that he was trying to learn its words. He had no comment to make about what's happened to the song since he left the country – for over ten years now, the Iraqis have been trying unsuccessfully to replace it, most recently in 2012, when the country's parliament announced that a poem called 'Peace on the Hills of Iraq' would become the anthem. It was written by Muhammad al-Jawahiri, 'the Iraqi Shakespeare', a man who fought against practically every government that ran his country to the point he once had to go into exile in Prague. It was a choice no one could disagree with; he was a friend of all ethnicities. But then Iraq's Kurds demanded a verse in their language. And its Assyrians did too. Then so did its Turkmen. And the initiative collapsed into another squabble.

Okay, so Iraq's not really a good example of how to use anthems to forge national unity, but it does give an idea of what else could have happened in Bosnia: any of the country's High Representatives over the past twenty years could have simply ignored the ethnic bickering and forced some words to be adopted, just as one forced the music on the country having realised it was the only approach that would get results (that man, Carlos Westendorp, unfortunately left the job a year later).

In other words, they could have acted just like Iraqis believe Paul Bremer did. Forcing words on people may ultimately do little to change their feelings of belonging to the country, but they would at least give people something to sing at football matches, meaning that the next time Bosniak fanatics tried singing 'Jedna si Jedina' over the top of Dušan's music, they wouldn't be heard, and for once they wouldn't be able to remind everyone just how split this country still is. It might not sound like much, but in Bosnia, it would be progress.

*

It's been over three years since I met Dušan Šestić, and he's been stuck in my mind ever since. Of all the people I've met while researching this book, he's the most memorable, though sadly for all the wrong reasons – he seemed so utterly beaten down, so weary and defeated, evidence of all the problems anthems can cause. So one January, I decided to go back to Bosnia to see how he was doing. I didn't expect to find him. He hadn't been answering his phone and his daughter wasn't responding to emails. And sitting on a bus from Sarajevo to Banja Luka, I feel sure I'm going to arrive to be met only by rumours: 'I heard he became a hermit and is living in a cave'; 'He just grabbed his violin one day and left town'; 'The old composer? My grandmother said he killed himself and now haunts anyone who plays his anthem.' But just outside the city, passing through a snow-covered gorge, I get a phone call from my interpreter, Dragan, saying he's somehow found Dušan and he's agreed to meet us at exactly the same slick bar as before.

We wait outside as we did last time, speculating about what he's going to look like, expecting a melancholy figure to come skulking towards us, hunched over, even more dejected than before. But the Dušan who appears is nothing like either of our memories or expectations. He's still old, yes. But he has a broad smile on his face and is dressed all in orange, a scarf louchely tossed over a shoulder; his white hair, which last time was shaved almost to stubble, is now long, sparkling with melting snow. He doesn't look like the composer of a failed anthem, more like the leader of a cult, or perhaps a Hare Krishna member about to pull out a tambourine and start dancing down the street. There are enthusiastic greetings – 'It's been too long!' 'You look well' – and it's a while before we're settled and I can ask what's changed.

'Not much,' he laughs, before outlining exactly how little: how the politics here are still crippled ('People think our politicians are incapable, but they're not, and that's the problem'); how his anthem's still 'just another currency' for people to gain from; how the plagiarism scandal has flared up again; and how he still hasn't been paid for the words he once wrote for the anthem ('I'm thinking of suing'). He also reminisces a lot about Yugoslavia and how that country, which 'was a paradise – really', has been 'sacrificed'. It is, in other words, the exact same story as the first time we met, it's just now he sounds . . . well, 'happy' is probably the wrong word, but he's certainly defiant, laughing at the absurdity of the situation he's found himself in rather than weighed down by it. Practically every remark this time comes with a knowing smile and a shrug afterwards, as if to say, 'You couldn't make this up.'

It's such a transformation I feel like a therapist bumping into a recovered former patient. 'What happened to you?' I feel the need to ask.

'At the height of my problems, I had a stroke,' he says. 'Not a heart stroke, but in the brain, whatever you call it. And it ended up pretty good. I'm alive! I'm here! And I decided that God loves me, takes care of me and keeps me for some reason. And I also decided that a man shouldn't pay attention to all the details. I accept more things than I did before. Where I can, I still bark at a tree, but where it doesn't make sense, I look past this life.' Oh, and he's retired, he adds. That's helped a lot. 'Now I just smoke, listen to music and paint.' He gets through seven cigarettes in our ninety minutes together, proving he's at least enjoying the first of those three things. 'My doctor told me not to, but . . .' He waves a hand dismissively.

His new-found outlook even seems to have affected his opinion of his anthem. We go back to the time he wrote it and he almost tries to rewrite history in front of me. He says he was really proud to have written it back then and that it was written with good intentions. Not national pride, obviously, but in the spirit of 'Let's make people come together as much as they can.' At one point he claims he didn't even need the money and I think of saying, 'Look, you're going too far with your revisionism,' but decide not to break the mood and so just ask about the fact his song's still wordless.

Adding lyrics would be a 'good, practical thing to do,' he says, 'a first stepping stone for bigger things later on, because if we can't solve this, who knows what else we can't solve.' A few inspiring lines might even increase people's feelings towards the country, he adds, although not in Republika Srpska, where we are. 'As far as I hear – and, as a musician, I've learned how to listen – most of the people would still like to separate. This bad memory of the war will not pass easily, even after twenty years.' I ask what he expects to happen to his song. He half expects it to be dropped, he says. If there's another war – something he bleakly doesn't want to rule out – it definitely will be. But then he says something so optimistic it seems to show exactly how much his personality has changed. 'I'm hoping for a victory of minds,' he says. 'The anthem's not really important. It's just a symbol like this.' He points to the Nike swoosh on his woolly hat. 'The hat's important; the emblem's not. You're going to wear it either way.'

أُمّتي قَدْ لاحَ فَجرٌ

('My Ummah, Dawn Has Appeared')

أُمّتي قَدْ لاحَ فَجرٌ فَارقُبي النصر المُبين
دَولةُ الإسلام قامَت بِدماء الصّادِقين
دَولةُ الإسلام قامَت بِجهاد المُتّقين
قدّموا الأرواح حَقًّا بِثَباتٍ ويَقين
لِيُقامَ الدّين فيها شَرعُ ربّ العالمين

—

My Ummah, dawn has appeared, so await the expected
    victory.
The Islamic State has arisen by the blood of the righteous,
The Islamic State has arisen by the jihad of the pious.
They have offered their souls in righteousness with
    constancy and conviction,
So that the religion may be established, in which there is
    the law of the Lord of the Worlds.

8

The Islamic State

ANTHEMS IN JIHAD

On 4 December 2013, a Wednesday, a song was uploaded to YouTube. It was tagged to its 'how to and lifestyle' section, a somewhat strange choice given its content. But anyone who stumbled across it that day – perhaps while searching for a clip explaining how to descale a kettle – would have felt at first like they couldn't have been luckier, as if they'd found an intensely beautiful piece of music.

Little more than an Arabic chant, it's sung by a man whose voice seems so relaxed you expect him to drift off halfway through, but he sounds timeless, the sort of singer who immediately makes you wonder how you've never heard him before. His melody has a gentle swing to it too, something you could easily imagine a jazz drummer playing behind to give it some oomph, and he soon starts multitracking his voice so it sounds like a whole choir's jumped in to trade lines, the song's impact only growing as the voices multiply.

But then, after two minutes and fifty-three seconds, some sound effects drop in.

There's the ring of a sword being unsheathed, the *stomp-stomp-stomp* of soldiers' feet, and some stuttering gunfire. And it's probably about this point that any of the people who did stumble across it twigged what they were actually listening to. The song uploaded that day is called 'Dawlat al-Islam Qamat', or, to give

it its English title, 'My Ummah, Dawn Has Appeared'. It is one
of the most popular songs in the Islamic State, and it is, arguably,
the world's newest national anthem. 'The Islamic State has arisen
by the blood of the righteous,' it goes. 'The Islamic State has
arisen by the jihad of the pious / . . . For victory will not return
except by the blood of martyrs.'

Ever since that song was uploaded, it has made appearances
in dozens of the Islamic State's videos: booming out of cars in
towns they control as if they are using it to demarcate territory;
blasting from PA systems at recruitment events; creeping out of
mobile phones on battlefields. It became so associated with the
group that rival jihadists banned it from being played in areas
they controlled, notably al-Shabaab in Somalia. Then, in January
2015, Boko Haram – the Nigerian terrorist group – used it to
open and close one of their propaganda clips and instantly the
song stopped simply being the anthem of a few tens of thousands
of jihadists in Syria and Iraq; it became the anthem of a self-proclaimed caliphate, its territories 4,000 miles apart.

*

If there were one type of society you'd think could do without
anthems, it would be Islamist ones. Anthems are meant to be about
praising countries, after all – and in many of them God, when he
features at all, is relegated to the second or third verse, simply asked
to 'Spare [a nation] conflict and tribulation' and bring it 'Peace. /
Rain. / Prosperity' (to take words straight from Lesotho's). Anthems
like that instinctively don't feel halal, as if they're turning the country
itself into an idol to be worshipped. Who needs paradise above
when you have it here on earth? (Several anthems actually call their
country a paradise, notably the Czech Republic's 'Where is My
Home?' and Wales's 'Land of My Fathers', which, if you've ever
been to Merthyr Tydfil, feels a bit of a stretch.) Islamist thinking
also doesn't seem to sit neatly with the idea of a nation state, due

to the belief that all Muslims are ultimately a single community (the *ummah*, as spoken of in the Qur'an) and that their goal should be to unite. In that sense, an Islamist group with an anthem almost seems to be admitting that goal is unachievable.

There's also a bigger reason why many people wouldn't expect anthems to be at the heart of any radical Islamic society: the perception that many Islamist scholars despise music, viewing it as a distraction from studying the Qur'an, and warning people to keep away from it as if dancing to a four-to-the-floor beat is a stepping stone to depravity. There has, it's true, been a long-running debate between Islamic scholars of all hues about music's status – some saying it should be avoided at all costs; others effectively saying, 'Don't be silly,' pointing out it's just a 'means of entertainment that may comfort the soul'.

However, the Western perception that Islamists reject music is mostly to do with one man: Ayatollah Khomeini, the stern yet charismatic leader of the Iranian revolution.

In July 1979, just a few months after he'd proclaimed the creation of an Islamic Republic and got rid of the shahs, the country's royal family, Khomeini sat down with a room full of the country's radio broadcasters and, fixing them with his intense stare, announced that music 'stupefies people who listen to it and makes their brain inactive and frivolous'; that it 'corrupts Iranian youth'; and that it robs them of their 'strength and virility'. 'A youth who spends their time listening to music can no longer appreciate realities, just like a drug addict,' he added, in case the DJs hadn't yet understood that they wouldn't be allowed to play the next Kate Bush single. 'It's just like opium.'

The next day, headlines around the world screamed that Khomeini had 'banned music'.

Khomeini's regime did, it's true, place some horrific restrictions on musicians – banning women singing solo in case it aroused men, requiring songs to be vetted, restricting concerts, and closing university music departments. Many of those restrictions are still in place today. But the Western newspapers created the impression that Khomeini – and so all conservative Muslims with him – was against music full stop; that he was railing against every note and melody, every harmony and chord. That couldn't be further from the truth. Khomeini might not have been a fan himself, but songs and music had been at the centre of his revolution, with the million-strong crowds who had woven their way through Tehran and called for him to save them, having sung and chanted continually. Khomeini obviously wasn't going to step in and tell those same people to stop singing – to stop praising him and his revolution. What he was against, though, was music he thought of as decadent and indecent: the pop songs that dominated Iranian radio in the shah's time; that godforsaken rock 'n' roll that seemed to be everywhere. He clarified these views just weeks after the supposed ban in an interview with an Italian journalist, Oriana Fallaci.

That interview is an incredible read. In it, Fallaci pillories Khomeini for all the freedoms he's restricted, especially for forcing women to wear the veil. 'If you do not like Islamic dress, you are not obliged to wear it,' he seethes at one point. 'It's for good and proper young women [not you].'

'That's very kind of you, Imam,' Fallaci replies, before pulling off her chador and throwing it to the floor, a move that led to Khomeini walking out in disgust (when the interview resumed, Fallaci immediately raised the issue of the veil again, causing Khomeini to burst into laughter at her cheek, one of the few times he's known to have ever laughed).

Eventually, Fallaci got round to asking him about the music ban. 'Why is listening to music a sin?' she said. 'Our priests drink and sing – even the Pope.'

'The rules of your priests do not interest me,' Khomeini replied. 'Music dulls the mind because it involves pleasure and ecstasy. Your music, I mean. It destructs our youth, who become poisoned by it.'

'Even the music of Bach, Beethoven and Verdi?' Fallaci asked.

'I do not know those names,' he said. 'Some of your music is

permitted. For example, hymns for marching . . . and music that
makes our youth move instead of paralysing them; that helps
them to care about their country.'

Unsurprisingly given those last few sentences, Khomeini seems
to have been very much in favour of national anthems. On the
eve of the Persian New Year in 1980, his government adopted a
new one, 'Lasting Iran'. 'The Islamic Republic has been established,' it begins.

> Through the Iranian Revolution,
> The palace of oppression has been overturned.
> …
> Under the Qur'an's shadow,
> May Iran be permanent, everlasting.

That march survived a decade until it was replaced with the
anthem still in use today (it's equally religious: 'Your message,
O Imam . . . / is imprinted on our souls,' it goes at one point).
Many think Khomeini's death prompted the change; it's actually
because the government realised his anthem went on too long.

Iran isn't the only strict Islamic country that has embraced
anthems. Saudi Arabia, a place where music isn't played in shopping centres for fear it might offend conservative Salafis, has a
sprightly anthem that cries out for Saudis to 'Glorify the Creator
of the heavens' and 'Repeat: *Allahu Akbar*.' In fact, the only Islamic
country that has ever refused them is Afghanistan under the
Taliban's austere rule. For three years, from 1999 to 2002, it was
the only country in the world without an anthem, although I
doubt anyone suffering there noticed that bizarre fact.

Afghanistan became a place where musicians had to bury their
instruments and where anyone found with a cassette tape that
didn't feature only religious chanting was thrown in prison. The
insides of the cassette itself would be hung from trees as a warning
to others. However, I have a sneaking suspicion that even under

that brutal regime there would have been something akin to an anthem being sung: a Qur'anic chant, perhaps, that was being heard more frequently than all the others; one that Taliban soldiers instinctively cried out at moments of joy when prayer just wasn't enough. The reason I believe that isn't because I'm an anthem obsessive desperately trying to prove the importance of these songs; it's because of what's happened in the Islamic State, and the prominence music has among every jihadi group in the Middle East.

*

'When you quote me, can you please make it clear I'm not a supporter of the Islamic State?' Behnam Said asks from his home in Hamburg. The plea seems somewhat unnecessary given his job – he's a member of the German intelligence service, and spends his days analysing jihadi trends – but his concern becomes slightly more understandable when he starts talking about jihadi songs, a topic he completed his PhD in. These songs are known as *anasheed jihadiya*, or *nasheeds* for short – a slightly annoying shorthand given it can also refer to a normal Islamic chant – and Behnam sounds so enthused when he starts talking about them it would be easy to get the wrong idea. 'The first time I heard "My Ummah, Dawn Has Appeared", I couldn't get it out of my head for about two weeks,' he says at one point. 'It touched me in a different way to other *nasheeds*. I mean, I'd sit on the metro and it would just come into my head. The melody's just so striking.' He pauses and lets out an awkward laugh. 'I do realise just how I sound right now. This is what happens to you if you listen to too many of these songs!'

The Islamic State isn't actually the first group to use *nasheeds*, Behnam says. Jihadi songs date back to the 1970s, when Islamic fundamentalists in Egypt and Syria – mainly members of the Muslim Brotherhood – started writing them to inspire supporters and get out their message. '*Nasheeds* as a genre of religious songs are as old as any other, but these groups started making ones that were political and rebellious against governments and that was entirely new,' Behnam adds. The groups would record them on to cassettes and hand them out to anyone they could, hoping to offer people an alternative to pop music. After clampdowns on the Brotherhood's activities in the early 1980s, its members fled to countries like Saudi Arabia and Kuwait and started teaching *nasheeds* in training camps, thereby spreading them further. They took advantage of any technological developments, using synthesisers as soon as they became available, for instance, then moving on to sound effects.

Immediately, of course, some scholars condemned the songs as un-Islamic – 'One wrote that the very idea of Islamic music made literally no sense, like Islamic democracy or Islamic communism,' Behnam says – but soon no one could stop them. Even a teenage Osama bin Laden founded and sang in a *nasheed* group in an effort to avoid being seen as 'too much of a prig'. By the late 1980s, Hamas, the Palestinian group, was including *nasheeds* in its official charter, admitting its members' 'souls will be bored' if they can't listen to some kind of music. Today, most Islamist scholars seem to have realised there is no turning back and have decided to say they're acceptable, at least at times of war. They've become a major propaganda tool for all jihadi groups, although they are seldom commented on in the West due to the fact they are in Arabic and so difficult for non-speakers to understand.

If you want evidence of the impact of these songs, you only have to look at the writings of jihadists, Behnam adds, before telling me about one al-Qaida member who wrote a piece for the group's in-house magazine (for want of a better term) that read almost like a music review, talking of being transfixed by one particular *nasheed* while driving across the Yemeni desert. 'I closed my eyes as the wind blew through my hair,' he wrote.

I try to get Behnam back to discussing the Islamic State's songs, but he's really more interested in the history of *nasheeds* than what they sound like today. But he has noticed one important thing about them. 'Older *nasheeds* tend to have been produced by groups that are small and clandestine and so they have a defensive message – "They can torture us, but we'll hold on to our beliefs," things like that. But the Islamic State's *nasheeds* are not defensive at all. They are about a hope to change the world for ever.'

*

'I do sometimes find myself having conversations with people about how catchy some of this music is then look back and think: What the hell was I drinking when I decided I liked this stuff?' laughs Phillip Smyth, a young researcher of Middle Eastern affairs and the person I've been reliably informed knows more about modern jihadi music than anyone else. Phillip's your typical 'beer-drinking, hot-dog-eating, politically incorrect American' (to use his description), but he's also one who happens to be obsessed with jihadi music, so much so, he regularly uses *nasheeds* for his ringtones, something that apparently 'scares the shit' out of the people he sits next to on his commute each morning.

Phillip once spent time with a former militia songwriter just so he could see how this type of musician works ('I sat in this guy's mother's basement, where he had a little keyboard and he put a whole song together in a week and a half'), and he knows these songs so well he can pick them out at any occasion. 'It's really surreal where you can find these jihadi songs being played,' he says. 'In Lebanon, you can be in these villages drinking arak, the aniseed liquor, just chilling out, dancing to some music, checking out the girls and whatnot, and then you'll suddenly hear a song from Palestinian Islamic Jihad. I don't even know how to start explaining how weird that is.'

Probably the most interesting thing about jihadi *nasheeds* today, Phillip says, is how different they sound depending on which branch of Islam the musicians belong to. Most Sunni jihadi groups, like the Islamic State, see instruments as haram (forbidden) and so take a bare-bones approach to their composition. Almost all their *nasheeds* are a cappella, the only accompaniment being the sound effects, which can range from galloping horses (symbolising the Prophet's time in the desert) to bombs going off. The only other ornamentation they have is a spoken-word intro in which someone dramatically says the Arabic word for 'Introducing . . .' like a judge on *The X Factor*.

In contrast, Shia groups like Hezbollah don't seem to have any such self-restraint. Many of their *nasheeds* are packed with drums, and sometimes feel as if they place as much importance on rhythm as rap or ragga tunes. Their singers also apparently cannot get through a verse without heavily processing their voices with Auto-Tune, while the videos for their songs are so packed with young men dancing they come across more boy band than militia. 'These groups will call their songs *nasheeds*, but sometimes they don't even fit in with their own ideologies,' Phillip says. 'If Ayatollah Khomeini was still around, he'd look at some of the techno stuff and go, "What the hell is this?" But the groups are all operating off some kind of religious guideline. They're all getting an ayatollah in who's saying, "Yes, this is halal. Go for it."'

Some might think the influx of Western fighters into the Islamic State's ranks would see the group's music move away from a cappella, but Phillip says that's never likely to happen – Western jihadi converts always wanting to appear even more fundamentalist than a group's founders (although they have released some songs in French that seem remarkably close to raps).

There are many groups producing music like the Islamic State's, but Phillip insists ISIS is operating on a level all its own. Most jihadis simply recycle old *nasheeds*, but the Islamic State has set up its own wing, the Ajnad Media Foundation, to produce new ones, and it churns them out on an almost endless array of topics. Some of these are little more than exercises in trolling – naming Iraqi politicians and saying they're coming after them, for instance – but there are others aimed at the people under the Islamic State's control, trying to convince them they've found a 'life of security and peace', or which try to encourage foreign groups to join the caliphate. There are also many that seem written simply to sate the bloodlust of the militants. 'Nasheeds have become a real comprehensive messaging strategy for ISIS. They know everyone in the Middle East's listening to them.'

No one knows who the people are actually writing the Islamic State's *nasheeds* – not their names, what they look like, or even their musical backgrounds – but Phillip says they'll be using a production line method with poets writing the words, then passing them to musicians to come up with melodies, before singers record them – a bit like a jihadi version of how Motown Records used to make its hits. Whoever is writing them, though, excelled themselves with 'My Ummah, Dawn Has Appeared', he says. 'The Islamic State isn't going to say, "This is our official song." But it's recognised by the fighters and the supporters as kind of like their anthem. It just spells out everything they stand for: the Islamic State has arisen, we've defeated so many enemies, we're going to keep on doing so. And it also sounds good. I mean, even for an infidel like me, it has a certain quality. It invigorates certain spirits.' Other *nasheeds* have risen in popularity among the groups for a few months at a time, he adds, but this is the one everyone keeps coming back to.

I ask Phillip if the Islamic State could ever officially adopt it as an anthem, in an effort to prove they are actually a state – whether in a few months they'll start sending copies to foreign embassies with official translations attached or handing over recordings to the International Olympic Committee. It's a flippant comment, I know – a bad joke, at best – but he takes it entirely seriously. 'There's always a possibility,' he says. 'Iran's technically an Islamist state – it supports the ideology of jihad – and it has an anthem. Is it possible that a Sunni state could do it too? Well, the Ottoman Empire had anthems, although I imagine the quote-unquote Islamic State would say, "That wasn't a real Islamic state, guys."'

*

It's winter 2014 and I've just written an article about 'My Ummah, Dawn Has Appeared' for the *Guardian* newspaper, and had the pleasure of reading several hundred comments people have posted about it online. Worryingly, several were from ISIS sympathisers thanking me for bringing their anthem to wider attention, but many are from people angry at me for having written the article at all. All these ask why – 'Why *in the world*', in fact – I'd give publicity to the music of murderers, several asking when I'd be booking my plane ticket to Syria to join them. That level of vitriol is a little understandable, as the article didn't actually explain why I thought the fact ISIS had an anthem was important. I didn't explain at the time, because I thought the answer was so obvious: the Islamic State's meant to be made up of the people who should most shy away from anthems – condemn them, in fact. But if it's got an anthem – if, deep down, even its leaders realise a song can help bond people together in ways few other things can – it doesn't just show the ongoing importance of anthems, it shows that ISIS is trying to create a sense of belonging among the people in its territory, rather than just frightening them into submission. It shows it's genuinely trying to create an actual state, with all the hallmarks that involves – and that's something that makes it all the more frightening. It's an uncomfortable conclusion to come to, especially as 'My Ummah, Dawn Has Appeared' is, in comparison to most anthems, a great song. And that's why every time I find myself whistling it, I have to remind myself what the words mean: '. . . victory is near. / The Islamic State has arisen. The dreaded might has begun.'

بلادى، لكى حبى وفؤادى
('My Country, You Have My Love and My Heart')

بلادى بلادى بلادى

لكى حبى وفؤادى (x2)

مصر يا أم البلاد

انتى غايتى والمراد

وعلى كل العباد

كم لنيلك من أيادى

—

My country, my country, my country,
You have my love and my heart. (x2)

Egypt! O mother of all countries!
You are my hope and my ambition,
And above all people,
Your Nile has countless graces.

9

Egypt

ANTHEMS AND FAME

To my eyes at least, Ma'adi, one of Cairo's southern suburbs, looks like paradise. Trees bend over the roads and flicker shadows across the tarmac; women, their necks heavy with jewels, sit in gardens sipping fruit juices; the usually grey Nile glistens as it flows past. Compared to the middle of the city – where there seems to be nothing but dust storms, drivers leaning on their horns and people demanding to know if I'm a spy ('Why would I be asking you about your national anthem if I was a spy?' I asked one. 'I thought you were just really bad at your job,' he replied) – it couldn't be more welcoming.

So it's rather annoying that Tarek Sharara, a composer in his mid-seventies who's giving me a tour, won't stop pointing out its faults. 'Look, there's another pothole,' he says, as we cruise down a street lined by fig trees. 'And another! And look at that one – I don't think pothole's even the right name for it; it's too large. These roads used to be pristine,' he adds, wistfully. 'They used to clean them every day with soap and water. They used to be so shiny you could see your face in them like mirrors!'

I ask when that was. 'The forties, fifties,' he says, at which point I finally realise why I was told Tarek is the best person in Cairo to speak to about Egypt's first ever anthem, a song that was thrown out after the country's 1952 revolution along with its British-supporting royal family: Tarek is nostalgic for Egypt's

past. Not for the time when it was ruled by globe-strutting presidents like Anwar Sadat, who brought peace between Egypt and
Israel, or Gamal Abdel Nasser, who led the revolution and then
tried to unify the Arab world. But further back, to the days of
that royal family. Or maybe earlier still, to the time when it was
ruled by the Khedives ('I actually know Khedive Abbas II's
grandson; a very charming man,' Tarek says at one point).

When I ask about his family, his nostalgia becomes somewhat
understandable. After the revolution, they lost everything. Land
was confiscated, money too, while his father was only allowed
to earn a set amount a year ('The money they permitted him
was what he used to spend on cigars!' Tarek exclaims).

We go for lunch in a restaurant that Tarek insists is the only
place I can still get a feel for what Ma'adi used to be like, back
in the fifties when Cairo was the Paris of the Middle East. It's
the sort of place where waiters gently slip cushions behind your
back if they think you might be uncomfortable and where food
comes out under silver cloches that are pulled away dramatically
to leave you gawping at what's below.

As we eat, I start to ask him about that first royal anthem, but
he corrects me before I can even finish the question. 'You
shouldn't say it's our first,' he says. 'It's the only anthem we've
ever had. You can't just change anthems. The sound stays in
people's hearts, in their memories, for generations. A country
should only ever have one, like it has a certain people, a certain
language. Maybe you update the words to it to keep pace with
the world; you don't want to look backward. But changing the
melody?' He shakes his head.

*

The Arab world's anthems aren't, obviously, something you can
just tick off by talking about the songs of jihadists, as I did in
the last chapter. Its anthems are just as diverse, and relate to each

other just as chaotically, as the nations themselves. Some are filled with religious devotion, of course ('Remember through my joy each martyr; / Clothe him with the shining mantles of our festival,' goes Yemen's), but there are others that spend most of their time praising sultans (Jordan's doesn't just start 'Long live the king', it also goes out of its way to flatter' him, its chorus claiming his honour is 'Talked about in the depths of books'). Others are simple calls to patriotism, such as Lebanon's 'All of Us, for Our Country, Our Flag and Glory'; then there are those that spend their short life just screaming for a fight (Palestine's 'Fida'i', especially, which goes, 'With my determination, my fire and the volcano of my vendetta, / With the longing in my blood for my land and my home,' leaving you in little doubt what it's talking about).

If you listen to all these it might seem as though they have nothing in common, but there is, in fact, a heart to the region's anthems: Egypt.

In the middle of the twentieth century, Egypt wasn't just the political centre of the Arab world, but its cultural one too: the place with the greatest musicians, the best bands and an elite happy to splurge money on their talent then take credit for anything they created. Its radio stations spread the country's music across much of the region; and its films and emigrants got wherever those couldn't. Because of all that, if you were an emerging nation at that time and you needed an anthem, there was really only one place to go: Cairo. Egyptian musicians are responsible for the anthems of everywhere from Libya to the United Arab Emirates, Algeria to Tunisia, Palestine to Saudi Arabia.

Every country seemed to knock first at the door of the composer Mohammed Abdel Wahab, a man who daringly brought Western rhythms into Arab music, but who would also happily churn out martial compositions for anyone as long as they didn't question the results (he wrote the music to Tunisia's, the United Arab Emirates' and Libya's anthems, none of which you can really tell apart). But the fact that Cairo was once the Arab world's anthem factory isn't what makes Egypt most interesting in the history of these songs; that's more the stories of its own – three songs that couldn't be more tied in with Middle Eastern politics (from Israel to the Arab Spring) and that, more uniquely, are entwined with celebrity in a way few other anthems seem to be.

*

'Of course people tell you the anthem's by Verdi,' laughs Tarek, sitting beneath a parasol in the garden of the Ma'adi restaurant, having finally stopped reminiscing and instead started talking about Egypt's first anthem, 'Alsalam Almalaky' ('Peace to the King'). He pulls out a memory stick and starts playing different versions of it on my laptop: one from a children's music box that twinkles like a fairy tale; another played on an oud that almost demands any men within earshot to link arms and dance (Tarek uses the table as a drum kit as it plays); a third, a traditional brass number, which Tarek sings over so I can hear the anthem's original, somewhat repetitive lyrics: 'For the king, hail for king. / Hail for the king, oh lion of protection . . . or something like that anyway,' he says. When he's finished I have to admit it's a fun tune, whichever way it's played – oddly like Chopin's 'Funeral march' if you put it in a major key – but at the same time it's hardly what you'd expect of a man of Giuseppe Verdi's stature. He was the man who wrote the music for *Aida* (the love story of an Egyptian military commander and an Ethiopian princess during the time of the pharaohs), for *Rigoletto*, for *La Traviata*. He'd surely have written something better than this if it were his anthem, as every Egyptian insists it is. Unfortunately for every Egyptian, every Verdi scholar insists it isn't.

Tarek tries to explain how the mix-up happened. In the late

1860s, Khedive Isma'il Pasha, Egypt's then ruler, commissioned Verdi to write *Aida* for the opening of his opera house – the first in Africa – lavishing him with 150,000 francs to do so (one of the highest fees any musician's ever received). The Khedive was so committed to getting Verdi's name associated with his opera house, he even tried to get him to conduct the opening performance, despite knowing full well that Verdi feared the seas. 'Is it possible to build a bridge to Italy?' the Khedive is meant to have said.

The production ended up opening two years late because a war meant the costumes got stuck in Paris, but the Khedive still loved the end result, and the attention it brought both him and Egypt – so much so, in fact, he then tried to commission Verdi to write an anthem, suggesting he could perhaps take one of *Aida*'s tunes and tweak it a little. But, Tarek says, by then Verdi was long fed up of working for the demanding, if well-paying, Egyptians and so politely declined. Some say another Giuseppe – Pugioli, an unknown composer then working for the Egyptian army – ended up writing the anthem instead and that's where the mix-up was made. 'But even that's not right,' Tarek says. 'So who was behind the anthem?' He gives himself a drum roll and mimes a trumpet salute before unveiling the answer that took him months of research to find out. It was an Egyptian, Mohammed Bayoumi Effendi, he says, a man who was in charge of the band on the Khedive's yacht.

'If it's so clear this Bayoumi's the composer, why does everyone here still think it's Verdi?' I ask. Over the past couple of days several people in Cairo insisted to me it was him, I add, and I'm pretty sure they didn't think I was a British spy they needed to give false information to. 'The famous Verdi wrote our anthem and no one else's!' Tarek laughs. 'That's how great Egypt once was – the mother of the world! We could have the greatest composer alive write to our whims. I'd want to believe it too.'

*

'I wish it was still the anthem now,' sighs Bahaa Jahin, sitting in the offices of the newspaper where he works, his hands resting gently on his bulging stomach. 'It was born with me – both of us came into the world in 1956 – so I grew up with it, and of course I'm biased towards my father's things, but I honestly think the words to it are far more poetic than any other anthem we've had. They're quite violent, yes,' he laughs, 'but so are many songs from that time.'

It's a few hours after meeting Tarek, and I'm starting to think that every person I'm going to meet in this country will be afflicted by nostalgia for a past time and a past anthem. Perhaps it's because Egypt's recent torment – revolutions, military coups and Muslim Brotherhoods – means people find it's easier not to dwell on today. The reason I've come to Bahaa is to learn about his father, Salah Jahin, and about one of his most popular songs, the brilliantly named 'Walla Zaman Ya Selahy' – 'Oh, My Weapon, It Has Been a Long Time'. That song replaced 'Alsalam Almalaky' as Egypt's anthem in 1960 (the tune of 'Alsalam' somehow limped on for eight years after the fall of the monarchy). And for the next two decades, it seemed to set the tone for the Egyptians as a people fighting for the whole of the Arab world.

Salah wrote it at a time when Egypt was being turned upside down. In 1952, when he was just twenty-two, a group of army officers ousted the British puppet king, Farouk, and shortly afterwards Gamal Abdel Nasser, a handsome postal worker's son, took charge. He soon started trying to build a socialist utopia while also cracking down on anyone he saw as opponents, notably the Muslim Brotherhood. 'My father hated Nasser at first,' Bahaa says. 'When the coup happened, he was of course happy – Egypt had won its independence after three thousand years of foreign invasion – but he saw him as one of those fascists. It was only when Nasser nationalised the Suez Canal that he saw the better side of him: the man who was ambitious for the country, who wanted to make Egypt better. It was then he started to love him and wanting to join his project.'

Nasser's nationalisation of the canal was one of the political masterstrokes of Middle Eastern history. On 26 July 1956, he stood in a square in Alexandria and announced that he was ending British and French ownership of this key trading route from Europe to Asia. 'The Suez Canal was dug by the sons of Egypt,' he said, going on to claim that 120,000 Egyptians had died in the process. 'Today we declare that property has been returned to us. It will be run by Egyptians,' he announced, shouting 'Egyptians' again and again to bring home the weight of what he was doing.

That one speech, replayed on news bulletins worldwide, transformed Nasser overnight: he went from being just another coup leader to the man who could stand up to the old imperial powers and win, an icon not just for Egypt, or the Middle East, but for the whole developing world. Britain and France weren't too pleased about the move, though, to put it mildly, and so conspired with Israel to retake control. Just a few months later, Israel invaded the Sinai peninsula – where Moses is meant to have received the Ten Commandments – and as soon as they did, Britain and France sent several hundred warships to guarantee the canal's safety. Egypt quickly agreed to an American-backed ceasefire, but Britain and France eventually bombarded Port Said, which sits at the northern end of the canal, and sent paratroopers in to capture it. They expected the city to rise up against Nasser, but instead found themselves fighting practically every one of its residents. They only withdrew after America basically ordered them to do so.

It was in the middle of this crisis that Salah Jahin came into his own. 'He was a young man at that time, twenty-five maybe, and like everyone he'd become very patriotic and enthusiastic about everything that was happening,' Bahaa says. 'So when the invasion started he wanted to go and fight. But he looked like me' – Bahaa points at his stomach – 'and they told him, "You're fat. You don't have the physical fitness. You can't fight." And he got very angry and said, "Okay, I'll fight with my words instead," and so, among lots of other things, he wrote this song.'

The words Salah wrote couldn't have been more appropriate for a country that had just been invaded. 'Oh, my weapon, it has been a long time,' it starts. 'I long for you in the struggle.' The verses then hammer that message home in every possible way. 'Who shall protect free Egypt?' asks one, almost guilt-tripping the listener into joining the army. 'Land of the revolution, who will sacrifice for her sake?' In case that approach hasn't worked, the final verse tries flattery: 'The people are mountains, seas, / A volcano of anger ready to erupt,' it goes, 'An earthquake that will dig the enemies into their graves.' Salah's songwriting partner, Kamal al-Tawil, put those words to music that couldn't have been more fitting, its chorus the sort of stirring march you'd expect, but the verses filled with rapid horn stabs, making it feel almost more like a rumba than a patriotic cry. During the war, it (and a couple of other songs about the war) was played on the radio like no other music mattered, sometimes repeated every ten minutes. Four years later, it was still well liked enough – reminiscent of Egypt's defiance and success – that Nasser made it his anthem. (Egypt was actually part of the United Arab Republic at the time, an alliance with Syria. The anthem was usually played with Syria's far less rousing anthem, 'Guardians of the Homeland', following it straight afterwards.) Its reach even extended outside the country – Iraq, encouraged by Nasser's pan-Arabic message, adopted the music as its (wordless) anthem in 1964.

I ask Bahaa why 'Oh, My Weapon' was such a success, cherished above all the other songs his father wrote. He initially talks about the words, the passion in them, their drama and patriotism, but then, off-hand, he mentions what I believe is the actual reason. 'Of course, it was also sung by the greatest female singer in the country,' he says. 'That helped.' He doesn't add her name, because he knows he doesn't need to. There is only one person it could be. She's 'the voice of Egypt', 'the Star of the East', 'the diva of Arabic music'. Her name's Umm Kulthūm.

*

You can count the number of famous musicians who have written anthems on one hand – unsurprisingly, really, given that most musicians are either anti-establishment and so might see anthems as an embarrassment to their art form, or they're sensible enough to realise that writing an anthem could easily backfire (imagine writing a song about your country's landscape one minute; the next seeing hooligans shouting it on the news). Haydn is the one name that immediately springs to mind with his melody for Austria's emperor that eventually became Germany's 'Deutschlandlied' (the fact many people regard it as the world's greatest anthem has, I'm sure, more to do with his authorship than the tune itself). The other name that always seems to grab attention is Rabindranath Tagore, India's great poet and the first non-European to win the Nobel Prize in Literature. He wrote the words for both India's 'Jana Gana Mana' and Bangladesh's 'My Golden Bengal' (a great tune that strangely sounds like a soundtrack for people promenading along French riverbanks and contains such wonderful, innocent lines as, 'The fragrance from your mangrove fields / Makes me wild with joy – / Oh, what a thrill!'). But both of those were adopted after his death so it isn't as if he wrote the poems specifically to be anthems. The only other 'name composers' to come close to writing an anthem are Dmitri Shostakovich and Sergei Prokofiev – ordered by Stalin to try writing the USSR's (they failed) – and Benjamin Britten, who in 1957 was asked to write one for newly independent Malaysia. However, his effort – each chord drenched in Britishness – was swiftly rejected in favour of the melody from a cabaret tune.

Leaving aside classical musicians, you could perhaps make a

case for the man who wrote Barbados's anthem. His name is Irving Burgie, and he has sold over 100 million records. But he wasn't a performer; he was a songwriter, responsible for most of Harry Belafonte's hits in the 1950s, songs like 'Day O' and 'Jamaica Farewell', and his name has never been written in lights like an actual singer. I visited him in New York once and he was quite happy to admit that even the children who play outside his apartment wouldn't know who he was.

But Umm Kulthūm, the woman who sang 'Oh, My Weapon', was an actual superstar. When she walked out of her house, she was mobbed. When she wore a new dress, people copied it. And when she sang, people listened and they cheered and they wept.

Umm Kulthūm (her name can't be shortened; Egyptians call her the Lady if they want something snappier) was born perhaps in 1898 or perhaps in 1904 – they didn't keep records back then – and grew up in a mud-brick house in a small village in the Nile Delta. She was the daughter of the local imam, who boosted his meagre income by singing religious songs at weddings with Umm Kulthūm's brother and a nephew. He used to teach the boys in his spare time and Umm Kulthūm secretly listened in, then copied them 'like a parrot'. When her father finally heard her sing, he was so shocked by the strength of her voice – she was a girl of about five – that he decided to teach her too and eventually began to take her along with him to weddings, where she initially sang disguised as a boy.

The novelty of this small girl who could sing better than a man (the disguise wasn't a very good one), and who could recite the Qur'an better than her father, ensured she was soon not just doing weddings, but private concerts for Egypt's richest families. Her father was gradually able to make ever-greater contractual demands – for transport, for refreshments, for money. He started managing her almost like a pop star and she soon moved into Cairo's theatres, into recording studios and into films, until, by the 1940s, she had sung herself into becoming the most famous person in Egypt, someone the public treasured more than any politician including, later, their president, Nasser. Her incredible – and incredibly long – songs of love and longing were inescapable, as was her face, every newspaper seemingly filled with photos of her in her trademark shades (she was sensitive to light). She was so popular that in 1946 one of the king's uncles even proposed to her, thinking that the rest of the royal family would surely see her as a suitable bride. They didn't. To them, she was still a common singer, one from the Delta at that, and the proposal was rescinded. Umm Kulthūm was left distraught.

It's almost impossible to understate just how big a name Umm Kulthūm was by 1960 when Nasser realised he was in need of a new anthem (he had until then been playing the old royal one under a new name). On the first Thursday of every month, she used to perform a concert, three or four hours long, that would be broadcast live across Egypt and many of its neighbours. Millions tuned in and there are tales of generals cancelling military manoeuvres just so they could listen, and of politicians giving speeches in the middle of them only to find out they got so little attention they had to pretend they had never happened and repeat them the next day. She was the sort of singer whom people loved to gossip about, and other musicians loved to complain about (she was once blamed for the death of a rival in a car accident).

You could say, then, that Nasser choosing one of her songs to be his anthem – and Umm Kulthūm accepting – is surprising; rather as if in 1958 President Eisenhower hadn't just drafted Elvis into the US military but asked him to record a new version of 'The Star-Spangled Banner' while he was there. But there's a crucial difference. Egypt's music scene at that time was unlike anywhere else – a place where musicians really wanted to write patriotic songs (which they called anthems), swept up in the fervour of the time just like everyone else. They were also used to their songs being used for political purposes. During the Second

World War, for instance, Germany, Britain and Italy all tried to commission Egyptian musicians to record songs that backed their cause. And after the 1952 revolution, most musicians raced to write songs backing it (Umm Kulthūm literally so, rushing from her summer house back to Cairo and recording a song called 'Egypt, Which Is In My Mind and In My Blood').

Patriotic songs went on to be written about practically all of Nasser's policies. There were ones celebrating his nationalisation of the Suez Canal and songs celebrating his plan to build the Aswan Dam every bit as patriotic as 'Oh, My Weapon'. Egypt became a country where musicians were actually expected to produce these songs. From 1960 onwards, for instance, Salah Jahin and Kamal al-Tawil wrote a song every year for the singer Abdel Halim Hafez to perform on Revolution Day. One year they decided they didn't want to do it, and were told they'd have their passports confiscated if they didn't change their minds. By then, Nasser had realised music could be a weapon for him – to help increase his popularity and that of his policies – and he made sure all such national songs were promoted, and also that he was photographed with stars at every possible opportunity, the stars more than happy to benefit in return. Given such propagandist motivations, maybe it's not such a surprise that Nasser chose one of Umm Kulthūm's songs to be Egypt's anthem rather than choosing some 200-year-old poem, or announcing a nationwide competition to find something suitable. Maybe the real surprise is that no other leader has done the same.

*

In the middle of his newspaper office, Bahaa lets out a big belly laugh. 'He did at least become a better father after that,' he says of his father Salah. 'I never saw him before then.' We're talking about the Six Day War of 1967, an event you wouldn't think would generate any kind of positive response in Egypt. That year, Nasser got reports that Israel was deploying troops on the Syrian border (it wasn't) and started to make increasingly aggressive statements pledging to 'exterminate [Israel] for all time'. He was probably just playing to the gallery, but Israel couldn't be sure that he wasn't being serious, and decided to strike first. On 5 June, at 7 a.m., its entire air force took off; half an hour later, Egypt's didn't exist. Within, yes, six days, Israel had taken the West Bank, Gaza, the Golan Heights, Jerusalem and the whole of Sinai. Nasser was never the same again – he died of a heart attack three years later – and nor was Bahaa's father. 'I didn't know him very well as a young man,' Bahaa says. 'He lived in the night with his friends. He was never home, always out smoking and drinking and writing. But 1967 hit him in the heart. He was not the same man who loved life and loved being with people afterwards. That was finished. He became a man who stayed at home and never left his study unless he had to. That's the Salah Jahin I know intimately.'

Salah carried on writing great patriotic songs and poems ('I love her when she owns the earth, east and west, / And I love her when she's down, wounded in battle,' one goes), but much of his work became infused with sadness and nostalgia ('Let the projectionist rewind the scene. / I want to see myself in the old days, young / among the ranks of the revolution'). He died in 1986, aged just fifty-five, from an overdose of painkillers (Bahaa says it was accidental).

Out of everyone involved in the anthem, the only person who really came out of 1967 better than before was Umm Kulthūm. She performed in Paris that year and donated all proceeds to the national treasury, as if she was going to single-handedly save the country. Soon she was doing similar concerts in Tunisia, Libya, Morocco, Kuwait and elsewhere. She was given a diplomatic passport (you can see it at a museum dedicated to her life in Cairo; its photo features her in jewelled shades). Most people saw her music as old-fashioned by then and preferred listening to pop, but despite that she stopped being simply the voice of Egypt, and became its face as well. When she died in 1975, some 4 million people filled Cairo's streets, the overpasses so crowded with those wanting to see her that it was feared they might collapse. At one point, the crowds took her casket from the pall-bearers then passed it around the city for three hours, as if everyone had to be given a chance to pay tribute. A band marched in front. It played 'Oh, My Weapon'.

*

Immediately after 1967, most Egyptians must have found singing 'Oh, My Weapon, It Has Been a Long Time' absurd, knowing full well that it hadn't been a long time and that Egypt's weapons had just proven wholly inadequate in its defence. But the song's power did creep back, especially under Egypt's new president, the fashionable, slim and moustached Anwar Sadat, who took office immediately after Nasser's death. Sadat is a man whose character is almost impossible to decipher. He was capable of bold, some would say irresponsible, actions – in his twenties and just a captain in the army, he tried to forge an alliance with the Nazis to throw Britain out of Egypt – but then he also had a habit of writing himself little self-help notes as if he lacked all self-confidence ('Be yourself, hopefully and happily' and 'Keep yourself healthy and young' are two I saw at his museum in Alexandria).

In 1973, Sadat restored much of Egypt's pride when he decided to send the Egyptian army back across the Suez Canal to reclaim Sinai. It should have been a suicide mission, especially as Sadat made no effort to hide from Israel what he was about to do, even telling journalists that 'everything in this country is being mobilised for the resumption of battle', but somehow the army got over the canal and then managed to survive long enough for a ceasefire to be negotiated (Israel did actually launch a counter-attack and go even deeper into Egypt than it had before, but the political victory was Sadat's).

During the next few years, however, Sadat became increasingly fed up with the state of the region – its aggression, its uncertainty – and so in November 1977 he suddenly announced that he'd be happy to go to Israel's parliament to debate with them about both Sinai and Palestine. He scheduled a visit for ten days later. As the day of his arrival approached, the shocked Israelis realised they didn't have any Egyptian flags to welcome him with; neither did their military orchestra have the faintest idea how to play Egypt's anthem. Its foreign office sent an urgent telegram to Chaim Herzog, Israel's delegate at the United Nations in New York. 'Send Egyptian flags, all sizes,' it read. 'Also Egyptian national anthem, scored for military band.' Herzog found the anthem in the UN library, bought a dozen miniature flags from its gift shop, then put them all on a plane. He later told journalists it was 'among the most pleasant' orders he'd ever received. 'I'd like to hope the music generates the tune and harmony for future relations,' he added, which certainly suggests he hadn't had the lyrics translated. In the end, it turned out he needn't have bothered sending the sheet music; the leader of Israel's military orchestra had taught himself the anthem by going out to the desert and listening to Egyptian radio, pen in hand.

On 19 November, Sadat touched down in Tel Aviv. Moments later, 'Oh, My Weapon, It Has Been a Long Time', a song written to encourage Egypt to repel an Israeli invasion, and sung for years by people baying for the country's blood, was played to welcome him.

Less than a year and a half later, Sadat landed at Cairo airport and waved his walking stick in the air triumphantly. He'd just been to Washington DC and signed a peace deal with the Israelis, guaranteeing the return of Sinai. That deal had angered most of the Middle East because it had done nothing for Palestine; it had angered many Egyptians too for the same reason, a lot of whom already disliked Sadat for pandering to America and dumping Nasser's socialism. Sadat didn't care, according to reports from the time. Anyone who complained was a fool who didn't understand the magnitude of what he'd achieved. He walked down the steps of the plane and was met by the sight of a military band fronted by Mohammed Abdel Wahab, the most famous composer of his age, the man who'd written the anthems of Libya, Tunisia and the UAE.

Sadat knew what was coming as Abdel Wahab raised his baton: a new national anthem was about to be played. Out with the violence of 'Oh, My Weapon, It Has Been a Long Time'. That wasn't appropriate for an era of peace, Sadat had decided. From now on, the anthem would be 'Bilady, Laki Hubbi Wa Fu'adi' – 'My Country, You Have My Love and My Heart' – more commonly known as 'Bilady, Bilady'. It was a song everyone in Egypt already knew and loved. It was by an old composer, Sayed Darwish, 'the father of Egyptian music' as everyone called him, but Sadat had thought it best to get Abdel Wahab involved, to modernise the song and give it some stardust. He'd even made him a general especially for this occasion. Abdel Wahab's baton came down and President Sadat straightened up to observe this new anthem of apparent peace.

The next morning anybody who picked up a copy of *Al-Ahram*, Egypt's biggest newspaper, found themselves greeted by a picture of Sadat with news that peace had arrived. On the same page there was an advert for toilets, which some of those who didn't view the announcement favourably may have felt was an appropriate juxtaposition. Over to the right, there was another story. 'Starting today,' it casually read, 'there is a new national anthem.' Some people would have got to the end of that article, put down the newspaper and thought, At least there's one thing he's done right. Everyone liked 'Bilady, Bilady' after all – its melody and words are simple enough for a child to learn. Others, though, would have felt cheated, as if the only reason Sadat changed the anthem was to sugar the pill that Egypt was no longer the Middle East's greatest country; that they'd traded Palestine's future for their own. Some of them might have even felt as if he was going against the whole meaning of that song.

★

When you talk to Egyptians about 'Bilady, Bilady', they always say you need to know about the time it was written and you need to know about its author. When people say that about a song, it's normally an indication it's not very good, but in the case of 'Bilady, Bilady' there is some truth to it. Sayed Darwish, the man behind it, was a revolutionary who probably wouldn't have liked his music being used by the establishment. He was born in 1892 in Kom el-Dikka, a slum right in the heart of Alexandria, the great city on Egypt's Mediterranean coast. His family, poor carpenters with no money to pay for his education, sent him to religious school to train as an imam, since it guaranteed he'd be fed, clothed and given a job. There he showed a remarkable – raw – talent for reciting the Qur'an, so much so that he was made a muezzin, a caller to prayer, at a local mosque.

His love for music was so strong that at the same time he also started singing in Alexandria's cafes, surrounded by men smoking *shishas* with probably one or two prostitutes present in dark corners. Unfortunately for him, one of his teachers walked past one of these cafes one night and saw him through the glass mid-performance – a muezzin in a place of ill repute – and promptly kicked him out of school (Sayed seemed to take that rejection rather personally, later writing a song called 'The Preacher's Anthem', which features some mullahs saying they are off to France to 'eye up white women whose flesh is like rice pudding').

Sayed had no choice after that but to pursue a career in music. He certainly had the looks to be successful, with hair that curled up wildly, almost like a quiff, and a fat, disjointed nose that made him unmistakable. But things didn't go well. His voice was quickly ruined by his love of drink and drugs and he also had a tendency to get distracted by belly dancers. But once he moved to Cairo in 1918, and started writing songs and plays for the theatre, something changed. He still drank and snorted and became infatuated with women, but in five short years, with the help of a librettist, Badi' Khayri, he turned Egyptian music upside down. He wrote songs about working-class Egyptians like porters, doormen and fruit sellers – something that had never been done before. He wrote songs that were short and catchy – something that had never been done before. And he wrote songs that were nationalist and political – something that definitely hadn't been done before. He was, in a way, lucky to come of age at the same time as Egyptian nationalism – in 1919 much of the country was in revolt in the hope of ending the British protectorate that ruled. Sayed wrote 'Bilady, Bilady' with the pure hope that it could boost the uprising – a motivation that's a far cry from the peaceful image Sadat later imposed on the song. He's meant to have based the words on a speech by Mustafa Kamil, Egypt's original nationalist ('If I had not been born an Egyptian, I would have wished to be one,' Kamil once said), which Sayed claimed to have witnessed as a child, its words somehow never leaving him in the years afterwards.

Sayed wrote other, more direct songs for the revolt too, of course, one called 'I'm an Egyptian', another named 'Rise Up, Egyptian' (just affirming someone's Egyptianness having significance back then). One of his plays even featured a song with the line 'Our army is coming with victory', which, given that his audience normally included a British officer or two, wasn't very wise. But Sayed was never one to care. If the British closed down the theatre where he was working, he'd just start again elsewhere. Sayed's rebelliousness and salaciousness probably annoyed as many Egyptians as it did British at the time, but no one could argue with his creativity. At one point, he even wrote the drum rhythm that's still used to mark the end of every wedding in Egypt. His musical future seemed assured; he had plans to head to Europe to study, then overturn that continent's music too.

But then in 1923, aged just thirty-one, he was dead.

In Cairo, I talked to several people about Sayed Darwish and all were obsessed with the circumstances of his death. 'He was killed by the king,' said Fathi al-Khamissi, a musician and scholar of Darwish's life, 'because he was a danger man, not just a musician. The king poisoned him with massage oils. I'm sure of it! Before then, Sayed Darwish had never expressed pain once in his life. Nobody had heard of him ever getting a headache; not even a cold. Then suddenly he's dead? Impossible!' Iman el-Bahr Darwish, one of Sayed's grandsons, a singer himself, insisted it wasn't the king who'd killed him, but the British. They had refused to let an autopsy take place afterwards, he said. He then asked me if I could go through the British government's records to see if they had any documents proving the murder. 'Please do,' he said. 'If it's true they killed him, it would be a great honour. It shows how important he was. It shows he was a hero, not just a musician.'

Unfortunately, neither story is likely to be true. Shortly before going to Egypt, I met a woman called Reem Kelani in London. A flamboyant British-Palestinian singer, Reem's devoted several years to recording Sayed's songs and researching his life (she gave me most of the information about him here). 'So the idea's either the British killed him or the king killed him,' she said. 'Then other people say it was his muse who did it – the queen of the belly dancers – but it was really a cocaine overdose. I'm sure of it. His family try to say he didn't even take drugs, but he even wrote a song for cocaine addicts saying, "I've ruined my lungs, I've ruined my life but still, if I have to [use more] I'll take the local stuff."'

The only other part of Sayed Darwish's life that caused this much division was 'Bilady, Bilady', especially how he would have felt about it being the anthem. Iman said he was sure Sayed would have been prouder than anyone could fathom – 'His patriotism was so big.' But then another of his descendants, who didn't want to be named, insisted he'd have been appalled especially at it being the anthem today. 'I think he'd be composing again for another revolution,' they said proudly. But it was Reem who was most verbose. Sadat 'hijacked' the song when he made it the anthem, she insisted. He knew all the associations both it, and Sayed Darwish, had with Egypt's fight against the British and he thought that by making it the anthem he could tap into those memories, and make Egyptians believe that peace with Israel was a kind of revolution too. 'Why didn't he just write a new song? "We Love Israel",' she said, only half joking. Sayed would have been more than appalled, she was sure.

I asked her if people had bought Sadat's revision of the song, and she pointed out that he'd been assassinated in 1981, just two years after making peace (he was shot by Islamist army officers during a military parade); the inference being the song clearly didn't convince many people that peace had been a good idea. 'Bilady, Bilady' didn't recover its true meaning, she added, until some thirty years after Sadat made it the anthem, when the Arab Spring occurred and it was sung at the protests in Tahrir Square.

*

Samia Jahin, bulgingly pregnant, is propped up on a sofa in her Cairo flat. She's Salah Jahin's daughter (and Bahaa's sister), and she's been chatting animatedly for the past half-hour about Egypt's anthems past and present. But for the last few moments she's drifted into melancholy, staring into the middle distance like I'm no longer there, as if she's picturing somewhere else entirely. 'Sorry,' she says, 'I can get lost thinking about it – remembering that there was a moment when we were just sitting in

Tahrir, not afraid of what would happen, just singing, chanting. How happy everyone was. It feels like it was another lifetime.'

It's 28 February 2015, the fourth anniversary of Egypt's most recent revolution – the day the Arab Spring succeeded here, when protestors in Tahrir Square brought down Hosni Mubarak, the general who'd ruled the country since Sadat's death in 1981. It was on that day that 'Bilady, Bilady' was sung in celebration louder than ever before, including by Samia who was one of the most vocal figures there (there were dozens of 'songs of the revolution', but everyone agrees the anthem was in the top handful). But, as Samia says, that day now seems like very long ago. During the last four years, Egypt has experienced government under the Muslim Brotherhood, a military coup, the election of the man who ran that coup (Abdel Fattah al-Sisi), and then a severe crackdown on all opposition, including multiple death sentences (Samia, who now works as a human rights activist, says she's been threatened with prison many times, her father's name the only reason she hasn't been locked up).

Cairo today doesn't exactly feel like a place of celebration as it was back then. The huge teardrop-shaped Tahrir Square is now surrounded by coils of barbed wire, ready to be pulled across the roads if needed; tanks sit menacingly outside the Egyptian Museum on its northern side, ready to roll into action, almost daring tourists to try to take a photo of them; while newspapers are filled with warnings about extremists and the 'foreign forces' behind them (that explains why people think I'm a spy). You only have to be in this city for a few moments to realise everything the Arab Spring hoped to achieve has failed.

It's because of that fact that Samia drops into a reverie whenever I ask her about Tahrir – even when I just ask if she sang 'Bilady, Bilady' while protesting there. 'Of course we sang it then. Every day. Many times,' she says. 'And when we sang it, it actually meant something, for the first time I think. I used to sing it all the time in school and it never meant anything, but singing it then when people were sacrificing their lives for the country – getting killed by the police – it felt different.'

'Didn't you feel like you were singing the anthem of the very government you were protesting against?' I ask.

'Yes, of course,' she says. 'But we were singing it to re-own it – to say "This is our country; not yours." We didn't sing it the gentle way they sing it. We sang it like "BILADY, BILADY, BILADY".' She shouts every word at me. 'We were taking it to a different place. Sometimes it felt like my heart was going to pop out of my chest when I heard everyone sing it, or my father's songs. But that's all another time now; that's the sad part.'

I ask how she feels about the anthem today. 'When it comes on the radio, we turn it off. Not just the anthem; all the songs we sang at Tahrir. We don't want to listen to them. That's how bad things have got.' She takes a deep breath as if to steady herself. 'This is not my country any more and this is not my anthem. Maybe you've caught me on a bad day, but I don't feel romantic about it now. I'm too hurt to feel that way.'

Samia knows that the majority of people don't feel as she does – about the country, or the anthem – even those who have every right to share her views. Earlier this morning, I'd got talking with the young owner of a washing machine shop, his gigantic beard and the deep prayer bruise on his forehead indicating he was a devout Muslim. He would have once been the now-banned Muslim Brotherhood's target audience. 'Things have changed since 2011,' he said. 'We' – he pointed at his beard – 'are looked on differently now. We're not to be trusted. But whatever happens, I'll love my country. I can't stop doing so. You want me to give you reasons, like one, two, three, four, five? I can't explain it like that. I'll always love Sayed Darwish's songs too,' he added. 'His music was about the normal people like me.'

I tell Samia about this man, but she just says that for her things have become 'too personal' to think like him. I ask how many of her friends were killed during the revolution. She stares off into the middle distance again. 'These weren't close friends,' she says, 'just people I got to know, that I respected.' She takes another deep breath. 'There's Mena, Ahmed . . .' a slight smile comes across her face as if she's just recalled something funny one of them did, '. . . Karika, Ali . . .' I look down and suddenly realise she's counting each person off on her fingers. '. . . Sheik Emad – that's his picture over there, they graffitied him on to one of the walls around the Square . . .' I can't look away from her hands. '. . . Mohammed, the son of a friend of mine . . .'

The list goes on.

*

It's a few days after meeting Samia, and I'm standing outside what I think is Sayed Darwish's house in Kom el-Dikka, the slum in Alexandria where he was born. I've come to see how the city remembers its most important son, the composer of its anthem. Unfortunately, the man at the doorway – silver-haired and stooped, smiling but sceptical – doesn't seem to want to let me in. He and my translator are deep in conversation. 'Does he think I'm a spy?' I'm about to ask wearily. Over the last few days, I'd been ordered out of a tube station while tying my shoelaces, had my bag searched while on a tram and even been asked to sing 'Bilady, Bilady' to prove I wasn't on the payroll of MI6, so I could quite believe this man assumed I was up to no good too.

Fortunately, my interpreter saves me from looking paranoid. 'It's his wife. She's inside and, y'know . . .' He mimes 'uncovered'. After a few minutes, we are let in and the man leads me up a rotten ladder to the roof, then points down at the building next door. 'Sayed Darwish,' he says, smiling. The tiny, square building where Sayed was born has no roof itself – it barely has what you'd call walls – and it's being used as a rubbish tip. It's actually quite colourful, filled with bright blue and green plastic bags, and with an old sofa collapsed in a corner like a drunk who can't get up.

It's a scene that should probably cause me to make a pithy comment, to say it shows that all anthem composers – even one as renowned as Sayed Darwish – are largely forgotten compared to their songs. But it wouldn't actually be true in his case. On my way to this flat, I saw graffiti of him near a football stadium, his lyrics sprawling out along the length of the walls. I also saw cafes named after him, while the city's opera house carries his name too, as does a nearby school, his unmistakable face – quiffed hair and disjointed nose – pictured on, or inside, them all. The reason his birthplace is so derelict has more to do with politics, as has seemingly everything else concerning Egypt and its anthems (most of the world's anthems too, really). Sayed's grandson, Iman, told me earlier he'd offered to turn one of Sayed's former homes into a museum, only to be rebuffed by the authorities, who preferred to demolish them all for new flats, almost as if his song's status was memorial enough, or perhaps as a subtle reminder that they could use his image and his song whenever they needed to, and that they could just as easily discard them.

I clamber back down the ladder and the man insists that my translator and I stay for tea. His wife, now covered, brings out some jam biscuits she's made. He takes us into their living room-cum-bedroom, which has water dripping down the walls, and proudly turns on his small black-and-white TV. The news is on. It's about President Putin's state visit to Cairo. There's a shot of Putin and al-Sisi, the Egyptian president, strolling along what I can only assume is a red carpet; then there's another of them standing before a military band. Then the Russian anthem starts up and I immediately start laughing. It's one of the worst renditions of an anthem I've ever heard. If this wasn't a Muslim country, I'd be sure the band had tried the orchestral equivalent of method acting beforehand and had a few vodkas each. Actually, scrap that: they sound as though they've definitely all had at least half a bottle. They wheeze in and out of tune, some going up in pitch while others go down, the melody falling apart more and more with each note. The screen cuts to Putin's face. He doesn't look happy. It's a national embarrassment. An inquiry has been set up to look into what on earth went wrong, the newsreader says. The band's rendition of 'Bilady, Bilady' was even worse apparently, and it doesn't look as if the channel can bring themselves to show it. I want to laugh some more, but everyone else in the room looks so stern, I have to just sit there with my jam biscuit, trying to imagine what Sayed Darwish would have made of it all. I think, to be honest, he'd be as amused as I am.

National Anthem of South Africa

Nkosi sikelel' iAfrika,
Maluphakanyisw' uphondo lwayo,
Yizwa imithandazo yethu,
Nkosi sikelela, thina lusapho lwayo.

Morena boloka setjhaba sa heso,
O fedise dintwa le matshwenyeho,
O se boloke, O se boloke setjhaba sa heso,
Setjhaba sa South Afrika – South Afrika.

Uit die blou van onse hemel,
Uit die diepte van ons see,
Oor ons ewige gebergtes,
Waar die kranse antwoord gee,

Sounds the call to come together,
And united we shall stand,
Let us live and strive for freedom,
In South Africa our land.

—

God bless Africa,
May her glory be lifted high,
Hear our prayers,
Lord bless us, the family of Africa.

God protect our nation,
End all wars and tribulations,
Protect us, protect our nation,
Our nation, South Africa – South Africa.

From the blues of our heavens,
From the depths of our seas,
Over our everlasting mountains,
Where the cliffs answer our calls,

Sounds the call to come together,
And united we shall stand,
Let us live and strive for freedom,
In South Africa our land.

10

South Africa

TRYING TO SING THE RAINBOW:
ONE ANTHEM, FIVE LANGUAGES

Nana Zajiji, large-eyed and crop-haired, has to be the most patient language teacher in Johannesburg. For the past ten minutes, she's been trying to teach me just one word: 'Xhosa' – the name of the language I've come for a lesson in – and she's somehow yet to swear or throw her arms up in defeat. 'Almost!' she shouts encouragingly, quickly following it with a 'Nearly' and a 'Keep trying', before going back to the start as if on a loop.

Anyone overhearing us would think I'm the most inept student imaginable, but in my defence the thing that's causing me so many problems is that 'Xhosa' starts with a 'click', one of those unfathomable sounds that make some African languages so beautiful. The Xhosa language features three of them: one you make against the top of your mouth; another against your front teeth; a third against your cheek. It's that last one I just can't get right. In theory it should be easy – 'It's just like saying giddy-up to a horse,' Nana says – but actually doing it is something else. 'Put your tongue to the side of your mouth,' she says at one point. 'Is it behind your teeth? Great, now . . . click.' I do as I'm told. 'What?' she cries. 'That was the top of your mouth! How did you manage that? It's like you've never used your tongue in your life.'

'Do I actually need to know how to click to sing the anthem?' I ask.

'Of course not,' she says, 'no white person would be able to sing it if it had clicks in,' and then, unprompted, she starts singing South Africa's anthem for me, the world's only one to feature five languages – that uniqueness the reason I've come here. *'Nkosi sikelel' iAfrika,'* Nana begins in Xhosa, *'Maluphakanyisw' uphondo lwayo'* ('God bless Africa, / May her glory be lifted high'). *'Yizwa imithandazo yethu, / Nkosi sikelela, thina lusapho lwayo,'* she adds in Xhosa's close relative, Zulu ('Hear our prayers, / Lord bless us, the family of Africa'). *'Morena boloka setjhaba sa heso,'* she goes on, speeding up as she jumps into Sesotho, another language entirely. She races through three more lines of that, but then suddenly grinds to a halt, only halfway through the song. There are still verses in Afrikaans and English to come. 'I'd prefer it if those verses weren't included, to be honest,' she says, embarrassed. 'I feel like . . . Well, the majority of people in South Africa are black, obviously. And also there's this terrible history here – of apartheid – and the lines in Afrikaans are from the old apartheid hymn. It just doesn't feel great, sorry.'

It would be easy for everyone to just learn the Xhosa, Zulu and Sesotho and leave it at that, Nana adds. 'I mean, it's not like they're hard to sing.' She asks me to parrot back the first line. *'Nkosi sikelel' iAfrika,'* she sings.

'Unkosea sickeleila eeeAfrica,' I reply.

'Er, yes. Let's not worry so much about your pronunciation for now,' she says. 'Let's just try to get all the way through.'

*

South Africa's anthem is one of the world's most important songs, let alone anthems – perhaps the only piece of music that has helped reconcile a country with its past, and bring it peace. It's actually a combination of two anthems: 'Die Stem van Suid-Afrika', the hymn that was South Africa's anthem during apartheid (a song detested by any black, coloured or Indian person who heard it – the three groups non-whites were split into) and 'Nkosi Sikelel' iAfrika', the African National Congress's anthem during those same years (a song some whites thought was a war cry against them). But it's not just the melding of those melodies that makes the anthem special; it's the five languages it contains, the way the anthem almost forces everyone in South Africa to engage with each other's cultures in a way they might otherwise not.

There are plenty of countries that have anthems in multiple languages, of course. Belgium's 'La Brabançonne' can be sung in French, German or Flemish, while 'O Canada' is singable in both poetic French or unpoetic English, depending on your preference (the French goes for lines like, 'Thy brow is wreathed with a glorious garland of flowers'; the English, 'The True North, strong and free'). But hardly any country seems to have had the confidence to mix multiple languages in a single anthem, as if doing so would undermine the whole project of nation-building – most people expecting a country's citizens to share a common language, after all. Pakistan's anthem, 'Qaumi Taranah' ('Blessed be the sacred land, / Happy be the bounteous realm'), is in Urdu even though it's only 8 per cent of the population's first language (it is the lingua franca, admittedly); similarly, Singapore's 'Majulah Singapura' ('Onwards, Singapore') is in Malay even though English is the language everyone there communicates in and Chinese dialects are the second most used (it's actually illegal to sing it in anything but Malay). Some countries have even used anthems to try to enforce a single-language policy, notably Sri Lanka, where in 2010 the government tried to ban singing of its anthem in Tamil, the language of 20 per cent of the population including those who fought against it in the country's long-running civil war. It justified the move by saying that 'in no other country is an anthem sung in more than one language'. Not long after the news became public, journalists asked the government if it had heard of South Africa, but the criticism was ignored, and an unofficial ban went ahead anyway. It was only lifted in 2015.

There is really only one country, in fact, that South Africa could have looked to for inspiration when deciding to adopt a multilingual anthem: Suriname. Its anthem, 'God Zij Met Ons Suriname' ('God Be With Our Suriname'), starts with a verse in Dutch, the old colonial language, heavy on lines about tilling soil, before it flows into a verse in Sranan Tongo, heavy on machismo ('If there's a fight to fight, we shall not be afraid'). But you wouldn't think that one song would be enough to reassure the politician who came up with the idea for South Africa's multilingual anthem that what they were doing was sensible. Two languages seems achievable, but *five*? If I were to ask you to guess who that politician was, you'd only ever give me one answer: Nelson Mandela. And you'd be right – the colossus of South African politics is at the centre of the anthem's story, just as he seems to be at the centre of every story you've heard about this country. But to talk about him now would be to get ahead of myself, because to understand the anthem, the first person you need to know about is someone who died before Mandela was even born.

*

Enoch Sontonga is a man it's almost impossible to learn anything about. There are only a couple of photos of him, black-and-whites from the late 1800s. In them, he's in a dapper three-piece suit, a bow tie more thrown than tied around his neck, his moustache looking like it's been waxed to points. He's running the chain of a pocket watch through his hand in one of them and looks more like a gold trader calculating figures than what he really was – a teacher at a Methodist school in what's now Soweto, as poor and unvalued as every other black in the country at that time. No one is clear about what Enoch actually taught at that school, but it's known he ran the choir and that he compulsively wrote songs for it, scribbling ideas down on scraps of paper between lessons. He eventually collected all his efforts into an exercise book, which he hoped to publish, but died before he had a chance to do so, in 1905, aged just thirty-two, of gastro-enteritis and a perforated appendix. He was thrown into the black section of Johannesburg's main cemetery, grave number 4,885. The cemetery's records listed him as Enoch Kaffir – christening him with a new surname, the derogatory Afrikaans word for black people. That, essentially, is all there is to say about Enoch; eight short sentences, the most interesting of them about what happened to him after he died.

Soon after arriving in South Africa, I spent an afternoon in Soweto desperately trying to learn more about his life, hoping to at least find the school where he worked so I could flesh out that minimal portrait, but even that proved impossible. I was led around the different parts of Soweto that Enoch might have lived in – Pimville, Nancefield, Klipspruit – by young woman after young woman, all of them holding parasols to protect themselves from the sun, making Soweto seem more like Edwardian England than the teeming city it is. In the end I was dropped off with a middle-aged woman, Olive, who I was told knew more about the area than anyone else. 'No need to sit down,' she said after hearing why I was there. 'This won't take long. You're in Soweto. Everything here was bulldozed during apartheid. You won't find a building more than forty years old. Haven't you read no history books?'

However, there is one other fact about Enoch's life that is known. One day in 1897 he grabbed a scrap of paper and wrote 'Nkosi Sikelel' iAfrika' on it. It was a short hymn, just a four-line verse in which a choir pray for the Lord to bless Africa, then a two-line chorus in which the singers repeatedly ask for the Holy Spirit to descend. When that chorus is sung, people echo each other until it sounds like hundreds are making the call, not just a handful of schoolchildren (some say Enoch took the melody from the hymn 'Aberystwyth', but only a Welsh nationalist who hadn't listened to both songs properly would insist on that).

Enoch only intended for the song to be sung by his choir, but the children couldn't keep such a haunting melody to themselves and soon schools and churches across Johannesburg were singing it (some school choirs did tours at the time, which obviously helped). Not long afterwards it was travelling through every Xhosa-speaking community in the country, reaching as far south as Port Elizabeth, as if people were being sent out in ox wagons just to teach it. In 1912, some of the most respected black men in the country met in Bloemfontein to discuss concerns that non-whites were losing the few rights they had. They were especially concerned about the planned Natives Land Act, which intended to ban blacks from owning land in 90 per cent of the country – the first real piece of legislation aimed at creating a formal system of segregation in South Africa. The men formed the South African Native National Congress to fight such laws and at the end of the meeting decided to sing a song together to sum up their hopes and what they wished it could achieve. They sang 'Nkosi'. By 1925, the SANNC had become the far-better-named African National Congress and 'Nkosi' had become its anthem.

*

Over the next seventy years, 'Nkosi Sikelel' iAfrika' was sung at every major event in South African history you might care to name: at times of happiness, of sorrow and of desperation. In 1952, when the ANC launched its first major campaign of civil disobedience, getting people to break any apartheid law they could – such as by using whites-only toilets and ignoring curfews – it was there, sung by people as they were carted off to prison. In 1957, at the Johannesburg bus boycott, it was sung at the end of each day, after people had trudged miles home to their township because they weren't willing to pay inflated fares. The boycott was a success. During the Treason Trial of 1956–61 – the event that brought Nelson Mandela to the world's attention, when he and 155 others were accused of plotting to overthrow the state – it was there too, sung during lunch breaks and echoing around the courthouse when they were finally acquitted. After the ANC and other groups were banned in 1960, it was sung by their members in exile, hundreds of homesick men and women joining in with that chorus and linking training camps in Zimbabwe and Botswana with meeting rooms in London and New York. As the anti-apartheid struggle grew more violent in the seventies and eighties, 'Nkosi' was sung every Saturday, at funeral after funeral of dead protestors. Sometimes it was sung so frequently on those days it was like it stopped being a song and became a continual dirge, a lament no one felt it was safe to stop singing. And, of course, it was also sung in the prisons, a final show of defiance by activists as they were marched to the gallows, and who tried to keep singing until the moment the trapdoor fell away beneath their feet.

The apartheid government bizarrely played its own part in promoting the song, when in the sixties it created the Bantustans – nominally independent countries whose real aim was to remove black people's claims to South African soil (the idea being that people became citizens of those countries, and lost their South African citizenship). Two of these, Transkei and Ciskei, were allowed to use 'Nkosi' as their 'national anthem', something I can only think the apartheid government signed off on because it felt the move would nullify the song's political power and end its association with the ANC. It did not. In truth, there was little the apartheid government could have done to stop the song's progress anyway. Even if it had made 'Nkosi' illegal and somehow made everyone so afraid of singing it they wouldn't even do so in church where it could be interpreted as just a hymn like any

other, it would have still leaked into the population's consciousness thanks to neighbouring countries taking it up. In 1961,
Tanzania adopted a Swahili version of the song as its anthem.
Zambia followed suit three years later, although it commissioned
its own English lyrics ('Stand and sing for Zambia, proud and
free'). Zimbabwe also used the melody of 'Nkosi' as its anthem
during the 1980s, while Namibia did for a short time after its
independence. (No one I spoke to had any problems with this
musical sharing; just like few Liechtensteiners I met really had a
problem with their anthem having the same tune as 'God Save
the Queen'.) By the 1980s, 'Nkosi' had also been taken up by
rebellious white teenagers throughout the country, who asked
to sing it in school choirs, knowing full well it would annoy their
parents. A white rock band, Bright Blue, even managed to
smuggle its melody into one of that decade's biggest hits,
'Weeping' – remarkably, the government's radio censors failed
to notice.

Of course, there were plenty of other important songs during
apartheid – many of which were far more emotional, inspiring
and fun than 'Nkosi'. While travelling around the country,
whenever I asked people what music they remembered most
from that time, the first thing they all said was the *toyi-toyi* – a
dance people would do in the townships, often while rushing
towards the South African army who'd come to control them,
while shouting 'Za! Za!' in mimicry of guns going off. Sometimes
they'd sing as they danced, largely about how they were going
to find some guns and kill the Boer.

But as all those songs came and went, 'Nkosi' stayed. It
reminded everyone just how long the fight had been going on
and it gave them hope God would eventually intervene on their
side. In 1996, Mandela opened a monument to Enoch Sontonga
– a huge granite block on the likely site of grave number 4,885
in Braamfontein Cemetery in Johannesburg – and tried to explain
what the song meant to him. Mandela wasn't normally a great

public speaker, to put it mildly, so long-winded and verbose at times his audience would drift off, but he got it right that day. 'What a hymn it is,' he said, 'this simple appeal for national redemption, for continental salvation . . . It is the torch that has lit our way . . . that even as we fall, we hand on, one to the other, to the end of time.' All right, he actually went on for several more minutes, repeating his point endlessly, the way only Mandela could, but you can see his deep love for this song; his belief that Enoch Sontonga gave the anti-apartheid struggle its voice.

Of course, while black South Africa had its anthem, South Africa itself had one too: 'Die Stem' ('The Call'). It was written in 1918 by Cornelis Langenhoven – a man who it's easy to get a horrendous impression of despite the almost universal acclaim he receives to this day. Cornelis was a lawyer, newspaper editor, politician and author whose main aim in life seemed to be to promote the use of Afrikaans; to first ensure its survival against English, and then to make it blossom. He had the bushy moustache, shining eyes and laugh lines of a favourite uncle, he thrilled people with the ghost stories and satire that he wrote, and he was renowned for his wit (he once said in parliament that 'half the people here are baboons'; when the Speaker ordered him to retract, he replied, 'Okay, half the people here are not baboons'). But he was also a drunkard and an adulterer, and he didn't exactly have an enlightened view on race relations – he was, for instance, the author of the 'Black Manifesto', one of the more infamous documents in South African political history, which warned of an 'impending flood of barbarism' and claimed the country was about to become a 'black Kaffir state'. Admittedly he was asked to write it by other politicians, but he gave their ideas such urgency and power that you could argue he's the reason some white Afrikaners saw racial segregation as so essential to their survival. (In Cape Town, I met Cornelis's grandson, a kindly ninety-year-old mathematician called Guillaume Brümmer, who told me at length about all of this, not trying to hide any of it it printed in the leading Afrikaans newspaper. 'Let it appear in this shape and then somebody can replace the music with something better, and once they've done that, somebody else can find better words.'

*

Contrary to his expectations, Cornelis's efforts couldn't have been better received – people wrote letters from all over the Cape praising them. Here was a song that perfectly summed up their feelings for the land, and their desire to be free of all vestiges of past British rule. Their only complaint about the words seemed to be that there weren't enough of them, and people begged Cornelis to add a fourth verse expressing their love for the Lord as well as country. They weren't so keen on the music, though, which, yes, was amateurish. Several composers soon tried to improve it, but Cornelis didn't like any of their efforts.

Only one of them persisted, a minister in the Dutch Reformed Church, Marthinus Lourens de Villiers. Marthinus is a far easier character to like than Cornelis. He was an eccentric who walked around the towns where he lived in a pith helmet, hitting golf balls for children to collect. He also invited coloureds into his church services, despite the whites frowning upon it. He didn't actually really want to be a minister – he was a frustrated musician who had only entered the Church to please his parents, who had promised God that he would do so after he miraculously recovered from a childhood bout of measles. One day in 1920, Marthinus was supposed to be occupied writing a baptism certificate, but he showed his true calling by suddenly shouting at his wife to come to him. 'I've got it! I've got it!' he's meant to have cried as he rushed to his piano. '*Uit die blou van ONSE HEMEL,*' he then sang as he played, raising the song's melody to reach the blue heavens of the sky; '*Uit die diepte van ONS SEE,*' he went on, dropping it to hit the depths of the oceans, and then he carried on, simply letting Cornelis's words guide his tune wherever it needed to go.

*

'Die Stem', once Cornelis had given his approval to Marthinus's music, was immediately sung by whites throughout the country as if it were South Africa's anthem, but it didn't become the official one until 1957, when the government threw out 'God Save the Queen' and the country's last remaining symbolic links to Britain with it. After that, it was everywhere – played before sports games and at cinema screenings; in schools and at political rallies. At the Currie Cup final, the largest rugby – and so sporting – event in the country, a white-gloved bandleader used to turn to the main stand and conduct the spectators through it, the crowd singing so loudly there was no point his band joining in. Surprisingly, given all that, the song's name doesn't appear much in the history of apartheid. There aren't tales of South African Defence Force soldiers singing it gloatingly at blacks; the government didn't even force non-whites to learn it in schools. In fact, the one major appearance it does make in South African history occurred after apartheid ended and Mandela had been released.

On 15 August 1992, South Africa was due to play New Zealand at rugby, which would mark the end of a sixteen-year international sporting embargo against the country. It was a day the white population had been longing for – most Afrikaners loving nothing more than sport and feeling that their national rugby team, the Springboks, epitomised everything about them: strong, unrelenting, unbeatable. Giving the match the go-ahead was a remarkable reconciliatory gesture by the ANC, but they only agreed to it on the understanding that none of apartheid's symbols would be used. That included 'Die Stem'. The anthem would not be played, the ANC said; instead there would be a minute's silence 'in support of domestic peace'.

Unfortunately, some Springboks fans didn't take too well to that news. They wrote to newspapers threatening to turn up with ghetto blasters to play the anthem themselves if it were banned, not seeming to realise or care that by doing so they would be pissing on the spirit of reconciliation that had led to apartheid ending without a civil war. Some papers fanned these flames; the editor of *Die Burger*, the largest Afrikaans newspaper, announced that the ANC didn't seem to 'have an inkling of the raw emotions they are touching among whites'. Everyone hoped it was simply bluster, but on the day some people did indeed walk into the stadium carrying bulky ghetto blasters, others clutching the country's orange, white and blue, soon-to-be-re-placed, flag. When the minute's silence came, the stadium launched into 'Die Stem' a cappella. They sang it through once, they sang it through again, and then, apparently to calm everyone down, the music was played over the stadium's speakers, so everyone got to sing it once more. 'As much as I can't stop the ANC from marching or singing what they wish to sing, they must give me the same right,' said Louis Luyt, the president of the Transvaal Rugby Football Union, and the man who apparently gave the all-clear to hit play. The incident somehow didn't cause much trouble – perhaps due to the fact there were few non-whites in the stadium to witness it, maybe more because the South African Rugby Football Union rushed to issue an apology, prom-ising it would never happen again.

The climax of the story of South Africa's anthem should, of course, be the event that is the climax of every story about South Africa: Mandela's inauguration in 1994 as the country's first post-apartheid president. It was on that day that the new anthem was unveiled, after all. Well, new *anthems*, plural, would be a better term – during negotiations over the country's future, it had been decided to keep playing 'Die Stem', but to immediately follow it with both 'Nkosi Sikelel' iAfrika' and then its Sesotho-language version, 'Morena Boloka', creating the world's first three-in-one anthem. Mandela was the driving force behind that decision. The rest of the ANC's leadership had pushed for 'Die Stem' to be treated like every other legacy of apartheid, but at a meeting Mandela scolded them: 'This song that you treat so easily holds the emotions of many people you don't represent yet. With the stroke of a pen you would take a decision to destroy the very – the only! – basis that we are building upon: reconciliation.' Mandela got his wish a few weeks later when he became president, getting the chance to stand hand on heart, face serious and taut, through all three songs. Mandela's happiness with the outcome is seen in his autobiography, *Long Walk to Freedom*. The playing of the anthems is almost the last thing he mentions in it. 'The day was symbolised for me by the playing of our anthem,' he writes. 'Although neither group knew the lyrics . . . they once despised, they would soon . . . by heart.'

But if that was where the anthem's story ended, I wouldn't have chosen to write about it at all, because what was unveiled that day wasn't an anthem that could really unify anyone – it was an endurance test. The playing of the three songs took five minutes and four seconds. Prince Philip, the Duke of Edinburgh, joked afterwards that he'd had to remove his hat for so long during them he'd got sunburn. It was clear to anyone impartial watching on TV that the decision was a disaster – not just because of the length of time it took to get through this tripartite anthem, but because of the fact you'd need weeks of rehearsals and language lessons if you were going to even try singing it. If, say, you were an Indian South African from Durban, who only spoke English and Zulu, you suddenly found yourself having to learn twelve lines of Afrikaans and an equal number in Sesotho. If you were a coloured from Cape Town who only spoke Afrikaans and English, you had a similar problem with the Sesotho, and also had to deal with thirteen lines of Xhosa and Zulu. If you were a black from Limpopo in the north who only spoke Venda, well, you'd probably be better off just giving up (an unlikely situation, admittedly).

Renditions soon became farcical, people mumbling their way through the songs, or just entirely ignoring the ones they didn't know. Mandela initially didn't seem to think the complaints were justified, and at ANC meetings he used to act like a disappointed father who knew better than his children and would force the anthems to be replayed again and again until everyone joined in. But after a few months even he began to admit it was 'quite embarrassing to have people standing for such a long time' and that he was left as much 'bored' as inspired. It was then he had his real anthem masterstroke: he decided he wasn't the man to come up with a solution after all, formed a committee and got them to sort it out.

*

Sitting in her office at the music department of Wits University in Johannesburg, Jeanne Zaidel-Rudolph doesn't exactly look like your typical post-apartheid hero. She's not black, for a start. She's not coloured or Indian either. She's a sixty-something Jewish woman, with bouffant hair and a love of pearl necklaces, someone who looks more like they should be showing visitors around a stately home than songwriting for a nation. I'm not the first person to leap to the wrong conclusion about her. In 1997, when her anthem was unveiled, most newspapers chose to ignore her role in creating the song and instead attributed it mainly to the chairman of the anthem committee, a black language professor and composer, James Khumalo. It's something she's clearly all too aware of, which I think explains why she spends the start of our meeting pulling out page after page of proof that it is indeed mainly her work. 'Look, here's a letter from the Ministry of Culture thanking me for writing it,' she says at one point. 'And here's a receipt showing how much I was paid. The grand sum of 3,350 rand [£190]! Can you believe that? If only we'd met at my house then I could show you this plaque I was given for it.'

Jeanne was actually one of the first people Mandela's government called to be on the committee to sort out the anthem, simply because she was one of the few musicians in South Africa capable of working with both African spiritual and Western classical music. She grew up in Pretoria, where her father ran a men's outfitting shop. Being Jewish, she quickly started to feel very uncomfortable with the apartheid system – 'I knew what prejudice means, let's put it that way' – but she was also helpless to do anything about it. 'I remember my brother and I cycling one day and we saw these police beating up these black men for no rhyme or reason, probably because they didn't have their passbook or something. And I'd often come home after seeing things like that, in tears, and say to my parents, "What can we do?" and my mother would just say, "There's nothing we can do. The government's too strong."' Jeanne's own early efforts to combat apartheid tended towards the whimsical, such as trying to get the family's maid to eat with them, much to the maid's horror.

However, as Jeanne grew up and she realised that she wanted to be a composer, the idea came to her that she could use music to fight the system in her own small way. It helped that she had become obsessed with African rhythms and was determined to use them in her work. 'When I was about eighteen, I started going out to a platinum mine to record the men playing on Sundays,' she says. 'Fifteen, twenty thousand men might be there at a time. And my mum used to beg me not to go because there were protests and riots – "Please don't, you'll be attacked" – but I really enjoyed it; they had the most incredible orchestra of xylophones and *mbilas* with ankle beads and drums and shakers. A lot of them were from Mozambique and Zimbabwe, not just here, and there was such virtuosity and speed. I think the miners thought I was a little bit mad. "What does this young white girl want to record our songs for?" But they were quite happy for me to be there and listen.'

For the next twenty or so years, Jeanne tried to make a distinctly South African classical music, although she jokes about whether she got anywhere near succeeding. 'In the seventies, I studied for a while under [Hungarian composer György] Ligeti, and I went through a phase of writing very unlistenable and avant-garde music, so the African feel may not have been so noticeable back then,' she laughs. This didn't apparently put off the people who mattered.

It was February 1995 when the anthem committee had its first meeting, squeezed around a boardroom table in an 'exceedingly bland' government building in the middle of Pretoria. 'The instruction was that we couldn't just do anything we wanted. We had to use the existing anthems,' Jeanne says. 'That was Mandela's wish. Don't scrap anything, be inclusive.' As the meeting started, several people put forward suggestions of what approach to take. The idea that gained the most backing was that the anthem should start with 'Die Stem' before moving into 'Nkosi', an idea that clearly wouldn't have worked as it would have given the impression that, musically at least, non-whites were still second-class citizens in the country. Jeanne realised she had to speak up. If this was going to be an anthem for a new, reconciled country, 'Nkosi' should be first, 'Die Stem' second, she insisted. You could bridge the change in pitch between the two by getting people to sing the words 'South Africa', she added. She made it all sound easy, more like joining a child's building blocks together than songwriting, and everyone went for it.

The task then just became one of cutting away as many lyrics as possible until the anthem hit a reasonable length. (The beautiful chorus of 'Nkosi' was one of the first things to go, some Muslims – about a quarter of South Africa's Indian population are Muslim – having objected to its references to the Holy Spirit. Surprisingly that caused less debate than some sentences in 'Die Stem', such as a line about ox wagons 'Cut[ting] their trails into the earth', which many blacks saw as a reminder of the initial

Tsonga- and Venda-speakers I spoke to – the only two of South Africa's eleven official languages not represented in some way in the anthem (Ndebele, Tswana, Swati and the Sotho languages are linked to either Xhosa, Zulu or Sesotho). 'Take it from me – take it from me! – nobody in Venda feels excluded because our language isn't in there,' said Nkhelebeni Phaswana, a linguistics professor and expert in Venda culture, when I asked him if he felt left out. 'We actually feel more – more! – united with the rest of the country, because everyone across South Africa is now singing the same song.

'You know Enoch Sontonga's original song is a hymn for Africa?' he added. 'Well, do you think he should have written it in hundreds of languages so that everyone in the continent felt included? Are you mad? What's important about a song is its message, not the language the message is in. We in Venda sang his song long before the end of apartheid and we'll keep on doing so for a long time to come.'

Plenty of others agreed just as strongly about the impact of the anthem. Most laughed that they did not know all the words, but they said that didn't matter. Johan de Villiers, Marthinus de Villiers's grandson, said he felt the anthem was the greatest 'conciliatory gesture' Mandela ever made. 'The emotional impact of keeping "Die Stem" is larger than anyone realises,' he said. 'Just with that, he won over the hearts of so many, many people he might not have done otherwise.'

I questioned him on this: surely whites weren't that averse to singing 'Nkosi' alone? It's hardly the most controversial song, what with its gently religious lyrics. But he put me straight, giggling his way through a story about when he formed a multiracial choir in the late 1980s. 'White people would phone our house and shout at me, "What would your grandfather say? He composed 'Die Stem'!" And I used to say, "He'd be delighted!"'

Edward Griffiths, the man who was in charge of South African rugby during the 1990s and forced the national team to learn

'Nkosi' before they hosted the 1995 World Cup (one of the great unifying post-apartheid events – the Springboks fans seeming to have lost some of their Boer nationalism of a few years earlier), said he thought the anthem wasn't just a success in South Africa but was proving influential abroad. 'New Zealand appear to have copied it – they now sing a verse of their anthem in Maori before a verse in English,' he said, 'and I dare say soon we'll have an Australian anthem with some lines of an Aboriginal language. It's been a really positive thing.'

However, after I spent slightly longer in the country, I realised my optimism about the song was somewhat misplaced. People started pointing me in the direction of the Economic Freedom Fighters, the country's third-largest political party, who have asked for 'Die Stem' to be dropped from the anthem unless 'it can be scientifically confirmed that its inclusion brings social cohesion'. 'Die Stem' was 'a musical . . . commitment to kill and die for the white supremacist state', its statements on the issue say. 'If languages were the issue, why couldn't there have been another Afrikaans song included to create a multilingual anthem?' Others pointed me towards Steve Hofmeyr, an Afrikaner pop star who still sings 'Die Stem' as if he were living in the 1950s and, by doing so, has angered more blacks than you would think possible. I initially dismissed both of them as extremists, but then I started speaking to more people about the anthem – friendly, everyday people you can't dismiss so easily – and realised just how widespread disappointment with it is.

In Melville, Johannesburg's trendy middle-class haven, a place filled with signs warning passers-by that armed response units patrol the area, Zethu Mashika, a film composer, told me, 'I feel so uncomfortable when I get to the part in Afrikaans, it's like something's crawling under my skin. We should just sing "Nkosi", or some completely different song.'

Another day I had a drink with Mondli Makhanya, an ever-laughing, middle-aged newspaper columnist. 'The anthem's not the progressive nation-building thing Nelson Mandela believed it was,' he said. 'All it's done is give the Afrikaners something to hold on to, a celebration of them-ness, and you see that every time there's a rugby game. When they get to the "Die Stem" part it's like the roof of the stadium blows off. Literally. There'll be some singing of the "Nkosi" parts, by the young people and the English-speaking whites who did not necessarily identify with "Die Stem" back in the day, but there's still this hard core and when they get to that part, they let their feelings [be] known.' He smiled awkwardly as if trying to decide whether to voice the thought that had just come into his head. 'I can never forgive Mandela for this – and he's the man who embodies forgiveness!'

Again, and again, from person after person, I heard comments just like those. And it wasn't just blacks I met who felt uncomfortable with the anthem – I met many whites and coloured people too who agreed with them, who said there were still too many divides in the country and that perhaps it was better to create a new anthem that transcended history rather than acted as a continual reminder of it. Even Jeanne Zaidel-Rudolph, the anthem's composer, who insisted it was uniting many people, said she 'half agreed' with complaints about it. 'It would be nice to have something completely new and ours,' she said, 'although don't ask me who'd compose it.'

*

'Argh, you've just been speaking with the wrong people,' says Lolla Meyer, a blonde, curly-haired thirty-something in a vampish red dress and equally vampish red lipstick, who's meant to be teaching me Afrikaans, the final language of the anthem I've got to learn. 'I've got lots of black students – Zulu-speakers, Ndebele-, Tswana-speakers – and they all love it. They know the past, but we just make a joke about that. Like today, I was teaching some the imperative, and our textbooks are from the eighties as no one's written a new one for so long, so all the sentences were things like "Stand to attention!" and "Go fetch my suitcase!" And we were all just laughing. I mean, "Go fetch my suitcase"? It's ridiculous. But that was the past; you can't ignore it.'

It's coming to the end of my time in South Africa and, as Lolla speaks, I allow myself to hope that maybe she's right – maybe I have just been talking to the wrong people and there are a whole host of black people out there who do love the anthem, even the Afrikaans lines. It helps that she's also making me wonder if it'd even be possible to change the anthem in the way many would like by just having 'Nkosi' and forgetting the rest. 'How would I feel if they cut out the Afrikaans?' she asks. 'Very pissed off, *ja*. But everyone would keep singing "Die Stem" anyway. There's enough people who're still proud of Afrikaans. Go to Pretoria. If you told half the people there they'd never be able to speak Afrikaans again, there'd be a war. It'd be the same if you went and told people in the Eastern Cape they can't speak Zulu.' She pulls out a sheet of paper and shows me the breakdown of the country's languages. There's Zulu at the top, 22.7 per cent of the population's first language. Xhosa comes in second at 16 per cent, then it's Afrikaans at 13.5 per cent. You can't take any of the languages away is her point. If you changed the anthem, you'd have to keep Afrikaans in somehow and if people objected, well, tough.

She starts telling me more about Afrikaans, its history, its use and unique characteristics – from swearing ('*Voetsak!*') to more swearing ('*Fukof!*') – as if trying to convince me it's the best language here and I should be on its side. She's funny and interesting during all of this, but then she starts saying Afrikaans is also an 'incredibly sexy language – you can have great pillow talk in it' and I realise things have gone a little too far. Lolla's clearly decided I'm gullible, that she can say anything about this language and I'll believe her. I mean, I've been in South Africa two weeks, I know as well as anyone that Afrikaans is a language that occasionally sounds like it's spoken with a particularly viscous piece of phlegm stuck in your throat. Don't tell me straight-faced it's sexy.

I decide to draw our chat to a close and say that perhaps it's best we get on with the lesson I'm paying for, so she starts to teach me the anthem's four lines of Afrikaans. The first two are easy enough:

> *Uit die blou van onse hemel,*
> *Uit die diepte van ons see.*

You just say what you see with a slight Dutch accent. But then we get to the last two – '*Oor ons ewige gebergtes,* / *Waar die kranse antwoord gee*' – and I come to an appalling stop. It's the 'ge' sounds that are the problem. They're meant to be guttural, almost like you're rolling your r's, and I can't do it no matter how much I try.

Lolla just smiles, tells me not to worry and says there is an easy way to learn. 'Just watch my lips,' she says, and I stare at her mouth as she says each word slowly, her tongue fluttering up and down between her bright red lips. 'Er, wig, ge, ge, berg, tes,' she says, breaking down the two hardest words, each syllable practically purring out of her mouth. I sit there silent for a moment, not sure how to react because dear God, this is almost, dare I say it, genuinely, yes, sexy . . . No, no, no, I tell myself, shaking my head clear. This can't be happening. She does it once more, then asks me to give it a go. 'Eurghweegergh gerhj-blerghterghs,' I gargle, several flecks of spit flying out of my mouth in her direction and abruptly, thankfully, killing the mood. 'Er, yes, perhaps we shouldn't worry too much about your pronunciation for now,' she says. 'Let's just try and get through to the end.'

*

The problem with researching an anthem like South Africa's is you're always looking for straight answers – either it's one that did inspire a freedom struggle and still is inspiring people today, or it's one that desperately needs changing. But after meeting Lolla, I came to the realisation that in South Africa things are just never going to be that simple. It's a messy country where awkward associations are a part of daily life – but that doesn't stop it being one of the most enthralling and uplifting places you can visit. It's the same with the anthem – it's a messy answer to a messy problem and some people are always going to be happy with it, others always uncomfortable. It can be both one of the world's great songs and one of the most overhyped at the same time, surely? But deep down I still wanted to come down on the optimistic side, as much because there seems to be so little positivity among anthems today as anything else, which was why I felt grateful every time I met someone who still genuinely believed in the song, and especially when I met Wally Serote, South Africa's original angry young poet.

In the 1960s, Wally was locked up for nine months in solitary confinement for his work trying to resuscitate the ANC (it had suffered after being banned, with many of its leaders jailed and many young people turning to the more radical, also banned, Pan Africanist Congress). 'They said I was a terrorist,' he told me, 'that I had the intentions of participating in a conflict. And they weren't wrong, really, because I did. All the training I went through, I felt, was preparing me for that. The ANC had no plans for it, but it would have been very irresponsible of someone to have given me a gun back then because I would have used it.' After being released from prison, he moved to America to study and – much to the relief of the ANC, I expect – channelled his indignation into poetry, churning out angry, ominous work after angry, ominous work ('I do not know where I've been,' goes one, 'but brother, / I know I am coming, / I come like a tide of water'). Within a few years, he was back working for the organisation in exile in Botswana, part of both its arts programmes and its armed wing, Umkhonto we Sizwe (Spear of the Nation), although his strongest memory of this time was learning 'the principles of non-racialism' from those around him. 'I would have been a racist myself if it were not for how the ANC educated me,' he told me at one point, as if to emphasise just how much anger he had within him at that time.

Unsurprisingly given that background, Wally fully expected 'Nkosi' to be South Africa's only anthem after apartheid. 'It had inspired us to want freedom in our life, to fight and to unite our people,' he said. 'You can never separate it from that context.' He was somewhat shocked, then, when it wasn't subsequently given pride of place. He was the ANC's head of culture at the time and it seems he only reluctantly accepted the decision to keep 'Die Stem' too. The way he described it, he only fully realised why the compromise was made when he heard it at Mandela's inauguration. 'I was standing there at the Union Buildings next to four, five, six Afrikaner women and when the anthem was sung they wept,' he said. 'And I mean *wept*. Then one of them said, "At least they've put our song in there." I heard that with my own ears. I'm not making it up. And when I saw them weeping I realised that's how all South Africans feel about these things, how important they are. You can imagine us, how we felt, when "Nkosi Sikelel' iAfrika" and "Morena Boloka" were sung. It was almost the same feeling when we saw the National Defence Force do the fly-past, knowing that at one time these planes were bombing us and now were saluting our president. You realised that these were all symbols of change and how important it is to include everyone in them.'

After he told me that story, Wally started to speak about the euphoria of the moment, but also about how such euphoria is difficult to sustain when you can't change things like inequality and racism overnight. I expected him to then say, like most of the other black people I'd met, that the anthem had had its time, that you can't have one created on a wave of euphoria twenty years after its moment. But instead he said this: 'If you say this anthem was created so that our people could be united, there's a simple way to gauge if its time has passed or not. If you still have people who can't sing "Die Stem", then that is a problem. If you still have people who can't sing "Morena Boloka", then that is a problem. If you still have people who can't sing "Nkosi Sikeleli", then that is a problem. And that problem can become deeper and create disunity. This song still has the potential to unite the country if everyone commits to it. I've committed myself – I sing the whole song – and to do that was a serious effort for me. It was a serious effort to sing "Die Stem". A serious *emotional* effort. But that's what everyone has to work out for themselves: how do you make that leap? A song can help us still. It can be a bridge so that when people are singing they only see South Africans, no matter their colour.'

*

After leaving South Africa, I thought it'd be Wally's comments that would stick in my mind longest: honest, realistic, but hopeful. But surprisingly, the words that I kept remembering were those of someone who couldn't have been more different – someone who I only met for a minute but who I could tell hadn't tried crossing many bridges himself. I'd been in Cape Town trying to meet the former president F. W. de Klerk to talk about his role in negotiating peace with Mandela, and to see if he had anything to say about the anthem. I failed miserably in that regard, but outside his office I spoke with a member of his security team. 'Nah, I'm not singing the anthem – that's their song,' he said, dismissively. The fact 'their' meant 'blacks' needed no spelling out. 'Why should I? It's got nothing to do with my culture,' he went on. I thought about reminding him I was a writer and that perhaps he should tone the comments done, but then he said the most hopeful sentence of my entire trip. 'Of course my kids sing it – sing the whole fucking thing, all the languages. But they're a different generation.' And he walked back inside shaking his head, as if his own children were unfathomable.

República o Muerte

A los pueblos de América, infausto,
Tres centurias un cetro oprimió,
Mas un día soberbia surgiendo,
¡Basta! dijo, y el cetro rompió.
Nuestros padres, lidiando grandiosos,
Ilustraron su gloria marcial;
Y trozada la augusta diadema,
Enalzaron el gorro triunfal. (Repetir las últimas dos líneas)

Coro:
¡Paraguayos, República, o Muerte!
Nuestro brío nos dio libertad;
Ni opresores, ni siervos alientan,
Donde reinan unión e igualdad. (Repetir las últimas dos
    líneas)
Unión e igualdad! (x2)

—

The peoples of the Americas, unfortunately,
Were oppressed for three centuries by a sceptre,
But one magnificent day, surging forth,
'Enough!' they said, and the sceptre was broken.
Our fathers, grandiose in battle,
Showed their martial glory;
And after smashing the august diadem,
The triumphal cap was raised. (Repeat last two lines)

Chorus:
Paraguayans: republic or death!
Our spirit gave us liberty;
Neither oppressors nor slaves exist,
Where union and equality reign. (Repeat last two lines)
Union and equality! (x2)

II

Paraguay

NATIONAL OPERAS

The *Armada Paraguaya* is not perhaps the first part of Paraguay's military you would choose to go to in search of blood-and-guts patriotism, it hardly seeming like the most threatening fighting force there is. From its headquarters in downtown Asunción – the country's capital – you can't actually see water unless you are looking at one of the paintings on its walls. The Paraguay river is only a few minutes' walk away, admittedly, but if the *armada* ever wanted to get out to sea from there, they would have to sail for a good three days downriver, first on to the Paraná and then, eventually, out to the Atlantic, hitting the ocean 700 nautical miles away just north of Buenos Aires – praying Argentina's far grander *armada* let them past en route.

You might, therefore, expect the Paraguayan military to view the *armada* less as an integral part of their operations and more a place to hide the worst of its recruits, hoping that they just while away their days in the heat and not get into any trouble. If that is the strategy, though, they got it horribly wrong with *capitán, comandante* and *jefe* Mariano González Parra, perhaps the most patriotic and dedicated person I have met in all my travels. He welcomed me at the *armada*'s entrance a few moments ago, gleaming in a freshly pressed white shirt, the handful of medals on his barrel chest jangling up and down with every shake of my hand. He then practically dragged me into his office, from where he oversees river navigation, as if he could not have been more desperate for a chance to talk about his country or its anthem, 'República o Muerte'.

'Of course the anthem means a lot to me,' he says, leaning forward so I can look right into his eyes and see how honest he is being. 'That sentiment of independence still means a lot to everyone here. We were under the yoke of Spain for three hundred years. Can you understand that? We had to struggle to free ourselves from slavery. Then once we had independence, other countries tried to take it away. Do you know the Great War against Brazil, Argentina and Uruguay? Mothers and children died defending our country.

'Today,' he adds, 'we're all still struggling to become a better nation, to be better people and have a better life. It's not like I have to look hard for reasons to be patriotic. If I forget all that struggle then it wouldn't make sense to sing the anthem, but every time I sing it, I remember it all.'

He talks just as enthusiastically about all the memorable times he's sung it: from the day he graduated from the military academy to anniversaries of past battles. And he happily jokes about his job; how even his friends think it's funny he works for a land-locked navy (I assume they were especially unforgiving when he trained in Antarctica, given that the only ice you see in Paraguay is in people's drinks). But as he continues happily chatting away, his smile growing wider and his laughs louder, I start to feel worse and worse, because I know what I have got to do. In a moment, I have to ask him the one question I arranged this interview for – one he is going to see as facetious at best; at worst, an insult. 'Mariano,' I finally say somewhat embarrassedly, 'would you do as your anthem asks and die for your country?'

'Would I *die* for Paraguay?' he says, as if to check he's heard properly. He looks at my translator to check I'm serious, realises that I am and pauses to think. One, two, three seconds I count, far longer than I would have thought a soldier would need over such a question. He clears his throat. 'I'm not really a person who supports wars and confrontations,' he says with an awkward smile. 'I'm not someone who's happy when there's conflict.' My heart sinks. He's going to tell me he's not patriotic after all, isn't he? He's going to apologise for misleading me earlier with all that talk of dying mothers and Spanish yokes. This isn't the man I need to be talking to at all. I start mentally packing my things up to go when he suddenly adds that most glorious of words: 'But . . . Of course I am ready to die,' he says. 'It would be an honour to give my life if the chance came. And not just for me, for every Paraguayan. We'd all prefer to die than be defeated.' I smile with relief. He gives me a look suggesting it is perhaps not the most appropriate gesture after such a solemn vow.

*

South America's national anthems are, as a group, easily the world's best. They are exuberant, passionate, over-the-top, hilarious, camp, majestic – everything anthems should be. You can try to find adjectives to describe them, as I am right now, but none will ever seem good enough. It is the music most people know them for, these songs that last five or six minutes and sound more like operas than national anthems, featuring seemingly as many musical twists as the composer could fit on to the score.

Just take Argentina's, for example. For the first thirty seconds or so, it sounds like an orchestra being wound into life, as if the conductor is having to turn the key in each of his musicians' backs. But then for the next thirty, it is as though he steps away, throws his baton into the air and just lets everyone spectacularly unwind, each section of the orchestra trying to outrun the others until they reach the cataclysmic finale. It is one of the most vivacious anthems there is, although it is somewhat ruined when the singing comes in and all the speed and vitality in the song drops away, as if the orchestra's limbs have slowed to a crawl, each player in urgent need of a rewind.

But it's not just musically that South America's anthems stand out. Just read some of their lyrics. They are like epics, setting down for posterity the entire history of their country and its people, the woes they suffered, the pain they bore, and which then swear, with all the weight of the Old Testament, that they will never go through such ills again.

It's not hard to work out who the villains are in these songs: the Spanish and Portuguese who once tried to control the continent. 'Don't you see them over sad Caracas / Spreading mourning, weeping and death?' goes Argentina's at one point.

> Don't you see them, like wild animals,
> Devouring all people who surrender?

Fortunately, heroes are at hand: '"Down with the chains!" / the gentleman yelled, / and the poor man in his hovel / for freedom implored,' goes Venezuela's, sounding more like a Dickensian novel than an anthem. 'For a long time the oppressed Peruvian, / dragged an ominous chain / . . . he quietly moaned,' adds Peru's in a similarly dramatic vein. 'But as soon as the sacred cry, / "Freedom!" was heard, / the slave's indolence shook / [and] his humiliated, humiliated, / humiliated neck rose up' – the word 'humiliated' repeated three times to fit the music rather than to ram home the message of quite how bad being Peruvian was under Spanish rule.

Soon it's not just the people who are stirring to throw out the oppressors; it's the very land itself, the gods too, the animals, every historical figure you can name, even the dead. 'The Inca are shaken / and in their bones the ardour [for freedom] revives,' goes Argentina's. 'Untameable centaurs / descend to the plains,' adds Colombia's, making you wonder why the Spanish and Portuguese ever tried to colonise their countries in the first place.

The anthems then tell of the battles that were fought for independence, the blood that was spilled and the revenge that was had. You would think that all that would be left to do after that would be to celebrate victory, but practically all South American anthems then make sure to warn people that the Europeans could one day be back; that 'the barbaric injustice of fate' might force new chains around people's wrists. If that happens, everyone must be prepared to fight again (Ecuador's anthem is one of the few that doesn't call for more fighting in that eventuality, instead asking for a volcano to erupt and turn everything to ash so there will be nothing for the Spanish to enslave, an approach I doubt many Ecuadorians would be happy with).

The only South American anthems that do not roughly follow this pattern are Guyana's and Suriname's – perhaps unsurprising given they were colonised by Britain and the Netherlands – and Brazil's, which is simply two verses rhapsodising about that country's beauty ('Thy smiling, pretty prairies have more flowers [than any other land]'), but that is probably because it only got words in 1909, long after independence had been achieved and the wounds of colonialism had begun to heal.

It is easy to get lost in the sheer eccentricity of these songs – every time I read Colombia's I end up gawping at a verse that starts, 'In agony, the Virgin / tears her hair out' – but there is a serious point to them that you shouldn't miss: South America's anthems get to the point of what *nationalism* is meant to be about better than any others. They all say, in no uncertain terms, 'This is my land and I'm prepared to die for it.' Chile's, for instance, has the chorus, 'Either the tomb of the free you will be / Or the refuge against oppression', while Argentina's screams, 'Let us live crowned in glory / or let us swear in glory to die.' Then there's Bolivia's:

> For the sons of the mighty Bolivar
> have sworn, thousands upon thousands of times,
> to die rather than see the country's
> majestic banner humiliated.

Of course there are countries outside South America whose anthems do this too – Italy's repeats 'We are ready to die, / Italy has called' so many times you worry that singing it counts as a binding contract – but in no other continent's anthems is this message so common.

The anthem that does it best of all, though, is Paraguay's. 'Republic or Death', it says in its very title, a message that could not be clearer if the anthem were called, 'Step On My Land and I'll Slit Your Throat'. '¡República o Muerte!', to use the Spanish, is three words that say more about what is meant to be at the heart of nationalism than entire books on the subject do. They encapsulate that desire to fight and die for your land; that putting up of barriers against others; that need to keep what's yours for ever, no matter how arbitrary or recent a creation your country actually is. It's because of those three words that I decided I had to go to Paraguay. I wanted to see if that message could still mean something today, when most other countries would baulk at singing anything like them (even most other South American countries, which now ignore the bloodier verses of their original anthems in an effort not to seem like they still hold grudges). The fact that those three words sum up everything there is to do with nationalism is also why, in a way, I knew this book had to be named after this song. Well that, and because it was the only national anthem that worked as a book title.

*

If you spend a few days walking around Asunción, there are some things you can't help but notice. The colours, for a start, especially on the buses, their windows decked out with Jesuses, their sides painted like rainbows as if the decoration is more likely to attract customers than any destination. There's also the almost clichéd pace of life: no one here ever seems too busy to turn down a chat over *tereré* – the ice-cold tea everyone drinks,

rapidly sucking it up a metal straw then handing the cup back
for a refill, in need of hydration (the temperature's normally over
30°C) as much as caffeine. And there's the poverty too; the shacks
you find right outside the city hall, children openly having bucket
showers in between them while music blares from stereos that
have been illegally connected to the electricity supply.

   But there is one thing you're only likely to pick up if you start
talking to people: the fact that history is closer to the surface
here than in practically any other country you could visit. If you
ask someone why all the graffiti around the city seems to feature
a flabby-cheeked, bearded man, his eyes burning at passers-by,
they'll be happy to tell you it's Mariscal López, one of the country's former dictators and the national hero. 'Why wouldn't we
want him on our walls? He's an example to everyone.' Ask
someone else where they're from, they'll reply something like,
'Piribebuy – you know, where the Brazilians burned down the
hospital with everyone in it.' Or if you ask them about politicians
today they'll tell you they wish Dr Francia would come back,
since he was the last politician who wasn't corrupt; you'll go
back to your hotel, look up Dr Francia and discover he died in
1840. It's rather like walking up to someone in London, asking
directions to a pub and suddenly finding yourself in a conversation about what Henry VIII would do if he were still in charge.
But then few countries have a history as dramatic as Paraguay's,
every move of which seems to play into the story of its anthem.

   Most histories of the country start with the Jesuits, who arrived
in 1607 and didn't just try to convert the existing population,
most of whom spoke a language called Guarani, but also tried
to take them out of the Spanish colonial system, which had been
treating them as a source of labour and women. The Jesuits set
up *reducciós* – villages, effectively – where as well as being taught
about the glory of Jesus they were taught skills including music.
Non-Jesuit Europeans were banned from entering. The Spanish
eventually came to see these enclaves as such a threat to their

imperialist project that the Jesuits were expelled from all of South America in 1767, the *reduccións* left to decay into picturesque ruins.

Other histories begin with the day Paraguay got independence, on 14 May 1811, when a handful of men slipped out of an alleyway in the middle of Asunción, took control of the main army barracks, then pulled eight of its cannons to the governor's house and demanded that he give up power. Like most people faced with eight cannons would, he promptly did so. The fact it only took a small group to achieve this, and they didn't even have to fire a shot, tells you all you need to know about what a backwater Spain considered this country.

However, the place Paraguay's history *really* begins is when José Gaspar Rodríguez de Francia y Velasco – Dr Francia for short – was voted to power in 1814 and soon afterwards became El Supremo, Paraguay's first dictator and the first of a long line of rulers who most people outside the country saw as lunatics. Maybe people should have seen it coming. Dr Francia had a long nose and cloak and would have looked more at home sweeping vampirically through the halls of some crumbling castle than living in the centre of South America.

Dr Francia acted in the impulsive way you expect of a dictator: he established a secret police to crack down on opposition; he banned anyone from standing within six paces of him, to foil assassination attempts; and he decreed that prostitutes should wear golden combs in their hair (both to show what a noble profession it was – Dr Francia being a great advocate of sex before, outside and instead of marriage – and to mock Spanish women who wore such combs as fashion accessories).

But he also went further than most dictators do and closed Paraguay off from the world. Literally. He shut its borders and banned anyone from going in or out, like a nineteenth-century North Korea. He was helped in this by Paraguay's geography – the tangled forests that then dominated its north, the deep rivers to its south whose currents few wanted to tackle, the arid Chaco to its west. He did it, most people think, because he wanted to create a self-sufficient nation, one that could survive without any influence from its giant neighbours, Argentina and Brazil, both of whom had designs on the country (Argentina didn't recognise Paraguay's independence until 1852). He did his best to achieve that aim, taking land from the aristocracy and Church and giving it to the poor, and diversifying the country's agriculture. If you were a Spanish merchant, you would have hated him for it, but if you were an illiterate peasant, what was not to like?

Dr Francia also put in place policies to ensure Paraguay's culture flourished, banning Spaniards from marrying each other so they had to integrate with the locals, and forcing people to speak Guarani. Those measures also apparently included declaring a song, 'Tetã Purahéi', as the country's first anthem. Some say the music for it has been lost, and that it must have sounded like a Paraguayan folk tune – one of the sad ballads known as *guaranias*. Others say it sounded like any other military march, apart from its chorus, which weirdly jumped into a waltz.

Regardless of the music, the lyrics have survived. They are in Guarani rather than Spanish, Francia apparently saying to a poet, 'I don't want it in the language of the Spanish foreigner; write it in the people's language,' but they are perhaps most important as evidence that Paraguay's culture has always been one based on fearless self-sacrifice. 'Our arms, our lives, are due to this country,' it starts, 'slaves we'll never be.' 'Brave Paraguayans, / Will you suffer insults / And lose your name and glory, / Or die a thousand times?' asks one verse. 'Die! Die! Die!' comes back the answer a verse later. In the late 1820s, Dr Francia was so worried about Argentina's designs on the country that he even had that message written into Paraguay's flag, ordering the words 'Long live the Republic of Paraguay. Independence or death!' to be embroidered on to all of them. It was stamped on to all official documents too.

Dr Francia became ill in 1840. Knowing he was to die, some say he burned all his papers and refused medical aid. After he died,

some of the country's old Spanish families apparently stole his
body, cut it up and threw it in a river, but by then the Spanish and
Guarani populations were so entwined, there was no going back.

*

Just four years after Dr Francia's death, Paraguay got its second
dictator, Carlos Antonio López. He was obese – 'a great sea of
meat' – with more chins than most portrait painters would feel
safe tackling. He had the looks, in other words, of a man who
would take Dr Francia's legacy and build something genuinely
cruel out of it. But he actually did the opposite, opening the
borders and calling in experts from across the continent and
Europe to help modernise the country. He became a president
of firsts, building Paraguay's first railway, its first shipyard and
foundry, and giving it its postal service. He boosted its intellectual
and cultural life too, opening its first theatre and its first secondary
school. He was a builder more than a tyrant, in other words.
And is he remembered for his achievements today? Barely, it
seems. I found one mural of him in Asunción, featuring him
staring out sternly from the site of the country's first newspaper,
the *Independent Paraguayan* (another thing he set up). No one was
giving it a moment's notice.

During his reign, López also modernised the anthem, deciding
it needed to be in Spanish. That was the language of the future
in South America, he realised, and of diplomacy too. It was the
one that foreigners understood – and they were, in many ways,
the real audience for this song, the people who López needed to
recognise the country's sovereignty as others tried to undermine
it. He translated 'Tetã Purahéi' himself, but, clearly unhappy, is
said to have reached out to Vicente López y Planes, the poet
behind Argentina's anthem, for words to act as a brand-new
anthem. It seems a somewhat wild story – López contacting an
Argentine who probably thought Paraguay should not exist – but

Vicente is meant to have asked for 1,000 pesos, an unbelievably expensive sum at the time, and so the matter was dropped. Fortunately for López, a Uruguayan poet, Francisco Acuña de Figueroa, heard about Paraguay's search and sent some words of his own, free, 'dedicated to the republic and its most worthy president' (he might have also been asked; the facts are disputed). He sent a whole seven verses, a song that somehow manages to take in tortuous references to Romulus and Remus, the founders of Rome, and include such direct lines as:

> There is no middle ground between free and slave,
> an abyss divides the two
> ...
> Sound the cry, 'Republic or death!'

In 1853, Carlos had the words printed in his newspaper. It is doubtful anyone realised just how prophetic they would turn out to be.

*

Paraguay's third dictator was López's son, Francisco Solano López – the man whose face you see sprayed across so many of Asunción's walls. His name is everywhere too – I got on several buses named the *Mariscal López* after him.

There are two things everyone will tell you about Mariscal López, who took charge after his father's death in 1862. The first is that his partner was an Irish prostitute, Eliza Lynch, who he met while in Paris trying to buy arms. Eliza's European ways were not welcomed by polite Paraguayan society, which in the twenty-two years since Dr Francia's death had not kept up his friendly attitude to prostitution. Madame Lynch's response to the elite snubbing her seems to have been to insult them right back. One day she invited dozens of Asunción's most notable women to a grand banquet on a boat then, just after it had set off, ordered all the food to be thrown into the river, the women forced to watch as the fish and meat, the sauces and fruit salads congealed across its surface, the food mocking them as they wilted in the sun.

Eliza also became infamous for throwing parties in the ballroom at her house, a room painted so it looked as if vines were crawling across the ceiling and flowers were blooming out of the walls (it is now the dining room of the Gran Hotel del Paraguay). It was at one of those parties that 'República o Muerte' was sung publicly for the first time, on 24 July 1860 – a whole seven years after it was printed, the delay clearly showing that it had been conceived more for diplomatic purposes than anything else. A visiting French pianist played it, and the room erupted into cheers and applause, the noise apparently so loud dozens of locals were soon gathered outside the house's walls, clamouring to hear this new song that Eliza's patronage had instantly made the height of fashion.

Aside from his choice of partner, Mariscal López is also known for seemingly taking the title of 'República o Muerte' as a mission statement. In 1864, Brazil backed a coup in Uruguay – a move he saw as dangerously altering the balance of power in South America. Mariscal López's father had always told him to solve problems with a feather, but he was stubborn, still acting like a spoilt child even as he approached middle age. He gave Brazil an ultimatum: to stop meddling in Uruguay's affairs or face war. Brazil unsurprisingly ignored him – it was a country of 12 million people, Paraguay one of 450,000 – and sent troops into Uruguay, but Mariscal López didn't come to his senses; instead he seized a Brazilian ship, then raided some Brazilian towns. He then sent troops to Uruguay, but Argentina refused to let them across their land, so he declared war on Buenos Aires too.

Paraguay soon found itself fighting three enemies (Uruguay by this point had declared war against it as well) hell-bent, in Mariscal López's words, on ending its existence. 'I am disposed to continue fighting until God . . . decides the definite fate of language he normally refuses to speak), insisted it was banned as soon as the fighting began, both because it was in Spanish and because it was written by a Uruguayan. But Diego Sánchez Haase, one of the country's leading conductors and music historians, was less certain that it disappeared so completely, wondering aloud if such a perfect symbol of Paraguay's spirit could have just disappeared overnight (although he did admit the country went back to Dr Francia's original anthem for those war years).

However, there is little argument that over the next few decades it became a proper anthem, as we would understand the term today, used in efforts to reinvent the country and move it on from its past. The Great War, as they call it, was not a defeat, the country's politicians and historians said, but unquestionable evidence of Paraguayan heroism; Mariscal López was not a madman whose name should never be uttered louder than a whisper, he was the one true patriot. The anthem played into both those myths. By the 1920s, the Instituto Paraguayo, the country's leading cultural body, was even taking the time to create an official version of it to stop the 'anarchy' that often occurred when it was played, there being so many different versions, all in different keys and time signatures, that half the time audiences would just throw each other confused looks as if they weren't quite sure what was going to come next (the institute's version, by composer Remberto Giménez, was officially adopted in 1934).

During that decade, and the early 1930s, the country's pride needed to be restored quickly because Bolivia was making increasingly aggressive moves on the Chaco region, which makes up much of the north and west of Paraguay. The two countries both thought the area contained oil (it still hasn't appeared), and ended up fighting a three-year war over its arid land from 1932 to 1935. Accounts from the time make it sound like the most hideous of conflicts – soldiers used to shoot themselves in the throat because they couldn't take the thirst any more, or beg their commanders to urinate in their mouths so they could have something – anything – to drink. Paraguay emerged victorious, but at the cost of around 40,000 Paraguayan lives. You'd have thought the government would have seen this as a national tragedy; but they seem to have focused more on the fact the country had at last won a fight.

*

The anthem really came into its own, though, during the time of Paraguay's fourth dictator, General Alfredo Stroessner, who ruled from 1954 all the way until 1989. He had leathery, tanned skin, a receded hairline and a tightly clipped moustache, and always wore a military jacket. He looked, in short, like every other Latin American dictator of that time. You could have put him next to Chile's Augusto Pinochet and you would have struggled to tell the difference.

Stroessner acted like those other dictators too, clamping down on all opposition under the guise of fighting communism, often with American support. Sometimes he even clamped down on people who weren't opposed to him, just to help boost his anti-communist credentials. In March 1955, just six months after he had been inaugurated as president, a colony of Ukrainians, Poles and Belarusians who had fled Stalin organised a celebration in the town of Fram, inviting every local dignitary they could think of. They sang the Soviet and Paraguayan anthems as a welcome, which turned out to be a mistake, given that they were already under suspicion for receiving letters in their native languages. Stroessner quickly turned the singing into evidence of a communist plot, and its 'ringleaders' were arrested, beaten, and tortured by having blocks of ice tied to them and being given electric shocks.

Other countries' anthems may not have been heard much in Paraguay after that, but 'República o Muerte' was, Stroessner relying on it to help heighten nationalist sentiment and to try to link his own image with those of both Mariscal López and

Dr Francia (Stroessner was one for personality cults; his name flashed over Asunción at night, although he never sought to rewrite the anthem like, say, Kazakhstan's Nazarbayev has).

It is interesting talking to people about Stroessner's time and seeing how few seemed to get swept up by the nationalism he tried to encourage with the anthem, or if they did, how swiftly that feeling disappeared by the end of his rule. In the south of the country, I visited Santa María de Fe, a former *reducción* consisting of some simple white-walled adobe houses around a square with a church to one side. Trees soared in between the homes, each filled with bright green parrots, the occasional monkey. There I spoke to a middle-aged man called Isabelino Galiano, who was anything but fond of the anthem. He told me it was a 'song for the military, not for the heart . . . During Stroessner's regime, every day you had to sing it – in schools, in the army, everywhere. And when you heard it, you had to sing the whole thing. You know it's got seven verses? You'd start it and you wouldn't be finished for fifteen minutes! The songbook was this thick, like a Bible.'

Isabelino's father was a member of the *Ligas Agrarias*, a religious peasant movement that tried to improve the lot of small farmers until Stroessner decided it was becoming too vocal and clamped down on its leaders. Isabelino's father was among those arrested, labelled a communist, tortured and jailed. Isabelino remembers police being stationed outside his house who demanded to know his every move and who warned people off talking to him. 'If it hadn't been for the [local] priests, I wouldn't have spoken to anyone growing up,' he said.

He told me that the true anthem of the Paraguayan people is actually 'Patria Querida' ('Beloved Homeland'), a song written by a priest in the 1920s to a French dance tune that was originally about soldiers flirting with a waitress. It is a far more optimistic anthem, he said, singing its chorus for me. 'Beloved country, we are your hope, / we are the flowers of your beautiful future.' I

Today, Paraguay is nothing like its past, of course, and that raises a big question for its anthem. What can 'República o Muerte' mean at a time when the country no longer has dictators to sing the anthem for, or invading neighbours to sing it against? When Paraguay is just another developing country, filled with welcoming people and a fascinating culture, but beset by poverty and corruption? I think it is fair to say that for the majority of people its title, at least, does still, deep down, resonate. I asked all kinds of people if they would die for Paraguay, and pretty much all of them said they would, 'if the cause was right'. Occasionally someone would instead say, 'It's easy to die for your country, what's hard to do is to live for it,' but the only reaction I got apart from those two was a woman who said: 'Why would I even want to think about the anthem's meaning? Could you imagine me explaining it to my children? We want you to *die*?'

But even if the majority say they would die for Paraguay, does that mean they actually identify with, or even like, the anthem itself; that they're stirred by its notes whenever it comes on TV? That I'm less sure about, and it didn't help that most people seemed to hold back from being totally honest with me. Paraguay is, after all, a place where it's frowned upon to be anything but patriotic – a country that still sees itself as put upon, a small country struggling for recognition in the shadow of its two giant neighbours. So when a foreigner asks you about your anthem, you have to be positive; you can't be seen to let the nation down. When I asked people to sing the anthem for me, they would often give the most stilted renditions, standing straight, facing forward, their eyes practically begging it to end, but afterwards they would tell me they loved it and couldn't think of a better song. It wasn't as if I had the element of surprise when talking to people about it either, as I learned one day while visiting some Jesuit ruins in the countryside. 'You want to know about my anthem? That's crazy,' a security guard said when we got talking. 'There's a British journalist who's named a book after our anthem and is over here talking to people about it. It's all over Facebook. You should look him up!'

*

'No, no, no, they're lying to you – nobody likes the anthem,' says Diego Darío Florentín Sryvalin, slapping his desk at the Universidad Nacional on the outskirts of Asunción, his voice spiralling upwards in annoyance. 'They say they like it because it's a patriotic symbol and they love their country – everybody loves Paraguay! – but they don't like the anthem. It's sad, it's long, it's too hard to sing. You need to be Plácido Domingo or Andrea Bocelli! Nobody even knows what it means!'

He pulls out a copy of the anthem's lyrics and points at the first two lines:

> *A los pueblos de América, infausto,*
> *Tres centurias un cetro oprimió.*

'The people of the Americas were unfortunately oppressed for three centuries by a sceptre,' it means, the sceptre a somewhat archaic reference to Spanish rule. Diego thwacks the words repeatedly with his thumb. '"*InFAUSto*"? Who knows the meaning of that? Nobody! "*CenTURias*"? Nobody knows what that means! We say *siglo* for "century". "*Cetro oPRIMió*"? Nobody! Four words in the first two lines, nobody here understands! Four words! Nobody!'

The reason I arranged to meet Diego is that he's the only academic I have ever heard of having done a grammatical analysis of his national anthem. I'd spoken to him on the phone before visiting and he told me that he spent his childhood ashamed of not understanding the song, fearing it meant he wasn't actually patriotic. He'd also been regularly humiliated by it. 'Every day we had to sing it at school,' he said, 'and if you were late, they made you sing it alone in the middle of the school. It was torture! They punished you with this song.'

Despite that phone call, I wasn't expecting Diego to be quite so exasperated by the words that Francisco Acuña de Figueroa wrote 160 years ago. 'Look at the grammar,' he booms, 'nobody can work out what is the subject and what is the object, or what adjective goes with what noun. It's ridiculous!' He starts explaining the poetic concept of hyperbaton, which basically means swapping words around in sentences to appear clever, something the anthem contains lots of. 'It's . . .' He flicks around on a translation program, looking for the English word to express his anger. 'It's stupid!' he says. His two office-mates stifle smirks, but by this point even Diego's laughing at the absurdity of just how much annoyance the song causes him. 'And look at this word, *"enalzaron"*. I had to contact the Real Academia Española [the guardians of the Spanish language] to ask what it meant. It's not in the dictionary. And they tell me it's from the 1300s. In a Bible. It's a name of God. Who's going to know that? No one knows!'

It takes him about half an hour to explain all his problems with the first verse alone. 'So what would you like it changed to?' I ask.

'Change the anthem?' he replies. 'How can you change an anthem? It's a national symbol. We might not understand it, we might not like singing it, but we love it.' I look at him confused, given he appears to be completely contradicting himself. 'It's like God, y'know? You don't know God, but you love God.' I don't look any less confused. 'Or like your wife,' he tries. 'You love her, but sometimes . . .' He starts laughing again. 'It's complicated!'

*

'Acuña de Figueroa could write about anything,' says Coriún Aharonián, a sprightly, bald musicologist, sitting among dozens of filing cabinets in his office in Montevideo, the capital of Uruguay. 'And I mean anything. He could write about very stupid daily things, like what is happening in the neighbourhood, to very important things, like God. And,' he says, pausing for effect, 'he was supposedly the author of a lot of pornographic songs, and he also blacked up so he could write in the jargon of slaves.'

I cough into my tea in surprise and he gives me a knowing smile. It is fair to say that I wasn't expecting those last two revelations when I walked into Coriún's office. I wasn't even meaning to talk to him about Acuña de Figueroa. I've travelled overnight 1,000 miles south to see him because I was hoping he could shed some light on why exactly the Paraguayan anthem sounds so operatic; why, in fact, most of South America's anthems do. Those were the two questions I had outstanding from my time in Paraguay. There, no one had been able to help, simply guessing – 'Wasn't Argentina's first? That's operatic. Maybe we copied it from them' – or pointing out that 'We are a very passionate people' as if that explained everything, and so I realised I had to come here, to the city where both the poet and musician behind Paraguay's anthem had lived.

Coriún had already started answering those questions. 'In the 1800s, we were still very much in a colonial world,' he said when I arrived, 'but what happened here and in Argentina, and eventually Paraguay, is the fashion changed. The cultural fashion. And everyone suddenly went from being kind of prisoners of Spain, musically speaking, to discovering Italy, opera especially.'

However, he added, I had to realise that the music wasn't the place to start with any South American anthem. The continent's governments never actually seemed that worried about the music. What was important to them at first was having some words written down, officially, on paper, in law, as if the anthems were just something to ruminate on in a library rather than hear. And if I was starting with the words to Paraguay's anthem, I needed to start with the pornographer.

*

Francisco Acuña de Figueroa, portly and with sideburns so bushy they seemed to double the width of his face, was not the sort of man you would expect to write one national anthem, let alone two. He was born in 1790 in Montevideo, the son of the Spanish royal treasurer, and he grew up devoted to the Spanish throne, admitting he felt like he had lost his 'country, employment and home' when the Spanish were eventually thrown out of Uruguay in 1814. He even went in exile to Rio de Janeiro for a few years afterwards, unable to cope with the new order of things, and so he could work for the Spanish crown from there. When he eventually returned to the city, his past somehow didn't get in the way of him becoming one of Uruguay's most important officials (he was director of the national library and museum) or one of its most popular poets and songwriters. He might not have been the best of those, but he was certainly among the most entertaining, and as Coriún delights in mentioning, he also did his best to serve people's baser needs.

He wrote one poem called 'Apology for the Penis', for instance, that consists of little more than a hundred synonyms for that appendage ('Sausage, trunk and sweet potatoes, eggplant, gun and schoolmaster'). This was apparently his way of proving the penis is better than the vagina ('For which there are only eight names, and none worth a damn'). How he went from one day writing that, to the next writing celebrated religious texts, is something no historian appears to have been able to answer. 'His life is a bad example for schoolchildren . . . but respectability is not a criterion for literary appreciation,' wrote one.

In the late 1820s, Acuña de Figueroa took a turn no one would have predicted, given his royalist past: he was afflicted by a bout of patriotism for his new nation and decided to write it an anthem. No one asked him to, he just decided, somewhat narcissistically, that he should be the one to do so, the only poet deserving of having such a place in Uruguay's history. The government rejected his offer, so he tried again, and then again. He made five attempts

over several years, in fact, until in 1833 one of his efforts was
finally deemed acceptable. 'Orientals, the fatherland or the grave!'
it goes, Orientals, or Easterns, just being another name for
Uruguayans (the country's full name is República Oriental del
Uruguay because it is on the east of the Uruguayan river). 'Liberty,
or with glory we die!' it then adds.

> This is the vow that the soul pronounces,
> and which we, heroes, will fulfil.

Some people attacked the song as being so full of 'poetic junk'
it wasn't worth singing (by its end, it's talking about 'the spear
of Mars' and 'the dagger of Brutus'), but it was clearly popular,
and when a few years later he wrote similar words for Paraguay,
the government there clearly thought they had something too.

Acuña de Figueroa didn't write the music for either anthem,
though, so the only thing that actually guaranteed that they became
operatic was their composer. Francisco José Debali was born in
Romania (then ruled by Hungary), and seems to have been something of a child prodigy as he soon moved to Vienna to study
under Franz Süssmayr, the Austrian composer who had an affair
with Mozart's wife and completed Mozart's Requiem after his
death. Debali eventually ended up in Piedmont in northern Italy,
where he worked as the director of several military bands. It is
there, you have to assume, that his taste for opera was formed and
where, less positively, he realised he would never become as
successful as the man he had studied under. He had a choice: to
carry on toiling away in Piedmont, or to try his luck elsewhere,
so in about 1837, already in his late thirties, he headed for Brazil.

Back then, Brazil was regularly described as a paradise – a land
where fruit was always within your reach and gold was never far
beneath your feet. It was also a country in desperate need of
musicians to entertain European settlers. But when Debali
arrived, all he found was yellow fever, and so he was soon on

another boat, this time to Montevideo, where he became music director of the city's theatre (photos from the time show him in the black tie you would expect of a conductor, but with thin, round spectacles more suited to an accountant). Little is known about Debali's life in the city, or about the music he wrote at that time – most of his papers and sheet music were destroyed while being used as an improvised barricade during a war with Brazil – but in 1846 he entered a competition to provide music for the Uruguayan anthem (thirteen years after Acuña de Figueroa's words were chosen). Debali wrote three entries. One ended up going down so well with the public it became Uruguay's anthem; another, Acuña de Figueroa eventually took to become Paraguay's anthem (he first suggested singing it to the same tune as Uruguay's); the third was lost.

A lot of people argue with that story, pointing out there's no sheet music for either anthem with his name on, and Debali didn't speak Spanish so couldn't have possibly written music to such words. The initial government decree for Uruguay's anthem also had the name of another musician on it, which Debali did not challenge until 1855, when he wrote in to a newspaper saying he hadn't realised the music had been for something so important because he was so 'ignorant of the language'. But Coriún says it is impossible to decide either way. There are points in both anthems where the music and words are such a bad fit that maybe they could have only been written by a confused foreigner.

Both Debali's anthems (we'll give him the benefit of the doubt) could not sound more operatic. Uruguay's is even regularly criticised for being a rip-off of the 'Prologue' of Donizetti's opera *Lucrezia Borgia* (the criticism seems a bit unfair since they only share nine notes – Argentina's anthem is far more reminiscent of one of Clementi's sonatinas and, as we have previously mentioned, there are plenty of other far more egregious examples of anthem-borrowing). But why did Debali choose that style? Coriún is adamant it was just fashion and that he was simply fitting in with the existing anthems on the continent. Argentina's, Chile's and Brazil's, all of which had been adopted by the time Debali arrived in Uruguay, were operatic too.

But I think that answer is a shame, as it makes it seem as if Debali was just a gun for hire, writing to other people's whims rather than his own. Why can't it be that this was the music he loved and he happened to write the best tunes, two songs so good that two governments felt compelled to make them their anthems? If he had loved military marches maybe the anthems would have ended up in that style instead. Most of the other composers of South American anthems were opera fanatics like Debali. Francisco Manuel da Silva, who wrote Brazil's, founded that country's opera academy; both Bolivia's and Colombia's anthems were written by Italians; Ecuador's by a Frenchman who only went to South America in the first place because he was touring with an opera company. Of course fashion influenced things, but I would prefer to give all these composers their due.

*

Writing the two anthems didn't seem to bring Debali any fame. A couple of days after talking to Coriún, I went searching for his grave in Montevideo's main cemetery with Julio Huertas, a pianist and expert on Debali's life. We walked around for a few minutes, past statues of famous bankers with angels at their feet and clucking hens who had made the cemetery their home, until Julio said, 'I think he was buried here,' pointing at some mud-covered yellow and black tiles on the ground. 'It was a communal grave. He was just thrown in with everyone else. He was foreign and the people back then didn't care much for foreigners.'

'You said he "was" buried there,' I said.

'Yes, he's not there now. His body was stolen by the owners of a soap factory across the road.' The soap magnates, Julio said,

had found a treasure map they believed would take them to gold
left in Montevideo by Garibaldi, the legendary general who
unified Italy. They dug a tunnel from their factory to where the
'X' marked the spot, but all they found were the remains of an
unloved composer and the many builders and craftsmen who
had been buried alongside him.

'Where's his body now?' I asked. Julio just shrugged, clearly
disappointed by how little people cared.

*

Uruguay's anthem has essentially the same message as Paraguay's:
its cry of 'The Fatherland or the grave' almost interchangeable
with 'Republic or death'. But while in the country, I was repeatedly
told that it did not have the same hold on people as Paraguay's
does and that there is only one day a year when it is sung with
any meaning: 20 May, when there is a march through the middle
of Montevideo in memory of the 192 'missing', the people who
disappeared during Uruguay's dictatorship of the 1970s and 1980s.
As one woman was telling me this in the old city hall, she suddenly
realised one of the leaders of that march worked as a repairman
there, which was why I soon found myself listening to Amaral
García Hernández, a forty-something who looked like he should
be fronting a punk band, his hair almost mohawked and his
T-shirt ripped, tell his desperately sad story.

'I've got many memories of my parents,' he said at one point,
'but they barely have any movement to them. They're almost
like photographs. Eating soup together around the table, the
three of us. Another time we were eating fish and a piece flew
into my eye from the hot saucepan. How I screamed! I haven't
eaten fish since.' He smiled and his eyes glistened. 'I have another
image of my father pulling up a tree by the roots, but it was
probably really a twig. And I remember my mother's long hair,
so sweet. And I remember when they were abducted.'

Uruguay became a dictatorship in the 1970s, the military using a clampdown on the Tupamaros – a left-wing guerrilla movement who started out simply pulling pranks but quickly moved on to kidnapping – as an excuse to take power. Amaral's parents were members of the group; his father missed his birth because he'd been jailed for his membership. When Amaral was six months old, his father was released on the condition that he left the country and so the family moved to Chile, then Buenos Aires. His parents tried to stay active in their opposition, but collaboration between all of South America's military governments at this time meant they were soon being looked for and had to continually move from house to house and assume false identities. On 20 December 1974, the family went to a birthday party. The food ran out and so his father left to buy a chicken. An hour passed and his mother guessed something was wrong. She swept Amaral up and started saying her goodbyes, but before she could finish, some men burst into the room. 'We already have your husband. Come with us,' was all they said. Amaral's parents were flown back to Uruguay on a clandestine flight. They were the first people 'disappeared' under Operation Condor, a US-backed campaign across South America to suppress communists. A few weeks later, they turned up in a ditch an hour outside Montevideo, 'riddled with bullets', according to the official report. 'My father's name was Floreal Gualberto García,' Amaral said formally, as if he needed to guarantee every letter was written down for the record. 'My mother's was Mirtha Yolanda Hernández.'

Amaral did not know his parents had been murdered, of course. He was three at the time of their abduction and he started being brought up in Argentina by the very member of the Argentinian secret service who had infiltrated his parents' group. He was renamed Juan and he lived as Juan, loved and cared for ('I won't deny I loved my new family dearly') until he was fourteen, when Uruguay's dictatorship collapsed and his parents' families were able to trace him. He had spent much of his early life in Argentina confused, he said, sure that he remembered his original parents. 'Every time I asked my stepmother about them, she told me it was a dream. But I thought it wasn't. Every time I brought them up, I could see in their faces, they were worried: what should they tell this child?'

As soon as Amaral found out who his parents really were, he of course asked what had happened to them; who had killed them and why; how had those people been punished; were they in jail; if not, what could he do to put them there? He didn't get any answers and he probably never will – a few years after the dictatorship ended, Uruguay passed an immunity law pardoning anyone who had committed crimes during the dictatorship. This was something it felt it had to do, since so many people had been involved with the dictatorship and so many others had been victims (one in fifty Uruguayans having been locked up at some point) that many felt it was better to pretend it never happened. Amaral said he feels lucky in some respects. 'My parents are dead; they are not missing. I don't have that double pain where you don't know.' But then he told me that some days he was still overcome thinking about them and who pulled the trigger. 'I don't go around asking people, "Did you murder my father?" But it could have happened that at one time I helped someone cross the street and that person was my father's murderer. Sometimes I want to know. Sometimes I ask myself, "Do I really need to know?" It's crazy.'

I asked Amaral about Uruguay's anthem, and he explained how it was used during the dictatorship. 'It's meant to be the most sacred song in terms of nation, country, culture, so if a military cop was beating you, you could start singing it and they had to stop,' he said. 'It had to be respected.' He started laughing at the image, before checking himself, worried that I might not share his dark sense of humour. 'Yes, some didn't give a fuck about it and kept beating the shit out of people even when they were singing at the top of their voice, but it did become this tool to try and fight aggression.' People also used the anthem to show their hatred of the dictatorship, he said. At any event where they were made to sing it, they would do so quietly until they got to the words '*Tiranos, temblad*' – 'Tyrants, tremble' – then they would scream that line, three times, as if hoping their very voices could bring an end to the regime.

I asked how he feels about the song now, when he sings it on the marches for the disappeared. If he were your traditional activist he would say how it moved him, that at those moments he remembers his parents and knows that even if the government doesn't want to give him justice, there are thousands calling for it with him. But things are never so simple. 'Yes, I sing the anthem,' he said. 'There are people on those marches who inspire me and I love those people and I don't want to disrespect them. And I feel that by singing I help them feel like we're not alone in this. But, well, the people who were in favour of the dictatorship also sang it and just as loud, so then what's the point?

'*Himno e hypnosis*,' he added – 'anthem hypnosis' – as if that was the best way to describe the effect of these songs. I got his point – that what anthems do is fool people into believing in something for a short space of time; that they lead people into negative nationalism just as much as they can make people act positively; that in themselves, in his country at least, they don't change anything. But at the same time I wanted to tell him I didn't see that entirely as a bad thing. I wanted to tell him that in Paraguay I had met people who genuinely believed in the message of 'República o Muerte' – a song they could not even understand the grammar of. I had even met people who told me they were willing to die for their country, and they meant that in a good way, to improve their country's situation, not a bad one.

In fact, worryingly, I felt that despite all the stories I had heard like his, of lives destroyed under regimes, the one thing I had really learned about anthems in South America was that the continent had actually got them right. It had decided to make them over-the-top, in both music and lyrics, to focus on people's enjoyment of them above anything else, and in that sense people were more likely to find something in them than they would in the anthems of, say, Europe or Africa, even if it was just a chance to jump up and down while shouting their introductions. In Uruguay, everyone I had met before Amaral had enjoyed singing their anthem for me, no matter whether they believed it meant something or not.

A few days later, Amaral sent me an email. He'd been thinking about a question I asked: what song he would choose to be Uruguay's anthem if he had to? He had chosen a 'somewhat hilarious' Uruguayan rock song from the mid-nineties. I gave it a listen. The final lines are:

> If there's no other choice than liberty or death,
> I'll be the first deserter.

*

Mariano González Parra doesn't seem to want to let go of my hand at the entrance to the *Armada Paraguaya* in downtown Asunción. He just keeps on shaking it, as if he can never thank me enough for giving him the chance to speak about how much he loves his country and its anthem. He makes me promise I'll return; a poor naval cadet is made to take photos; another is sent off to try to find something to give me as a gift, coming back, slightly embarrassed, with a Paraguayan navy pen. It feels like I'm never going to be allowed to leave, so when I finally do manage to extricate myself and get into my part-time interpreter Silvia's car, I start to joke about it – until I realise she's crying. So much so, in fact, that she seems to be having trouble even getting the key into the ignition.

'I'm sorry,' she says. 'I can't help it. They're happy tears, I promise. It's just you don't know how much I'm enjoying my job right now. I find it so inspiring meeting someone like that, someone who cares so much for this country. This place is filled with so much corruption and we should be so much better than we are, but most people don't seem to care, so to meet someone like him, who does care, who is patriotic . . .' She wipes her eyes with the back of her hand, managing to start the car at last.

'I had an argument last night with my flatmate about you,' she says as she pulls out into the road. 'She said, "Why's he coming here? The people who that anthem's about – the Lópezes, Dr Francia – they died a hundred years ago. Doesn't he realise there are no heroes any more? No one believes in that message." And I said to her, "What do you mean? I'm a hero. Every day, I die a little bit for this country. I could be working abroad, but I choose to work here as a teacher and every day I go to school and it's hard, but I want to improve this country; I want it to meet its potential. So the anthem might not mean something to you, but it does me."' She pulls up to some lights and I reach into my bag. 'It's okay, I don't need a tissue,' she says, and I have to stumble out an apology as I wasn't ever reaching for one, but for a notebook so I could write down everything she just said: that national anthems do still mean something; that every day Silvia dies a little for the Republic of Paraguay.

Nous sommes la Suisse

Une croix blanche sur la poitrine,
En chantant cet hymne, nous avançons,
Traversent nos vallées, et montagnes,
L'égalité et le respect en tout, pour tout le monde,
Renforçons démocratie, liberté et paix,
Vous avez vos guerres, le sang, (x2)
Mais nous sommes, toujours, la Suisse! (x2)

—

A white cross upon our chest,
By singing this hymn, we go forward,
Across our valleys and mountains,
Equality and respect in everything we do, for everyone,
To strengthen democracy, freedom and peace,
You have your wars, your blood, (x2)
But we are, always, the Swiss! (x2)

Epilogue

HOW NOT TO WRITE A NATIONAL ANTHEM

I didn't appreciate quite how hard it is to write a national anthem until I tried it for myself. The nation (un)fortunate to be my subject in this was Switzerland, a place I had, up until that point, spent all of a week in, most of it falling face first into snow.

I hadn't just picked it at random; on 1 January 2014, the Swiss Society for Public Good had launched a search for a new anthem, having decided that the country could go on no longer with the 'Swiss Psalm'. That song was written in 1841, and it says absolutely nothing about Switzerland today, the society said. They had a point – the 'Psalm' sounds more like a biblical weather forecast than anything else, being filled with lines like, 'When the Alps grow bright with splendour, / Pray, free Swiss, pray.' Someone at least needs to write new words to the old tune, the society said, and so it set up a competition to pick some.

Since by then I probably knew more about national anthems than most of the people who wrote them, I decided to give it my best shot. So I sat down, pen in hand, and tried to think of something – anything – original to say about Switzerland's scenery: those mountains that you never seem able to lose sight of; those lakes that seem to beckon you to run off the nearest pier and jump straight into them. What's a good word for those? I asked myself. 'Glistening'? 'Luminescent'? I flicked through a rhyming dictionary, stared at a thesaurus, but after three hours,

I had got nowhere. I just had a page of clichés – words like 'glistening' and 'luminescent' – with 'THIS IS RUBBISH' scrawled across them.

In the afternoon, I gave up on that approach and decided to try to conjure a few lines based on the life of William Tell, the only legendary Swiss figure I could think of – the man who shot an apple off his son's head, then promptly shot another into an Austrian bureaucrat, single-handedly creating Switzerland in the process. His was a story so filled with drama it could surely inspire anyone, so I started trying to turn it into a call to arms for the Swiss today, urging them to 'grab their crossbows' and fight for his ideals. A few moments later, I realised that most Swiss couldn't grab a crossbow even if they wanted to, but I persevered. About five hours after that, I looked at my pad. There, in poor French, was the result of a day's work. It amounted to three lines:

> We no longer have crossbows,
> And our names aren't Tell,
> But his spirit's in us until the end.

I read it again. It didn't get better.

*

I put myself through this ordeal partly, as you would hope, to better understand the world's anthem composers and what they had achieved. But, let's be honest, I also did it for the prize money; 10,000 Swiss francs was on offer to the winner – a fortune in anthem terms, given that most composers get nothing. The competition's entry form didn't make writing an anthem sound too difficult, either. Anyone could enter, whether they were a Swiss goatherd or an Angolan fisherman, it said. All they had to do was conjure a song that was easily singable in French, German,

Italian or Romansh – the last a language spoken by only 60,000 people in the south-east of the country. It had to be based on the values in the Swiss constitution, such as respecting diversity and realising that 'the strength of a people is measured by the wellbeing of its weakest members'. Oh, and it had to be 'stylistically and artistically timeless'. I decided I'd jump that final hurdle when I came to it.

I didn't take the task of writing this anthem lightly. After my first appalling attempt, I travelled to Switzerland so I could get a better idea of what the country was like and ask the competition's judges exactly what they were after ('We'll consider anything as long as it's not racist, sexist or too nationalist' was the slightly unhelpful reply). I also spoke with people in the street there to find out just what they wanted in a new anthem. When I asked a teacher in Zurich what he most liked about his country, he stared out over the city's lake for such a long time I thought he'd forgotten the question. But then he finally turned around, inspired. 'I really like this lake,' he said, proudly.

'So how would you get that into an anthem?' I asked. 'What would be its first line?'

'Er . . . "Oh, lovely lake"?' he said. 'Would that work?'

However, none of that research seemed to help when, a few weeks later, I sat down to try writing the anthem again. I stared at the blank screen on my laptop and it stared back, the cursor flashing impatiently. The biggest problem was that there seemed to be nothing dramatic in the Swiss constitution to write about. I read and reread it and couldn't find anything to latch on to. I mean, an anthem about the Swiss being 'resolved to renew their alliance . . . in a spirit of solidarity and openness to the world' or being 'conscious of their responsibility to future generations'? Where's the fun in that? Where's the excitement? Where are the wars, the blood? That is what all the best anthems are about. It's hard to rally a people together when there's nothing to rally against. Why can't the Swiss dump their blessed neutrality and be a bit more aggressive?

And then it hit me – that frustration is exactly what I should put into the song. I immediately started typing. '*Vous avez vos guerres, / Vous avez votre sang,*' I wrote, almost without thinking. '*Mais nous sommes la Suisse. / Nous sommes la Suisse!*' You've got your wars, you've got your blood, but we are the Swiss. We are the Swiss! All right, it wasn't much better than what I'd written before, but at least with a bit of tweaking I could make it fit the tune and it did say *something* about Swiss values, namely that they don't like killing people. I could even picture crowds screaming, 'We are the Swiss!' at sports events. It was a shame there were five more lines to go.

*

When I first heard about the Swiss contest, I thought it was a fantastic idea. Here was a country getting rid of an unloved anthem for once, rather than miserably holding on to it and quietly hoping a revolution would come along to force a change. I also admired its desire to modernise the anthem, to in effect create the first for the twenty-first century – one that is not so much about a country, but about its people's values. If the organisers were successful, they would end up with a song that couldn't be dismissed by anyone as just banal nationalism. Who could argue against an anthem that called on people to be tolerant and to care about their environment, rather than telling them the scenery outside their window is nice or that God is watching over them?

The problem was, the more I thought about it, the more I realised that Switzerland had next to no chance of producing a decent anthem this way. The world's greatest anthems weren't chosen through competitions or written by committee; they emerged by accident. They were composed on the spur of the moment, in a single night or over a few exhausting days, written by people panicking that their country was about to be overrun, or breathless with excitement at having seen the last of some long-despised regime. It's exactly because they're written at such times that they have melodies that crawl into your gut and words so vivid you're almost afraid of singing them. That's why people always come back to the best anthems, whether they are Brazilians throwing Molotov cocktails while protesting against bus prices or Tunisians kick-starting the Arab Spring. It's much harder to conjure such passions when you're writing to a deadline or trying to make a song comply point by point with a set of rules.

(Yes, some of my favourites – like Nepal's – were written for competitions, as were other much-loved anthems like Turkey's, but even those were written at critical times in those countries' histories; moments that could inspire anyone. They weren't written during any ordinary year.)

The other nagging problem I started to have with Switzerland's quest was the very thing that had made it so appealing in the first place: that focus on values and that desire to write an anthem open to the world rather than closed off from it. I'm just not convinced that people actually enjoy singing about the values they hold. In every country I travelled to for this book, I asked people to sing their anthem, and the place people enjoyed doing so most was the one where the anthem was most anachronistic: France. 'La Marseillaise' waits six whole verses before talking about France's cherished *liberté*; another three before mentioning *égalité*. *Fraternité* doesn't even get a look-in. You could argue they simply enjoyed singing it because the tune is fantastic, but that music demands the words it has – a melody as aggressive as 'La Marseillaise' wouldn't work if it had, say, the words to Swaziland's anthem over it, everyone praying to God 'to grant us eternal wisdom without deceit or malice'.

There has been one previous attempt to write a modern anthem. In 1971, U Thant, then Secretary General of the United Nations, asked W. H. Auden to compose one for the organisation's twenty-fifth anniversary, saying the world had enough war songs already. 'Let music for peace / be the paradigm,' it goes.

> For peace means to change
> at the right time,
> as the world clock,
> goes tick and tock.

It was performed at the anniversary celebrations. It wasn't brought out again twenty-five years later.

*

When I started this book, I set out to find out if anthems were important – even I-M-P-O-R-T-A-N-T at that. I wanted to know if they really had been at the centre of global events, wars and revolutions, to discover if protestors were managing to hold back police just by singing them and, likewise, if police were keeping people in jail just for playing with their words. But deep down I feared that what I'd actually discover was that anthems are meaningless – sung solely through force of habit by bored schoolchildren and drunken sports fans – and that the only function they now serve is to gently remind the forgetful of where they were born. I worried that if that were the case this book would end up simply as a collection of anecdotes with a title like *The Wacky World of Anthems*. It would be filled with fascinating but ultimately inconsequential facts, such as that Greece's anthem is based on a 158-verse poem (luckily for every Greek, its government only adopted two of them for the official version).

The highlight of that book would have been a few pages outlining the (admittedly brilliant) story behind Mexico's anthem – the only one written out of lust. In 1853, Mexico's government launched a contest for words for a new anthem and a woman called Guadalupe González del Pino begged her poet fiancé, Francisco González Bocanegra, to enter. He, however, didn't fancy it – perhaps he was afraid his poems weren't good enough, or perhaps he just wasn't very patriotic – so one day she is meant to have taken him to her parents' house, whispered suggestively in his ear at the kitchen table and dragged him to a bedroom. The couple paused at the door, Pili – as she was known – pulling Francisco close for a kiss and beginning to untuck his shirt. But just as he was about to grab her dress, she kicked him inside, slammed the door and bolted it shut. Francisco looked up to find himself in a room covered with paintings of Mexican military victories, piles of dead Spaniards everywhere. Pili shouted through the wood that he wouldn't be let out until he had written an anthem, and stomped off. Francisco sullenly slipped ten verses under the door four hours later.

As entertaining as such stories are, I feared that if they were all I could find to talk about, I would be forced to conclude that anthems aren't important at all, merely curiosities that should be filed away in museums' sound archives along with the half-remembered speeches of dead politicians and old television theme tunes.

But gradually, as I travelled from place to place, that fear lifted. The more I looked into these songs, the more I realised just how much they still say about countries – their characters, their history, their politics – and also just what an impact they've had. Armies *have* fought wars while singing these songs. Protestors *have* used them to help bring down governments. Some of the most important figures in recent history have toyed with them in an effort to manipulate voters, while others have tried using them to heal bitter divides. For a good few hundred years, they have either been at the centre of world events or reflecting them in ways you wouldn't believe minute-long songs could.

But I don't think it's that which really drove home the importance of anthems to me; instead, it was learning the personal impact they have had. These are songs that have ruined some people's lives, weighing families and communities down like the worst of tragedies. You only have to go to Japan or Bosnia to realise that. But they have also inspired people, made them dream about what their countries could be – should be, in fact – encouraging them to take stands and risks I could never take myself, or just to work harder and treat their neighbours a little better. Just think of Paraguay's anthem, or even South Africa's. It's not just hard-core nationalists who find worth in these songs either – your stereotypical flag-waving bigots with their allegiance literally tattooed on their chests – it's everyone from teachers to heroin addicts to the most arrogant of rappers. And when I saw all the ways these songs have influenced individuals I had to decide, with a little relief, that, yes, anthems are a little bit I-M-P-O-R-T-A-N-T after all.

This doesn't mean I've become an evangelist for them and that I think people should stand and bellow them at every opportunity. Far from it. I still think my own is ludicrous. If you asked me to sing 'God Save the Queen' right now, I would probably just laugh, a little embarrassed, search though my pockets as if my phone had started ringing, then run out of the room. But I do think we should be taking these songs a bit more seriously: asking if they are what we want to represent us after all. I don't mean that just lyrically; most of the world's countries really need to ask why their anthems sound so much like Anglican hymns and nothing like the music you hear in their streets.

I admit that asking people to do that might be going a bit far, so perhaps I should set my sights on something smaller instead and ask people to just give some more thought to the men and women who have written anthems, because for songs that are so ever-present – played every day in schools, in sports stadiums and on TV and radio, used as shorthand to represent countries, joked about and mocked, celebrated and praised – it is perverse how unknown the poets and musicians who have written them are. These are people who have tried to give their countries songs of hope and ambition, love and devotion, and in return most have just got a road named after them, normally hidden away on some industrial estate, the street sign rusting, litter piling up below it. Some anthem composers are among the most thoughtful and fun people you could come across; others so dubious I would advise you never go near them. But all deserve more than they have got. And, who knows, if the composers were celebrated, perhaps countries would get better entries the next time they run a competition to change their own.

*

It's January 2015 when I find a letter from Switzerland sitting in my hallway. '*Monsieur*,' it begins, 'in the name of the Swiss Society for Public Good, I want to profoundly thank you for participating in the project to create a new Swiss anthem.' I can hear the 'unfortunately' coming with every word. Yes, there it is: 'Unfortunately, your contribution could not be taken forward.' Bugger, I think. There goes my shot at 10,000 Swiss francs and the chance of having a road named after me in a Zurich business park. But as I keep reading, another sentence catches my eye. 'Despite our decision, we wish to encourage you to carry on pursuing your artistic activity and utilise, if possible, your effort in another manner.' Hang on. Doesn't that mean they think my song could be anthem material after all? That it might not be good enough for Switzerland, but with a little tweaking, a line changed here, a different adjective there, it could be perfect for someone else? There'll surely be some new countries popping up soon. Catalonia, Darfur, Wallonia, perhaps. Maybe I can give it to one of them.

> You have your wars.
> You have your blood.
> But we're the Walloons.
> We are the Walloons!

That has a certain ring to it. Right?

Acknowledgements

An almost overwhelming number of people helped me write this and, if I had space, I would thank everyone I met or spoke to over the years researching it, from those who gave hours of their time to tell me the stories of these songs to those who just gleefully sung me their anthem after I cornered them in the street (then ran away in case I tried to get them to do anything else). But clearly I owe the biggest thanks to the people who wrote these songs – the poets and composers – for making anthems so intriguing that I wanted to investigate them in the first place. I am grateful to every one of those people that I met, as well as to their families and descendants.

I should also apologise to those I spoke to, but was unable to fit in to the final book: Kenrick Georges, who wrote and composed Saint Kitts & Nevis's 'O Land of Beauty!'; Jean-Georges Prosper, who wrote the words to Mauritius's 'Motherland'; Henri Lopès, who wrote the words to 'Les Trois Glorieuses', the anthem of the People's Republic of Congo from 1970 to 1991; Pa Benedict Odiase who wrote the music for Nigeria's 'Arise, O Compatriots' and sadly passed away in 2013; Sota Omoigui who co-wrote the words to Nigeria's anthem; and Mido Samuel who helped write 'South Sudan Oyee!', and spoke to me in pitch darkness a few days before his country gained its independence, as he had no electricity. You all played a huge part in my thinking.

I also owe enormous thanks to my sister, Jenny, and to Peter Robins, who happily read every chapter of this book even when it looked like it'd be nothing but a vanity project; and to Dominic Curran, although he was lucky enough to get away with only reading about a quarter of it. They all gave fantastic suggestions and dealt with a stream of annoying queries, although I owe them most simply for their encouragement without which I would never have got to the end.

I'm grateful to all my friends and family for their encouragement too, especially those – Kensuke Takaoka! – who ended up acting like a hotel, translation and problem-solving service, somehow without complaint. Thanks to Alex and Claire Whittaker, Tom and Ele Perkin-Brown, Paul and Caroline Hailey, Tricia Mundy, Ed Yong and everyone else from Pembroke, Ben Musgrave, Mark Willingham, Anthony Dhanendran, Seb Skeaping and the rest of the City journalists, Simon Evans, Francois Le Goff and Margaret Curran for their help with the Swiss anthem entry, and Alan and Tricia Marshall who for some reason let me steal their lives for the Nepal chapter.

Some people went out of their way to help me in each of the countries I visited, especially the many interpreters who worked for me seemingly more because they were interested in the subject than for any other reason. I would recommend the following to anyone: Dragan Markovic in Bosnia; Miki Wada, Izumi Kano Guisando and Yukiko Sadaoka in Japan; Artur Lyubanskiy in Kazakhstan; Ram Tiwari in Nepal; Aldo López, Silvia Terol and Silvia Sánchez di Martino in Paraguay; and Mariana Giménez and Frederico Casal in Uruguay. Other people I am particularly indebted to include Chika Yoshida at the Foreign Press Centre in Tokyo for securing so many interviews; Aleck Skeie for his help in Sera; the Nashville Sounds for letting me audition; and Ati Metwaly and Reem Kelani for so many contacts in Egypt.

I am also, of course, indebted to my agent, Jon Elek at United Agents, for seeing the strength of this idea in the first place, and to my editor, Harry Scoble-Rees, and everyone else at Random House Books and Windmill, for doing so not long afterwards and then working so hard on it. I also owe Harry enormously for all his suggestions that have much improved the book, for his enthusiasm and, probably most of all, for not insisting I went to the Islamic State to give that chapter more of a travel narrative!

Finally, thanks to you for reading it. This book is a snapshot in time; please visit the countries mentioned and explore them for yourself.

Bibliography

Anthems are one of history's most neglected subjects, many historians seeming to have decided they are simply a novelty. That means much of the information in this book comes from interviews – not just with the people mentioned, but countless others who generously gave me their time. I could not be more grateful for their help, but any errors in here are entirely mine. However, there are some books, articles, websites and radio programmes that I found particularly useful and here are some of those, arranged by chapter.

Prologue

De Bruin, Martine, 'Het Wilhelmus Tijdens de Republiek', *Volkskundig Bulletin*, 24 (1998), pp. 16–42

Malcolm, Noel, *Kosovo: A Short History*, 1998

Jobbins, Siôn, *The Welsh National Anthem: Its Story, Its Meaning*, 2013

France

Association Louis-Luc pour l'Histoire et La Mémoire de Choisy-le-Roi, *Rouget de Lisle et la Marseillaise*

Carlyle, Thomas, *The French Revolution*, 1837

Leconte, Alfred, *Rouget de Lisle: Sa Vie, Ses Oeuvres, la Marseillaise*, 1892

Schama, Simon, *Citizens: A Chronicle of the French Revolution*, 1989

Tulard, Jean, *Napoléon et Rouget de L'Isle*, 2000

Nepal

Hilton, Isabel, 'Royal Blood', *New Yorker*, 30 July 2001, pp. 42–57 – the source for many of the details of the royal massacre and the events surrounding it

Hutt, Michael, 'Singing the New Nepal', *Nations and Nationalism*, 18 (2) (2012), pp. 306–25 – the source for many details of the anthem competition

Whelpton, John, *A History of Nepal*, 2005 – the only real English-language history of the country and source for much about the Maoist uprising

America

Ferris, Marc, *Star-Spangled Banner: The Unlikely Story of America's National Anthem*, 2014

Hildebrand, David, *Broadside to Anthem: Music of the War of 1812*, 2012 – a radio documentary on the music from the time when the anthem was composed

Scott Key, Francis, *Poems of the Late Francis Scott Key*, 1857

Svejda, George, *History of the Star-Spangled Banner: From 1814 to Present*, 1969

Vogel, Steve, *Through the Perilous Fight: Six Weeks that Saved the Nation*, 2013

Japan

Aspinall, Robert and Cave, Peter, 'Lowering the Flag: Democracy, Authority and Rights at Tokorozawa High School', *Social Science Japan*, 4 (1) (2001), pp. 77–93 – the source for much of the detail of the Tokorozawa incident

Aspinall, Robert, *Teachers' Unions and the Politics of Education in Japan*, 2001

Buruma, Ian, *Inventing Japan 1853–1964*, 2004

Cripps, Denise, 'Flags and Fanfares: The Hinomaru Flag and Kimigayo Anthem', in Goodman, Roger and Neary, Ian (eds), *Case Studies on Human Rights in Japan*, 1996, pp. 76–108

Dower, John, *Embracing Defeat: Japan in the Aftermath of World War II*, 1999 – the source for the story that Japanese soldiers turned and faced the country when singing 'Kimigayo' abroad

Imamura, Akira, 'John William Fenton (1813–1890) and the Japanese National Anthem Kimigayo', in Japan Society, *Britain & Japan: Biographical Portraits*, 9 (2014)

Tsukahara, Yasuko, 'State Ceremony and Music in Meiji-era Japan', *Nineteenth-century Music Review*, 10 (2) (2013), pp. 223–38

Kazakhstan

Aitken, Jonathan, *Kazakhstan: Surprises and Stereotypes After 20 Years of Independence*, 2012

Aitken, Jonathan, *Nazarbayev and the Making of Kazakhstan*, 2009 – hagiography, but Aitken has had more access to Kazakhstan's president than any other researcher

Hersh, Seymour, 'The Price of Oil', *New Yorker*, 9 July 2001, pp. 48–65 – tells the story of Kazakhgate, which includes allegations surrounding the country's oil deals

Howard, Keith, 'North Korea: Songs for the Great Leader, with Instructions from the Dear Leader', in Orange, M. (ed.), *Cahiers d'Études Coréennes 7: Mélanges offerts a Li Ogg et Daniel Bouchez*, 2001, pp. 103–30

Huang, Natasha, 'East is Red': A Musical Barometer for Cultural Revolution Politics and Culture*, 2008

Locard, Henri, *Pol Pot's Little Red Book: The Sayings of Angkar*, 2005

Robbins, Christopher, *In Search of Kazakhstan: The Land that Disappeared*, 2007

Short, Philip, *Pol Pot: The History of a Nightmare*, 2005

Liechtenstein and the UK

Bateman, Stringer, *The Strange Evolution of 'Our Illiterate National Anthem' from a Rebel Song . . .*, 1902

Buckmaster, Herbert, *Buck's Book*, 1933 – the source for the quote about my great-grandfather

Connelly, Charlie, *Stamping Grounds: Exploring Liechtenstein and its World Cup Dream*, 2002

Cummings, William, *God Save the King: The Origin and History of the Music and Words of the National Anthem*, 1902 – along with Percy Scholes' book (see below), one of the two main studies of the British anthem

Cummings, William, *Dr Arne and Rule Britannia*, 1912

Davies, Norman, *The Isles: A History*, 1999

Frommelt, Josef, *Die Liechtensteinische Landeshymne: Entstehung, Einführung, Veränderungen*, 2005 – Josef's study of Liechtenstein's anthem also comprehensively tells the story of Britain's

Frommelt, Josef, 'Jakob Josef Jauch (1802–1859), Ein Unverstandener Neuerer', *Balzner Neujahrsblätter*, 17 (2011), pp. 23–38

Hans-Adam II, *The State in the Third Millennium*, 2009

Scholes, Percy, *God Save the Queen! The History and Romance of the World's First National Anthem*, 1954

The Gentleman's Magazine, 1745 editions

Bosnia

Malcolm, Noel, *Bosnia: A Short History*, 2002

slavkojovicicslavuj.blogspot.com – the blog of the former politician Slavko Jovičić, a Bosnian Serb. Very useful for his memories and views on Bosnia's anthem contests

The Islamic State

aymennjawad.org – researcher Aymenn Jawad al-Tamimi's website. He was the person who first posted an English-language translation of 'My Ummah, Dawn Has Appeared'. Along with jihadology.net it is one of the main Western websites collecting jihadi *nasheeds*

Baily, John, '*Can You Stop The Birds Singing?*': *The Censorship of Music in Afghanistan*, 2001

Fallaci, Oriana, 'An Interview with Khomeini', *New York Times*, 7 October 1979

Otterbeck, Jonas, *Battling Over the Public Sphere: Islamic Reactions to the Music of Today*, 2007

'"Our Music Needs Innovation": Dr Hassan Riyahi, Composer of National Anthem of the Islamic Republic of Iran', ecinews. org, 18 July 2011 – an interview with the composer of Iran's anthem and the source for the reason why Khomeini's anthem was replaced

Said, Behnam, 'Hymns (Nasheeds): A Contribution to the Study of Jihadist Culture', *Studies in Conflict and Terrorism*, 35 (12) (2012), pp. 863–79

Talbot, Margaret, 'The Agitator', *New Yorker*, 5 June 2006, pp. 58–67 – a profile of Fallaci and the source for the story about Khomeini laughing

Egypt

Danielson, Virginia, *The Voice of Egypt: Umm Kulthūm, Arabic Song and Egyptian Society in the Twentieth Century*, 1997 – the definitive English-language study on Umm Kulthūm and the forces that shaped her

Gordon, Joel, *Nasser: Hero of the Arab Nation*, 2006 – the source of the story about Salah Jahin being threatened with losing his passport

Gordon, Joel, 'Stuck with Him: Bassem Youssef and the Egyptian Revolution's Last Laugh', *Review of Middle Eastern Studies*, 48 (1–2) (2014), pp. 34–43 – although largely about recent history this is also a great study on Egyptian 'anthems' during Nasser's time

Kelani, Reem, *Songs for Tahrir*, 2012 – a BBC radio documentary on the Tahrir protests and Sayed Darwish's songs

Osman, Tarek, *Egypt on the Brink: From Nasser to the Muslim Brotherhood*, 2013

Teltsch, Kathleen, 'For Israel, a Banner-Hunting Day', *New York Times*, 18 November 1977 – the source of the story about how Israel obtained the music to Egypt's anthem 'Oh, My Weapon, It Has Been a Long Time'

Wright, Lawrence, *Thirteen Days in September: Carter, Begin and Sadat at Camp David*, 2014

South Africa

Carlin, John, *Playing the Enemy: Nelson Mandela and the Game that Made a Nation*, 2008 – an invaluable resource, including for Nelson Mandela's quote to the African National Congress about the anthem

Coplan, David, *In the Township Tonight: South Africa's Black City Music and Theatre*, 2008

Kannemeyer, John, *Langenhoven: 'n Lewe*, 1995

Keller, Bill, 'Flags, Anthems and Rugby: A Volatile Mix for South Africa', *New York Times*, 18 August 1992

Mandela, Nelson, *Long Walk to Freedom*, 1994

The Southern African Music Rights Organisation (SAMRO)'s archives, which include minutes of the South African anthem committee meetings and letters by its chairman to government

Woods, Donald, 'A South African Poet on his imprisonment', *New York Times*, 1 May 1983 – the source for the story that people sang 'Nkosi Sikelel' iAfrika' while being executed

Paraguay

Aharonián, Coriún, *'Que el Alma Pronuncia': Aportes a la Confusion General en Torno al Himno Nacional y Sus Autores*, 2012

Ayestarán, Lauro, *El Himno Nacional,* 1974

Haase, Diego Sánchez, *La Música en el Paraguay,* 2002

Lambert, Peter and Nickson, Andrew (eds), *The Paraguay Reader: History, Culture, Politics,* 2013 – the best history of the country, filled with everything from first-hand accounts of wars to excerpts from novels. The source of, among other things, the story of Ukrainians singing the Soviet anthem after moving to the country

Romero, Roberto, *El Himno Nacional Paraguayo: En el Proceso Cultural de la República,* 1986

Slonimsky, Nicolas, *Music of Latin America,* 1972

Sryvalin, Diego Darío Florentín, *El Himno Nacional Paraguayo: Un Estudio Morfológico, Sintáctico y Semántico,* 2010

Weschler, Lawrence, 'The Great Exception', *New Yorker,* 3 April 1989, pp. 43–85, and 10 April 1989, pp. 85–108 – fascinating and disturbing story of Uruguay's dictatorship, its downfall and the political fallout

General

Billig, Michael, *Banal Nationalism,* 1995 – the classic academic text on how people's sense of national identity is reinforced every day by things like newspaper headlines. Surprisingly makes little comment about anthems, but its conclusions can easily be read across

nationalanthems.info – my favourite website on anthems, featuring instrumental renditions and background information

Nettl, Paul, *National Anthems,* 1967 – showing its age, but one of the only books before this one to try to survey the world's songs

szbszig.atw.hu – a Hungarian website containing many vocal renditions of anthems, some wrong, but the easiest place to find them

Audio Guide

If you'd like to hear any of the music mentioned in these pages, a chapter-by-chapter audio guide is available at:

republicordeath.com

It includes all the anthems mentioned, as well as numerous other songs, photos and videos to help you delve further into the countries and the book's arguments. It will be updated if any of the anthems change – you can never trust them not to.

Index